WAL

21ST

CENTURY

LONDON

21ST CENTURY LONDON

THE NEW ARCHITECTURE

KENNETH POWELL

MERRELL
LONDON · NEW YORK

CONTENTS

At the turn of the new century, before the failure of the New Labour experiment, before the optimism fuelled by the election of 1997 evaporated, London's mood was one of expansive confidence. Life for many Londoners remained difficult: a shortage of affordable housing, failing schools, a transport system chronically in need of upgrading, and a public realm (the modish term for the spaces between buildings) that was too often depressingly squalid were the flipside of the boom of the late 1990s. The IRA bombings of the City of London in 1992 and 1993 had caused serious damage to buildings (wrecking the Baltic Exchange, for example, and in the process creating a site for Norman Foster's 'Gherkin' at 30 St Mary Axe; pp. 294–95), and for a time added to the gloom of recession. But the 'ring of steel' that was created to foil future car bombers turned out to be of enormous benefit to the City, reducing through traffic and stimulating the creation of pedestrian-friendly spaces, which the City had conspicuously lacked.

By the early years of the twenty-first century a building boom was gripping the Square Mile. The voting in of Ken Livingstone as the first elected Mayor of London – he effortlessly won a second term in 2004 – at first worried business interests. But Livingstone turned out to be the developers' friend, encouraging commercial development as a generator of employment and particularly favouring high-rise office buildings as a marker of London's significance in the global financial sector. The Blair government, in the person of deputy prime minister John Prescott, wavered but then backed the Livingstone line, and approval was given for the Heron Tower at 110 Bishopsgate (pp. 298–99), the brainchild of fearless entrepreneur Gerald Ronson, and a series of City towers. The opposition of English Heritage (the government's adviser on the historic environment) did not derail Renzo Piano's 'Shard' at London Bridge, set to be the tallest of London high-rises (pp. 326–27), and controversial schemes for Vauxhall and Lots Road, Chelsea, also secured consent.

The 'Gherkin' itself was completed in 2004 and was an instant popular success, its unusual form being recognized as a symbol of London alongside the Tower and Big Ben. It was one of a string of City office projects designed by Foster + Partners, now one of the leading players on the office scene. The largest of these projects – offices for insurance giant Willis – was completed in 2007 on the site of the 1958 Lloyd's Building at 51 Lime Street, across the road from Richard Rogers's iconic 1980s replacement. Rogers's London masterpiece is likely to be further jostled by another large new office building, across the road on Leadenhall Street, an innovative design by his own practice, Rogers Stirk Harbour + Partners.

As the City office market boomed, many of the buildings erected as part of the post-war reconstruction of the 1950s and 1960s disappeared: Richard Seifert's Drapers Gardens tower of 1967, for example, arguably

Opposite, top
New City towers: Twenty Fenchurch Street, by Rafael Viñoly, in the foreground (also opposite, bottom), with Kohn Pedersen Fox's Pinnacle behind.

one of his best buildings (although hopelessly obsolete in terms of twenty-first-century office technology); and Victor Heal's slightly dull but beautifully crafted New Change complex of 1960 immediately east of St Paul's, flattened for an office and retail scheme designed by French architect Jean Nouvel for Land Securities.

During the 1980s and 1990s British architects, with Norman Foster and Richard Rogers in the lead, were a major presence globally; in fact, Foster did not complete a major building in London until his ITN headquarters of 1991. Now, architects from elsewhere are focusing on London: Nouvel at New Change, Renzo Piano at London Bridge and St Giles Circus, and Rafael Viñoly on Fenchurch Street, not to mention Herzog & de Meuron's continuing involvement with Tate Modern, where a major expansion project is proceeding in difficult times (pp. 100–101). When the old-established Rothschild bank decided to rebuild its headquarters at the heart of the City, housed in a decent 1960s block by Fitzroy Robinson (now Aukett Fitzroy Robinson), it engaged the hugely fashionable OMA practice, headed by Dutch architect Rem Koolhaas, a commission that would probably have been inconceivable even a decade earlier.

Nationality counts for less and less on the world architectural scene. Foster + Partners, for example, employs staff who speak thirty or more languages between them. London architecture schools attract students from around the world, and many stay to work for London practices: one of the leading figures currently working from London is Iraq-born Zaha Hadid – winner of the Stirling Prize in 2010 – who, in common with many other 'star' architects, studied at the Architectural Association School of Architecture. Since the mid-1980s London has been the European base for a number of leading American practices, among them Skidmore, Owings & Merrill (SOM), HOK and Kohn Pedersen Fox (KPF). (In 2009 five of the founding principals of KPF left to found a new London-based practice, PLP Architecture.) Canary Wharf, London's second financial centre after the Square Mile, was masterplanned by SOM, and most of the buildings have been designed by Americans, creating an environment that is weirdly North American in character and, for all its success, alien to London.

London, more than any other European capital, has always been a business centre as much as a seat of government. It is also a world cultural hub. The launch of the National Lottery by John Major's government – less creditably the author of the disastrous railway privatization programme – provided the funding for a series of *grands projets* to rival those completed in Paris under François Mitterrand. They included the reconstruction of the Royal Opera House by Dixon Jones and Arup (a project launched in the 1980s), the Queen Elizabeth II Great Court at the British Museum by Foster + Partners, and Tate Modern by Herzog & de Meuron, as well as significant additions to Tate Britain, the National Portrait Gallery, the Wallace Collection, Somerset House, the National Maritime Museum, the Science Museum and other institutions. National Lottery money secured the site for the new Wembley Stadium (pp. 152–53). The most controversial of all Lottery projects was the Millennium Dome, with its collection of costly follies housed in a – remarkably economical – container designed by Rogers partner Mike Davies. Today, however, the Dome has been reborn as the O2, one of the most spectacular events venues in the world (pp. 138–39).

The National Lottery continues to be a major backer of sporting, arts and 'heritage' projects nationally, but the days of £50,000,000-plus grants seem to be over; too many hugely expensive projects outside London were disastrous failures (witness the £40,000,000 Earth Centre, Doncaster, now closed), and recently the Lottery has been milked to provide funding for the 2012 Olympics. Typical of the more modest schemes the Lottery has backed in the last few years is the highly intelligent refurbishment and extension (completed in 2009 by Flemish practice Robbrecht en Daem Architecten) of the Whitechapel Art Gallery, to which the Heritage Lottery Fund made a grant of £13,500,000 (pp. 108–109). More than £90,000,000 of Lottery cash went into the not uncontroversial refurbishment of the Royal Festival Hall by Allies and Morrison (pp. 92–93), yet the rest of the South Bank Centre remains apparently in limbo, with too little of the Rick Mather development plan of 1999 realized.

The economic climate of the New Labour years favoured the accumulation of private wealth, and there were plenty of clients for expensive one-off private houses designed by Caruso St John, Keith Williams, David Adjaye, Alison Brooks, Eldridge Smerin and others, and buyers for flats in such developments as Rogers Stirk Harbour's One Hyde Park, where the most expensive flat was reportedly priced at £140,000,000. One of the most disconcerting characteristics of present-day London is its role as a playground for the super-rich of the Middle East and Russia. Middle Eastern money, from Qatar, funded One Hyde Park (one of a number of developments in London promoted by the Candy brothers), and has been pouring into other London projects, including that

St John's Therapy Centre in Wandsworth provides a comprehensive range of health services for the community in a stylish building.

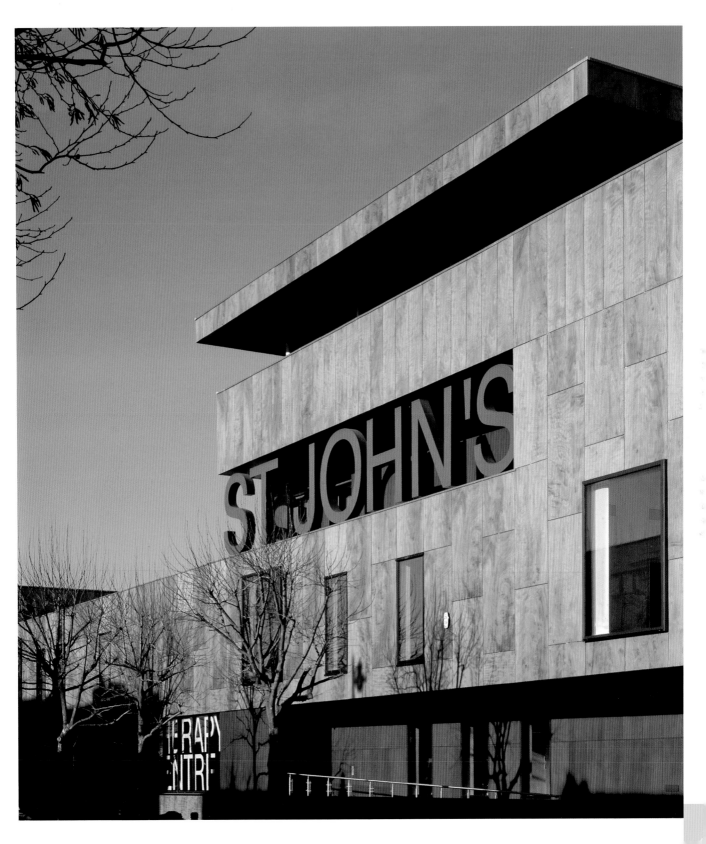

for the Chelsea Barracks site, where the alliance of the Candys and the Qataris has resulted in a court battle.

As well as a booming market in luxury homes, however, the first decade of the twenty-first century saw a healthy revival of investment in 'social' housing: schemes by Ash Sakula, Niall McLaughlin, Sergison Bates and Peter Barber are equally exercises in urban repair and enrichment. Coin Street Community Builders continued its ongoing development programme on the South Bank with affordable housing and a community centre by Haworth Tompkins (pp. 244–45), although its proposed tower on Doon Street – which will be visible from the great court of Somerset House – generated fierce opposition. The Doon Street project, designed by Lifschutz Davidson Sandilands, provides flats for sale at high prices, but is linked to the provision of a new leisure centre and swimming pool for the community in this part of the borough of Lambeth (pp. 116–17).

New Labour was also able to boast of major investment in health and education projects. The £1,000,000,000-plus reconstruction of the Royal London and Bart's hospitals by architect HOK is certainly spectacular in scale (pp. 148–49). Equally significant, however, was the provision of community health facilities: for example, the Kentish Town Health Centre

designed by Allford Hall Monaghan Morris (pp. 126–27), the St John's Therapy Centre in Wandsworth (2007) by Buschow Henley (now Henley Halebrown Rorrison), or the health centre at Vassall Road, Brixton, linked to a housing scheme by Tony Fretton (pp. 272–73). (Ironically, the building that, three quarters of a century ago, provided a model for projects of this kind, Berthold Lubetkin's Finsbury Health Centre, faced likely closure in 2010.)

One of the first actions of the coalition government in the summer of 2010 was to announce the scrapping of Labour's Building Schools for the Future (BSF) programme. Many of the new schools already generated under BSF were of poor quality, and the general assumption that well-built schools of Victorian or early twentieth-century vintage were obsolete and ripe for demolition was clearly misguided and scandalously profligate. (Such projects as the extension of Clapham Manor Primary School, completed in 2007 by dRMM, or Gumuchdjian Architects' additions to St Marylebone CE School, demonstrated the potential for extending and upgrading existing schools; pp. 168–69 and 202–203.) However, the best of the new schools, including those in Hampstead and Hackney by Feilden Clegg Bradley Studios (pp. 178–79 and 200–201) and the ingenious 'vertical schools' designed by BDP (pp. 160–61 and

The new American Embassy will be located on a highly secure riverside site in Battersea, downstream from Battersea Power Station.

176–77), offered a new vision of educational provision for London.

London's role as a global provider of higher education powered major development projects at the London School of Economics and Political Science, Imperial College, University College London, Queen Mary, University of London, and the Royal College of Art. One of London's major art schools, Central St Martin's, now part of the University of the Arts London, is scheduled to move to a site in the former goods yard of King's Cross station in 2011. Its new home, a mix of converted warehouses and new buildings, is designed by Stanton Williams (p. 32). Together with the Kings Place scheme by Dixon Jones (pp. 76–77) and the impending reopening of the former Midland Grand Hotel and St Pancras Chambers (as a flagship Marriott Renaissance five-star hotel; pp. 150–51), the project augments the dramatic regeneration of the King's Cross area. That process of renewal was underpinned by the opening in 2007 of St Pancras International station as the terminus for Eurostar services to the Continent (pp. 40–41). The dramatic reinvention of W.H. Barlow's great train shed as both a rail terminus and a high-quality shopping and restaurant complex – what other London station is a destination in its own right? – is perhaps the most

significant architectural project in London in the last decade. The adjacent King's Cross terminus is the subject of a comprehensive development scheme by John McAslan + Partners (pp. 34–35), providing a striking new concourse to the west of the listed 1850s train sheds and replacing the universally despised 1970s station concourse on Euston Road with a new public square. This could form part of the great boulevard into which, as part of a visionary proposal by Terry Farrell, Euston and Marylebone roads may be transformed.

While redevelopment proposals for London Bridge and Euston stations seem unlikely to move forwards rapidly, a number of long-delayed rail projects in London are finally happening. The London Overground project has cleverly linked the long-underused North London line (which formerly terminated in the City at Broad Street station, demolished in the mid-1980s) to the former East London line of the Underground. An extension to Clapham Junction in 2012 will be the final component in a system that already extends from Watford Junction to West Croydon. The merits of the project, which has been achieved so far on schedule and to budget, are undermined only by the lack of architectural vision for the new and revamped stations; they are generally of mundane character, and there is

nothing of the aspiration to create a permanent legacy for London seen so vividly in the Jubilee line extension stations completed at the end of the last century. Nor does the (hugely beneficial) expansion of Thameslink, allowing more frequent and longer trains to cross London from north to south, promise much in terms of architecture: Will Alsop produced remarkable designs for the new Blackfriars station, which will span the River Thames, but what is being built is no more than competent, with none of the visual thrills promised by Alsop. At least Thameslink is being sensitively slotted into the Borough Market area, allowing the market to continue business while construction proceeds. Vastly more ambitious – and costly – the Crossrail project (pp. 24–27), due for completion in 2017, will require the construction of seven new stations along the underground section of the route from Paddington to Canary Wharf, and one station above ground. Details of the proposed designs have emerged only slowly, and several stations have already passed through the hands of more than one practice. Former schemes for Paddington station, for example, include those by Alsop and John McAslan. Predictably, Canary Wharf is likely to be one of the more striking, with a scheme by Foster + Partners.

Transport connections are clearly the key to regeneration. Their absence has long stymied plans for London's most conspicuous historic building at risk, Battersea Power Station, where current proposals by Rafael Viñoly sensibly omit the grotesque 'eco-tower' put forward in 2008. The perceived development potential of this oddly isolated quarter of London may be increased by plans for a new United States embassy at nearby Nine Elms. An architectural competition for the new embassy – limited to American practices – was won by Kieran Timberlake in 2010. The scheme, characterized (perhaps a little unfairly) as 'a moated fortress', was condemned by Richard Rogers and Peter Palumbo, members of the competition jury, as reflecting a negative image of the USA; Rogers and Palumbo backed a rival submission by Thom Mayne of Morphosis. The decision to move the embassy to Battersea, welcomed by Mayfair residents, leaves the future of the existing Eero Saarinen building in Grosvenor Square, now listed, uncertain; a residential conversion is most likely.

One perennial player on the London architectural scene over nearly thirty years has been the Prince of Wales, whose campaigning activities began in earnest with the saga of the National Gallery extension in the early 1980s. The Prince's influence can be seen in the extension Venturi, Scott Brown and Associates eventually added to the gallery, and in Paternoster Square, next to St Paul's, where Whitfield Partners' masterplan, if not the buildings around the square by Eric Parry, MJP and others, is firmly traditionalist (pp. 334–35). The Prince's intervention in the planning process for the Chelsea Barracks site was highly controversial: he presented himself as the champion of the local community against the developers while others, including the President of the RIBA and Richard Rogers (whose firm's proposals for the site were subsequently scrapped) condemned his intervention as undemocratic and a misuse of his position. In any case, the Qatari owners of the site went on to commission a new masterplan from consultants Dixon Jones, Squire and Partners and landscape designer Kim Wilkie Associates. Across the road from the barracks site is, perhaps not coincidentally, a building – the Margaret Thatcher Infirmary of the Chelsea Royal Hospital (pp. 136–37) – by a practice admired by the Prince, Quinlan & Francis Terry. In the 1980s, when Prince Charles made Paternoster Square a battleground in the traditionalist/modernist confrontation, Terry and others working in the traditionalist mode seemed to be in the ascendant. Terry's practice has completed several commercial projects in London (in Baker Street and Tottenham Court Road; pp. 304–305), and fellow classicist Robert Adam was responsible for an office and retail scheme on Piccadilly (pp. 300–301), yet these practices still seem more at home with houses and the occasional college building. In fact, Terry's infirmary is a quiet and unobtrusive design that does not challenge the dominance of Christopher Wren's original building.

These adjectives could not be applied to the designs by Liam O'Connor for a Bomber Command memorial at Green Park. The memorial commemorates 50,000 airmen lost in Second World War bombing raids, but its bombastic form is entirely at odds with any notion of remembrance and reconciliation. How much more dignified and moving was Edwin Lutyens's approach to the design of the Cenotaph (which actually commemorates the British dead of all wars).

Winning the 2012 Olympic Games for London was seen as one of the triumphs of the Blair years. Not every Londoner is now convinced that the Games are of benefit to the city, especially when the residents are being presented with a significant bill for the privilege of staging them. Architecturally, the most spectacular legacy of 2012 (pp. 16–19) will undeniably

be Zaha Hadid's Aquatics Centre, her first major work
in this country. The Energy Centres by John McAslan +
Partners and the substation by Nord look promising, and
the Olympic Village draws together work by some highly
competent practices. In contrast, the International
Media Centre looks large, dull – and very costly.
The Olympic Stadium, designed by Populous, is
unremarkable – a temporary-looking, far from
impressive structure that may end up as home to one
of London's less notable football clubs. It remains to be
seen whether the Olympic site will develop, post-2012,
as the focus of regeneration for the further stretches of
the East End. The vast Stratford City project, developed
by Westfield and including a 175,000-square-metre
shopping centre linked to the new Stratford International
station, may be more significant for the future of east
London (pp. 44–45).

By 2012, some of the uncertainties that preoccupied
Britain at the beginning of a new era of austerity may
have been resolved. London will acquire more office
towers, shopping centres and lacklustre housing, and
much of its infrastructure will remain in need of renewal.
But the energy that has made it a true global capital of
architecture will continue to produce buildings worthy,
at their best, of a unique world city.

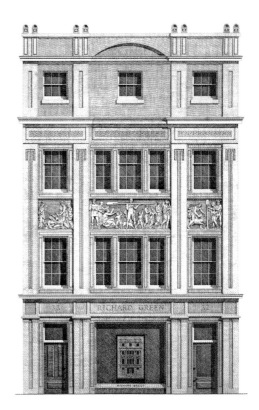

INFRASTRUCTURE AND PUBLIC SPACES

CAMDEN

ISLINGTON

7
11 8

4
10

14

4

4

4

12

6

5

15

1   2012 OLYMPIC AND PARALYMPIC GAMES

2   CANARY WHARF UNDERGROUND STATION

3   CITY OF LONDON INFORMATION CENTRE

4   CROSSRAIL

5   EXHIBITION ROAD

6   GOLDEN JUBILEE BRIDGES

7   KING'S CROSS CENTRAL

8   KING'S CROSS STATION

9   MILLENNIUM BRIDGE

10 NORTH GREENWICH STATION AND
    TRANSPORT INTERCHANGE

11 ST PANCRAS INTERNATIONAL STATION

12 SOMERSET HOUSE

13 STRATFORD CITY

14 TERMINAL 5, HEATHROW AIRPORT

15 WESTMINSTER UNDERGROUND STATION

WESTMINSTER

LAMBET

HACKNEY

TOWER
HAMLETS

SOUTHWARK

Aerial views show the Basketball Arena (left, centre), the Velodrome (left, top), Zaha Hadid's sculptural Aquatics Centre (opposite, bottom) and the Olympic Stadium (opposite, top).

In the run-up to the 2012 Olympic and Paralympic Games, their long-term benefits for London remain uncertain, not least in terms of their architectural legacy. What is certain is that they have generated no single iconic building to match the 'Bird's Nest' stadium designed by Herzog & de Meuron for the 2008 Beijing Olympics. The London Olympic Stadium by Populous is an altogether more straightforward structure, which has a rather temporary look. In fact, the upper levels are designed to be dismantled after the Games to reduce the seating capacity from 80,000 to 25,000, possibly for use as a football stadium. The architectural star of the Games – which is centred on the Olympic Park at Stratford – is clearly the Aquatics Centre by Zaha Hadid Architects, its dramatic undulating roof inspired, it is claimed, by 'the fluid geometry of water in motion'. With engineering input by Arup, the building certainly has landmark qualities, despite the cutbacks imposed on the project in the face of a rocketing budget. It surely has the potential to become a permanent resource for East London.

The future of other structures on the site is less certain, despite promises that the Games will play a major role in the regeneration of the East End. Hopkins Architects' Velodrome, with its sweeping timber roof, is clearly another building of distinction, but has no obvious use after 2012. The International Media Centre, costing more than £300,000,000, is little more than

a vast shed that could be the distribution depot for a supermarket chain. It has been the subject of fierce criticism, with claims that it has no practical use post-Games, and is likely to be demolished.

The Olympic Village, designed to accommodate 17,000 athletes and officials in 2012, will supposedly provide about 2800 homes for Londoners after the Games, but it is unclear whether the site will attract future permanent residents; student housing is one alternative. The architecture of the village is generally of high quality – Patel Taylor, Glenn Howells Architects, Panter Hudspith Architects and Penoyre & Prasad are among the practices involved, within a masterplan by Fletcher Priest Architects – and the landscape is equally far from routine. It is the location of the village that tells against it. Other sporting venues (for basketball, hockey and water polo, for example) are intended to be temporary, with a vague hope that elements of the structures might be reused somewhere in Britain.

Some of the best 2012 architecture derives, in fact, from strictly practical briefs: the Energy Centres designed by John McAslan + Partners and the already celebrated substation by Glasgow-based practice Nord are examples. Away from the Olympic Park, Wembley Stadium (pp. 152–53) is to be used for football, with equestrian events taking place in Greenwich Park (despite claims that the historic landscape will be gravely damaged).

Whatever the legacy of the Games to Londoners – who are paying heavily for them – architects and consultants of all kinds have certainly benefited from the spending splurge they have generated (at a time when public spending is being slashed). More significant for the long-term future of the Stratford and Lea Valley area is the development of Stratford City, with its colossal retail centre (pp. 44–45), and the opening of Stratford International station on the cross-Channel line from St Pancras.

Below and opposite, top
The Olympic Stadium is designed to be reduced in size after the Games.

Opposite, bottom
The Basketball Arena is the third largest building on the site, but will be dismantled and its parts used elsewhere after the Games. It will also house handball, wheelchair basketball and wheelchair rugby events.

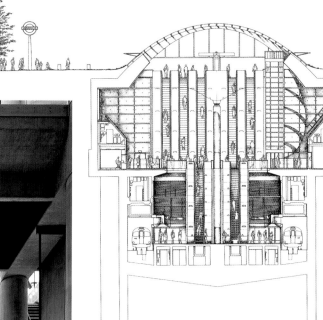

Canary Wharf station has the grandeur of a mainline rail terminal and the sleekness of an international airport, embodying all the expertise that Foster + Partners has developed in the design of public buildings and infrastructure over the last forty years. Yet, for all its monumental grandeur, Canary Wharf is a link in the chain of the Jubilee line extension from Green Park to Stratford, one of a series of eleven new (or largely rebuilt) stations commissioned by the extension's architect-in-chief, Roland Paoletti.

Work on developing the Canary Wharf 'office city' began in 1987, and the buildings started to come on-stream on the eve of the recession in the 1990s. By 1999, however, the project housed 25,000 workers, and within a few years this figure would more than double. As existing transport connections, notably the Docklands Light Railway, were stretched to breaking point, the Jubilee line extension arrived in the nick of time. The new station was designed to cope with future growth (40,000 passengers hourly), and is now working at capacity.

The site for the station is a former dock basin just south of Canada Square, the heart of Canary Wharf. A huge concrete box, 300 metres long, contained within diaphragm walls, was sunk into the drained dock and rooted into the waterlogged ground with deep piles. On top of the station box, a park was created – a valuable amenity, but also a vital practical device to prevent the station from floating upwards. If the engineering achievement involved in the project was heroic, it is the potency of the architectural expression, however, that places Canary Wharf firmly among Norman Foster's major works (where other recent buildings at Canary Wharf by the practice regrettably do not belong).

Externally, the station has a discreet presence. The glazed entrance canopies are a development of those Foster designed for the Bilbao metro system. The experience of descending the banks of escalators into the 265-metre-long concourse is as memorable as any found in contemporary London architecture. Natural light floods in and there is a clear and direct route down to the platforms. Ticket offices and other service spaces are rigorously marshalled along the sides of the concourse, and lighting and other services effortlessly integrated. Considering the demands on the structure, the lightness of the architecture is astounding. Slim, elliptical columns support the roof, from which a mezzanine is suspended. Architecture and engineering are, in the great Foster tradition, in complete harmony.

One of the remarkable features of the Jubilee line extension is the variety of its stations: Southwark is complex and reflective, North Greenwich (pp. 38–39) expansive and populist. Canary Wharf triumphs through sheer rationality: the inevitability of function expressed in noble form. The miseries of Camden Town or Tottenham Court Road stations seem part of another world.

Opposite, top left
The station's majestic concourse level.

Opposite, right
Cross section, showing the structure sunk into the former dock.

Opposite, bottom left
From the platform level there is a clear day-lit route towards the exit.

Below
Station entrance, with glazed canopy illuminating the escalators.

Left and below
Replacing a pavilion of 1951,
Make's information centre is
close to St Paul's Cathedral.

*Opposite, top, centre
and bottom left*
The form of the building is
highly expressive, with a prow-
like roof that extends to invite
in passing tourists.

Opposite, bottom right
The centre is constructed
from coated metal and glass,
a contrast to the historic
buildings that form the context.

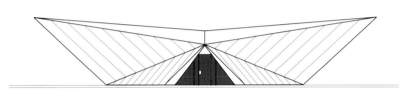

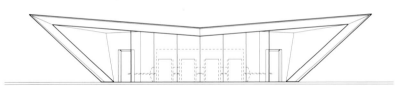

Make's pavilion replaces one of rather different character, originally designed by the City Architect for the Festival of Britain in 1951. The commission to Make (a practice founded by former Foster partner Ken Shuttleworth in 2004 and now established on the commercial scene) was part of a concerted campaign to improve the setting of St Paul's Cathedral. Strategically located near the Millennium Bridge (pp. 36–37), the new pavilion is a somewhat self-conscious piece of form-making by a practice that has become known for its exuberantly sculptural approach to design. Whether that is appropriate for such a sensitive location close to the cathedral's south transept remains an open question.

The triangular pavilion is clad in stainless steel on a steel frame, a piece of folded architecture with (says the architect) 'the lightness and aerodynamic profile of a paper aeroplane'. The 140-square-metre building opens out with a glazed façade to the north to address the cathedral. It is claimed to be impressively ecologically sound, with a high degree of insulation, cooling using water from a borehole, and the recycling of rainwater to flush WCs and irrigate the surrounding garden. Although not a building for strict rationalists, the pavilion adds an element of lightness and even frivolity – in the best tradition of 1951 – to the City scene.

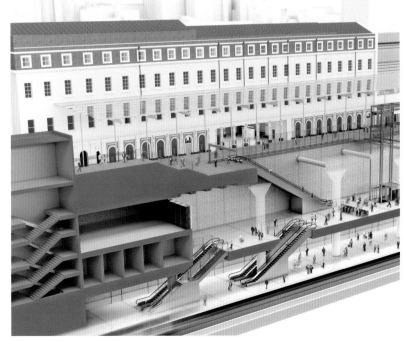

Opposite, top
Foster + Partners' station
at Canary Wharf will be six
storeys deep and sunk into
a former dock basin.

Opposite, bottom
The station at Paddington
by Weston Williamson
sits alongside the present
mainline terminus. The design
allows daylight to penetrate
down to the platforms.

Below
One of the dramatic new
entrances to the station at
Liverpool Street, designed
by Wilkinson Eyre.

Crossrail, the project to drive a mainline railway through
twin tunnels under the centre of London from east to
west, costing £15,900,000,000 and involving a large
team of architects and engineers, will use existing
tracks and stations on the outskirts of the capital.
But of its total of thirty-seven stations, seven are new
subterranean stations to be constructed along the
21-kilometre tunnelled section of the route, which
extends below the West End and the City to Docklands.
    Comparisons will inevitably be drawn with the
inspirational commissioning programme of the Jubilee

line extension (JLE), completed at the millennium with Roland Paoletti as chief architect (see pp. 20–21, 38–39 and 48–49). A number of the architectural and engineering practices working on Crossrail stations – Weston Williamson at Paddington, John McAslan + Partners at Bond Street, Wilkinson Eyre Architects at Liverpool Street and Foster + Partners at Canary Wharf – are veterans of the JLE. But the Crossrail project is more clearly engineering-led than the JLE; there is, for example, to be a common vocabulary for all below-ground areas, with Grimshaw as architect-in-charge.

The Crossrail stations are, in fact, very different in character from any of those on the Underground system, not least because they are designed to handle full-length mainline trains – at least twenty-four an hour at peak times – which demand platforms 260 metres long. Each new station will be a point of interchange, whether with the Underground or Docklands Light Railway (as at Tottenham Court Road or Canary Wharf, for example), or with the Overground or other mainline rail services (as at Whitechapel and Liverpool Street).

Large stations demand large sites, and Crossrail has already made its mark on London, with substantial areas of demolition around Tottenham Court Road and Soho, Bond Street, Moorgate and Farringdon. The new station at Paddington is being sunk beneath Eastbourne Terrace, west of the Grade I-listed terminus by Isambard Kingdom Brunel. At Farringdon (architect: Aedas) the Crossrail project will produce London's busiest station, with more than 140 trains per hour on the Crossrail, Thameslink and Underground systems; the impact on that area of London is likely to be dramatic. At Liverpool Street, Wilkinson Eyre's new station will be located beneath the existing Liverpool Street and Moorgate tube stations. The new platforms at Whitechapel (architect: BDP) will be in deep tunnels, but a strikingly modelled above-ground ticket hall and concourse, complete with a 'green' roof, will provide vastly improved access to the Underground and create a new pedestrian route across the site. The station box at Canary Wharf (its architect, Foster + Partners, also responsible for the spectacular JLE station there; see pp. 20–21) will be sunk in the North Quay of the former West India Dock, with four levels of retail space above, the whole complex topped with a lightweight timber-lattice roof. The station will underpin the ongoing development of North Quay as an extension to Canary Wharf's office city.

Royal Assent was given to the Crossrail Act in 2008, and preliminary work was undertaken during 2009. In the autumn of 2010 the government confirmed that Crossrail was to go ahead, and work began in earnest on the central section, with the first trains due to run in 2017.

Opposite, top
The station at Tottenham Court Road, by Hawkins\Brown, is located below a major new commercial development.

Opposite, bottom
John McAslan + Partners' Bond Street station also involves substantial new above-ground development, designed to complement the surrounding conservation area.

Right
At Whitechapel, BDP's new ticket hall and concourse extend over the Underground platforms, incorporating a new pedestrian route across the site.

Opposite, top, and right
Dixon Jones's proposals
for Exhibition Road create
a new pedestrian spine for
'Albertopolis', one of London's
prime cultural quarters.

Opposite, bottom
The project removes the
existing road and pavement
and associated clutter in
favour of all-over paving
with extended tree-planting,
providing a coherent and
pleasant route between
South Kensington station
and Hyde Park.

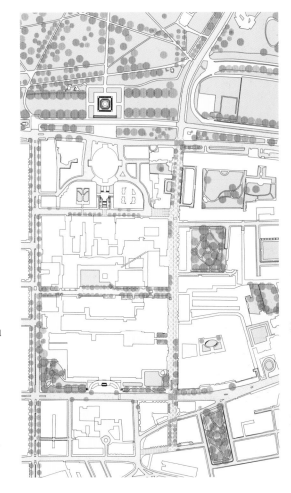

Exhibition Road is the spine of 'Albertopolis', the cultural and educational quarter in Kensington developed with the proceeds of the Great Exhibition of 1851 under the inspiration of Prince Albert. The Victoria and Albert and Natural History museums flank the southern end of the road. The Science Museum, Imperial College, Royal Albert Hall, Royal College of Art and Royal College of Music are located to the west. Every year, more than 11,500,000 people come to visit the museums and other institutions here. A high proportion of them arrive via the nearby South Kensington Underground station, which handles 30,000,000 passengers annually.

The inadequacy of the public realm around these institutions has long been recognized. The narrow pavements and heavy traffic are unattractive and often unsafe. The Royal Borough of Kensington and Chelsea, with project partners Westminster City Council and Transport for London, is transforming the streetscape of Exhibition Road in good time for the surge of visitors expected during the 2012 Olympic and Paralympic Games. A £28,000,000 project, designed by Dixon Jones and supported by Mayor Boris Johnson as part of his London's Great Outdoors manifesto (set out to improve public spaces in the city), is in progress to reduce traffic congestion and provide residents and visitors with more pedestrian space and better access to the museums. The project provides for a broad new pedestrian route extending from South Kensington station to Hyde Park,

with new crossings on Cromwell Road and Kensington Gore. Although still open to traffic, Exhibition Road will be paved as a single granite surface along its entire length, with kerbs removed – a strategy designed to limit vehicle speeds. Pedestrian space will be doubled, with visual and tactile delineators installed to help people distinguish between the 'safe zone' and the 20 mph 'traffic zone'.

In 2009, as part of the project, a number of traffic-management improvements around South Kensington station were completed, including unravelling the outdated one-way traffic system and creating a spacious pedestrian area for people using the station. At the end of the project Thurloe Street, which connects the Underground station to Exhibition Road, will be reserved largely for pedestrians.

Lifschutz Davidson made the clumsy Hungerford Bridge pedestrian-friendly by adding footbridges on both sides of the railway tracks. Their minimalism contrasts with the heaviness of the Victorian structure and recalls the elegance of the long-lost suspension bridge by Isambard Kingdom Brunel.

Hungerford Railway Bridge, built in 1864, is widely regarded as one of the worst eyesores in London – yet it seems destined to survive for many years to come. In 1986 Richard Rogers's visionary 'London as it could be' project proposed to replace the heavy and utilitarian Victorian railway bridge (which replaced an elegant suspension bridge by Isambard Kingdom Brunel) with a lightweight structure carrying a footbridge and monorail link, while closing the existing Charing Cross station. Terry Farrell's Embankment Place scheme subsequently cemented the station in place by covering the tracks with profitable office space, although the opening of the Jubilee line link to London Bridge and Waterloo makes Charing Cross an even more superfluous terminal.

The realized project was generated by the ongoing campaign to revitalize the South Bank arts centre site and to improve its connections to central London. Lifschutz Davidson's scheme, designed with structural engineers WSP, seeks to make the best use of the elephantine nineteenth-century structure, which carried a narrow pedestrian walkway on its eastern edge. Two new bridges flank the existing bridge, so that, for the first time, pedestrians are able to enjoy a view of Westminster from the Hungerford Bridge. The structural approach is as economical as that of the Victorians was cumbrous, and it evokes the spirit of Brunel and the 1951 Festival of Britain. The *in situ* concrete bridge decks are suspended on supporting steel rods from inclined 26.5-metre steel pylons sunk into the river bed. On the south side of the river, the bridge decks link directly to the terraces of the Royal Festival Hall (pp. 92–93).

Pragmatic rather than visionary, this project addresses a practical concern – that of encouraging people to cross to the South Bank – in a straightforward but incisive fashion. But the problem of Charing Cross remains: one day it should be closed and the tracks across the River Thames torn up.

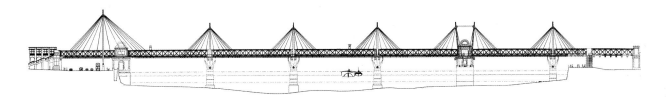

The site by the railway to the north of King's Cross station has been the subject of ambitious development proposals for nearly twenty-five years, after the closure of the huge goods depot that once occupied it. In 1987 plans to redevelop the area primarily as a new 'office city' became public, and London Regeneration Consortium, in conjunction with Foster + Partners (then Foster Associates), was selected to develop the masterplan. Their project for a large public park at the centre of the old goods yard, ringed by offices and blocks of flats and with landmark towers to the north, was killed off by the recession of the early 1990s.

In 2001 developer Argent, known for the successful Brindleyplace development, a mix of office and residential buildings by various architects on a brownfield site in central Birmingham, commissioned Allies and Morrison and Porphyrios Associates to prepare a new masterplan for the goods-yard site. It takes into account the new St Pancras International station (pp. 40–41) and the ongoing redevelopment of King's Cross by John McAslan + Partners (pp. 34–35), but its approach is far removed from that of Foster. The great park and towers have gone: this is to be a new city quarter linked to the districts surrounding it, a place of streets, squares and urban gardens in a recognizable London tradition. Connectivity is the principle, and new routes north from Euston into Camden Town and Islington traverse the site. The aim is to create that ever-elusive 'sense of place', with a balance of public and private spaces. The listed buildings, the most important of which is a magnificent granary by Lewis Cubitt (completed in 1852), are to be 'embedded' in the new fabric, not conspicuously preserved. The granary is being converted by Stanton Williams for use by Central St Martins, part of the University of the Arts London.

The masterplan, which won outline planning approval in 2006, provides for a mixed-use development, with offices concentrated to the south and housing to the north, with extensive retail space. Buildings are low- to medium-rise. The indications are that this scheme, one of the largest urban regeneration projects in Europe, will be in the Brindleyplace tradition, representing many styles and schools of thought; as many as sixty architects will be appointed to design buildings within the discipline of the masterplan. King's Cross Central will be judged not on its architectural variety, however, but on the degree to which it reinvents a tradition of urban design established in the nineteenth century by John Nash and the Cubitts.

Right and below
Stanton Williams' project for the University of the Arts London includes the conversion of a granary dating from 1852, as well as a complex of new buildings.

Opposite
The King's Cross Central masterplan will transform the former goods yard into a new urban quarter.

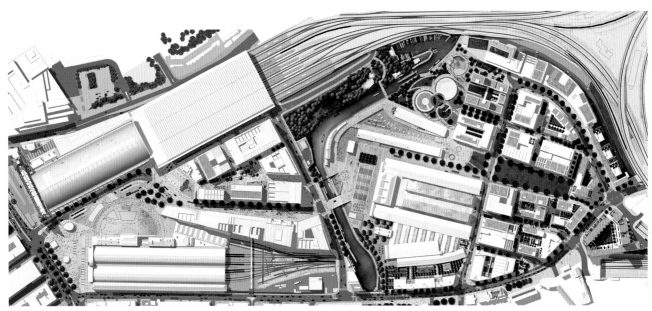

Below
The redevelopment includes
the remodelling of the
cluttered and claustrophobic
Underground station, with
reorganized circulation,
double-height spaces and
clean, pared-down finishes.

Opposite
The new western concourse
forms a broad arc extending
towards the reconstructed
St Pancras International
terminal and incorporating
the listed Great Northern
Hotel. Its lightweight roof
is a modern version of the
great Victorian station roofs.

This is one of a number of major development schemes
for London's historic railway termini. The reconstruction
of the adjacent St Pancras station (pp. 40–41) as the
terminus of the Channel Tunnel Rail Link and departure
point of the express shuttle to the 2012 Olympics site has
given impetus to the scheme. At the same time, King's
Cross Central (pp. 32–33) looks set finally to realize
the development potential of the former railway lands
immediately to the north of the station, the subject of
abortive planning proposals for nearly twenty-five years.

King's Cross is the terminus of the east-coast main
line from Scotland and the North. The station was built
in 1851–52 to designs by Lewis Cubitt, its severely
functional form contrasting – in a way that met with the
approval of modernist critics – with the ornate mass
of Sir George Gilbert Scott's later Midland Grand Hotel .
(St Pancras Chambers; pp. 150–51). The original diagram

of the station placed departures on the western side and arrivals on the eastern, with the space between used as sidings for railway carriages. Even after the addition of more platforms, the layout of the station presented operational challenges, and passenger facilities were minimal. In the 1970s the clutter of temporary buildings that had developed at the southern end of the station was replaced by a new concourse that – although improving on the existing accretions – was banal in design and a poor addition to the Grade I-listed Victorian station.

John McAslan's project removes the 1970s concourse and opens the splendidly austere southern façade fully to view. A new concourse on the western side of the station incorporates the listed Great Northern Hotel and provides connections to St Pancras and the rebuilt King's Cross St Pancras Underground station. Developed in partnership with Arup, the roof of the new concourse is a structural tour de force: extremely lightweight, column-free, and a worthy successor to the great station roofs of the nineteenth century. Cecil Balmond of Arup, who advised on the designs, describes it as 'a retina of diamond cells, capable of opacity, transparency, and a widening and narrowing horizon as the curvature changes from outer rim into plunging interior tunnel. As the roof converges, the pattern closes and slips down like a mantle to the station entrance.' The site of the 1970s concourse is laid out as a new public square, and the previously busy road in front of the station is narrowed and tamed. Inside the station, public spaces have been extended and the entire structure renovated.

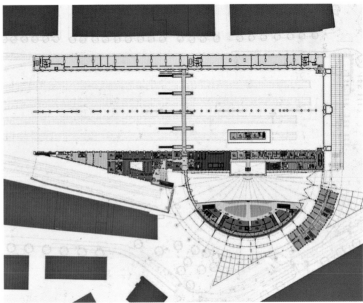

Opposite
The spare structure of the bridge has a sculptural elegance that contrasts with the solidity of Tate Modern.

Above, left
Structural detail, with a view up the River Thames towards Blackfriars.

Above, right
The bridge links the City and St Paul's Cathedral with the regenerated Bankside area around Tate Modern.

Norman Foster's victory in the competition for this bridge, which connects St Paul's and the City with Tate Modern (pp. 100–101), seemed effortless, part of his sure hold on key London millennium projects. Developed in collaboration with Arup and the eminent sculptor Sir Anthony Caro, the bridge was scheduled to open early in 2000 to service the new Tate. It did open – for a weekend – but was then closed for more than a year while significant technical adjustments were carried out to counter a pronounced wobble that occurred when large numbers of people crossed it on its inaugural weekend. Foster's detractors crowed and there was an element of *Schadenfreude* in some of the other criticisms made of the scheme.

Yet the problems of the bridge flowed from the high technical and aesthetic ambitions that underlay the project. This was to be the first new Thames crossing since the completion of Tower Bridge more than a century before, and the first Thames bridge ever to be purely for the use of pedestrians. The Thames is a big river, far wider as it runs through the City towards the sea than Dublin's Liffey or Paris's Seine. Foster's design capitalized on the thrill of being suspended high above the water, in the midst of a 320-metre span.

The basic form is that of a suspension bridge, with two Y-shaped armatures supporting cables that run alongside the 4-metre-wide aluminium deck, which is engaged by means of steel transverse arms. The cables rise no more than 2.3 metres above the deck, so that the effect is very different from that of the typical suspension bridge: Foster aimed to create a thin ribbon of metal, a direct statement of the act of bridging the water. By night, the goal was to make the bridge a blade of light. Those crossing were guaranteed uninterrupted views along the river, while the slenderness of the structure addressed the criticisms of those who feared that it would intrude on these precious views. In the quest for maximum structural economy, the design was perhaps too finely tuned. Foster's daring has, however, been vindicated, now that the bridge has successfuly been brought into use.

The integrated transport facility at North Greenwich was planned and commenced long before the emergence in 1996 of plans for the Millennium Festival and Dome. Initially, the new station was intended to serve Port Greenwich, a huge residential and commercial development by British Gas of the former gasworks site on the Greenwich Peninsula, but that project fell victim to the 1990s recession and was never resurrected. The decision to proceed with the Jubilee line extension connection was fortuitous: it made the Dome (now the O2; see pp. 138–39) possible and serves as the hub for the regeneration of the peninsula and for public transport links to a wide swathe of south-east London and north Kent.

Will Alsop, then working with his former partner John Lyall, was approached in 1990 to develop proposals for what is one of the largest stations on the extension: it is 358 metres long and has three platforms. The practice developed the project with engineers Robert Benaim & Associates, with detailed design development and construction overseen by the in-house team of the extension's architect-in-chief, Roland Paoletti. However, the station bears all the marks of Alsop's approach: colourful, strongly modelled, flamboyant and with a potent popular appeal. It is probably the Jubilee line extension station that has won the most plaudits from the travelling public.

The first idea was to build a station in an open cutting, surrounded by a green square and with the concourse suspended in the void. It would have been stunning, but the decision was made to give the station a lid. Construction began in 1995. The original concept was developed in the revised scheme, with the ticket hall becoming a great steel-clad 'boat' hanging in space, with views down to the platforms, which are accommodated within a spectacular train hall. The roof is supported on twenty-one pairs of 13-metre-high in situ concrete columns in V formations, clad in blue mosaic. A huge wall of backlit cobalt-blue glass provides intriguing reflections of escalators, people and trains.

The station has no expression at ground level. The logical course might have been to commission the surface-level bus station from the same architect, but it went to Foster + Partners as late as 1996 and was built in little more than a year. Tony Hunt's structure cantilevers off column supports on the edge of the station, with the 6500-square-metre roof supported on steel 'trees'. The image is that of a great bird. Although Foster and Alsop have very different approaches, their respective contributions at North Greenwich work well together, and the bus station, along with that at Canada Water designed by Eva Jiricna, represents a move towards civilizing travel conditions for London's long-suffering bus users.

Below, left
The blue motif that runs through the scheme is expressed in the mosaic applied to the wall surfaces and V-shaped columns.

Below, right
At platform level the underbelly of the passenger concourse is clearly visible.

Opposite
The industrial aesthetic of the service staircase contrasts with the backlit cobalt-blue glass wall behind.

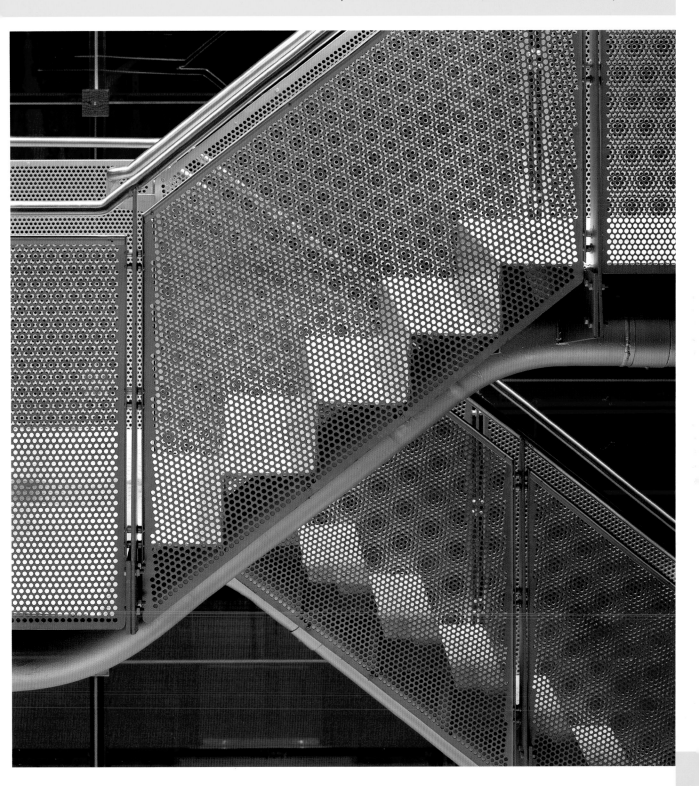

After seven years of construction, two years late and heavily over-budget, the Channel Tunnel opened in 1994, carrying Eurostar rail services from Paris and Brussels to Nicholas Grimshaw's Waterloo International station. On the English side of the Tunnel, Eurostar trains used existing tracks, rather than dedicated high-speed routes, which had been created on the Continental side. The decision to route Britain's own high-speed link to the east of London, serving a new station at Stratford and terminating at either King's Cross or St Pancras stations, was made as early as 1991, and subsequently confirmed by the governments of both John Major and Tony Blair.

The regeneration of the East End and the Thames Estuary was seen as a major spin-off of the proposal (which originated in studies by Arup), and there was also the possibility of providing through services to the Midlands and the North, although this seems to have been abandoned. The Channel Tunnel Rail Link (CTRL) was procured by the Private Finance Initiative route, and the London and Continental Railways (LCR) consortium won the bid to build the 108-kilometre link, which involved extensive tunnelling and other engineering challenges. St Pancras was confirmed as the final destination of Eurostar in 1994, with the abandonment of Norman Foster's proposal for a station below King's Cross, to be partly funded by development of the disused goods-yard site to the north (now the site of King's Cross Central; pp. 32–33).

Designs for an extended St Pancras were produced by Nick Derbyshire, who had led the British Rail architectural team for the rebuilding of Liverpool Street station. The plans were subsequently developed

in a new masterplan by Foster + Partners, the principle being that of a straightforward, flat-roofed shed 220 metres long, extending north of the arched shed designed by W.H. Barlow and completed in 1876. Foster's proposals were taken to detailed design and construction stage by the Rail Link Engineering (RLE) team, which – led by Alastair Lansley (who worked on the Liverpool Street project) – was responsible for the construction of the entire £5,000,000,000-plus CTRL project. Construction work began in 1998, and late in 2007 Eurostar services were transferred to St Pancras International.

A genuine piece of railway architecture, impressive for its scale and generous natural light, the new train shed may nonetheless seem a little prosaic alongside Barlow's magnificent creation. But the strategy for adapting the latter for its new role was both highly imaginative and rigorously logical. The platforms at St Pancras are elevated above street level as a result of a decision made in the 1860s to route the new Midland line above Regent's Canal rather than under it. The station's vaulted undercroft, originally used to store beer barrels brought from Burton upon Trent, houses check-in facilities for Eurostar, with the Channel Tunnel trains running the full length of the extended train shed above. A cut-out section allows views down into the undercroft. Trains serving the Midlands and suburban services, including fast Kent commuter trains using the CTRL route, are restricted to the new shed. The Underground station that serves both King's Cross and St Pancras has been reconstructed in line with this strategy and in anticipation of the reconstruction of King's Cross station (see pp. 34–35).

With a direct, express rail service from the new station to the 2012 Olympics site, St Pancras is emerging as the focus of a regenerated London quarter.

Opposite and far right
The single-span iron-and-glass roof of W.H. Barlow's arched train shed has been painstakingly restored, its trusses painted sky-blue as they would originally have been.

Right, top
The new train shed extends the existing structure to the north.

Right, bottom
The public spaces have been reorganized, with a new entrance complete with lightweight canopy.

SOMERSET HOUSE WC2

London is a city where, beyond the green expanses of the Royal Parks, there are few oases of quiet away from the noise of the streets; the squares of the West End, for example, were traditionally private places. In common with the British Museum's Queen Elizabeth II Great Court (pp. 86–87), the Somerset House project is about turning underused private spaces into a major extension of the public domain. The project has also created impressive new spaces for the display of works of art, making Somerset House the nucleus of a new cultural and educational campus.

Somerset House was never strictly a public building. Sir William Chambers's monumental complex of 1776–96 looks like a royal palace but was intended as offices for civil servants, with the fine rooms facing the Strand planned as accommodation for the newly constituted Royal Academy and Society of Antiquaries (which subsequently moved to Burlington House). There were no other grand interiors, and the impressive central court and riverside terrace were used only by those who worked or (in the case of the Navy commissioners) lived in Somerset House. Chambers's grand plan was completed long after his death with the construction of new wings to the east (for King's College, which opened in 1829) and west (designed by Sir James Pennethorne in 1856 for the Inland Revenue).

The University of London's Courtauld Institute of Art and Galleries moved to Somerset House in 1990, occupying the fine rooms and other spaces along the Strand frontage. In 1997 the Somerset House Trust was established with the aim of gradually bringing the remainder of the site into public use as, potentially, London's Louvre. By the end of 2000, a series of major elements within the overall masterplan had been achieved.

Peter Inskip + Peter Jenkins Architects' galleries for the Gilbert Collection occupy the monumental spaces below the riverside terrace and part of the basement of the South Building, and can be accessed via Chambers's Great Arch (once a water gate, but now beached on the Embankment) as well as from the Great Court. The design strategy combines restoration of the original structure with unequivocally contemporary interventions in a broadly high-tech manner. The economy of this approach provides an appropriate showcase for an extraordinary range of objects, ranging from the exquisite to the kitsch.

Donald Insall Associates' reworking of the Great Court included major below-ground works – lavatories are provided, for example, for large audiences attending open-air concerts – as well as the resurfacing of the court with setts, replacing institutional asphalt on what was a civil-service car park. In the South Building, a restaurant, bar and shops have been provided as well as galleries. Until 2007 these displayed a rotating selection of works from St Petersburg's State Hermitage Museum, and they are now used for temporary exhibitions.

Dixon Jones's fountain, which forms the magical centrepiece of the Great Court, was commissioned in 1998, and its choreographed battery of fifty-five water jets is a stunning invention, enjoyable and elegant. Less successful is the same firm's terrace cafe: its mannered woven acrylic canopies are flimsy on a windy day, and the bridge link between the riverside terrace and Waterloo Bridge shows little regard for the geometries of Giles Gilbert Scott's bridge abutments.

The Inland Revenue continues to occupy the Pennethorne block and wings along the west sides of the Great Court, but the east side of the court is now occupied by King's College, which sought expansion space as part of a development plan by Inskip & Jenkins. It took the determination of François Mitterrand to banish the French foreign ministry from the Louvre: who has the clout to clear the tax inspectors out of Somerset House?

The terrace cafe and the choreographed fountains in the Great Court are among the most striking interventions in this historic ensemble.

Below
The project will include new waterside public spaces and parks, providing suitable surroundings for those expected to flood into the area for the Olympic and Paralympic Games, and lasting improvements for residents.

Opposite
Stratford City transforms neglected industrial land into a mixed-use quarter, focusing on the new International station.

The 73-hectare Stratford City site is one of the most extensive exercises in urban regeneration in Europe. The planning application lodged in 2004 and subsequently approved was the largest ever submitted in London. Developers Stanhope, Multiplex and Westfield, partners with London & Continental Railways in the development consortium for the site, proposed 1,200,000 square metres of residential, retail and commercial development. More than 30,000 people are likely to work there, and there will be homes for 11,000.

The impetus to develop the site west of Stratford town centre, which was formerly occupied by a railway works and freight yards, came from the routing of the Channel Tunnel Rail Link (CTRL) through Stratford (which already has mainline, Underground and Docklands Light Railway connections). The focus of the project is the new Stratford International station, which is served by Eurostar and will also act as the principal means of access for spectators at the 2012 Olympic Games. London's victory in July 2005 in the contest to stage the Games created fears of a conflict of interest between the developers of Stratford City and the Olympic organizers (now the Olympic Delivery Authority), who were charged with masterplanning the selected Games site in the lower Lea Valley, extending from Stratford to the Thames (pp. 16–19). An agreement between the two parties, however, neatly integrated the Olympic Village with the residential element of Stratford City, so that construction of the athletes' housing (with accommodation for 17,000 competitors) could begin promptly.

The masterplan by Fletcher Priest Architects, Arup and West 8 is based on the idea of a series of distinct neighbourhoods, and has involved the commissioning of a number of architectural practices, with the emphasis on high-quality architecture and landscaping. The latter was modelled early on in the project using the huge amounts of spoil excavated from the CTRL tunnel and

Stratford station box: if spread evenly, it was estimated, it would raise the ground level across the whole site by about 6 metres. Good connections, mixed-use provision and the creation of generous public spaces are the stated aims; provision is made for a boulevard to connect the international railway station to the existing town centre. By the autumn of 2010 many of the retail units had been handed over for fit-out, and the whole scheme was expected to open in September 2011.

This page
The terminal includes impressive new public spaces and convenient links to public transport, which will be the principal means of access for travellers.

Opposite
Rationally (although conventionally) organized, Heathrow's new Terminal 5 is a spectacular shed in the tradition both of Richard Rogers's earlier work and of nineteenth-century rail termini.

Richard Rogers's new terminal at Madrid's Barajas Airport, winner of the RIBA Stirling Prize in 2006, opened eight years after it was commissioned in 1997. In comparison, the period of twenty years from commissioning to opening at Terminal 5, Heathrow Airport, seems to underline the perversity of the British planning system. There were widespread objections to a new terminal and also to the expansion of air traffic into London, but a hugely expensive public inquiry, convened in 1993, resulted in approval for the project being given in 2001.

The character of the project has changed radically over time. The single-level terminal proposed in Rogers's competition-winning scheme of 1989 was abandoned after the public inquiry ruled against the use of greenbelt land, beyond the A3044, for parking. A redesign produced a scheme in which arriving and departing passengers were segregated on two levels, with 'canyons' (a device used also at Barajas) drawing natural light into the heart of the building. By 1999 these, too, had been removed in favour of a 'shed' in the tradition of the Centre Georges Pompidou in Paris by Rogers and Renzo Piano, completed as early as 1977.

The Heathrow scheme, recognizing the reality of air travel in the twenty-first century, caters for the dramatic changes that will inevitably arise as security tightens, airlines come and go, new check-in technology is introduced, larger aircraft are put into use, and retailing – the prime source of income for airport operators – expands inexorably. Shops, offices, passenger lounges and other facilities in the new terminal are conceived as free-standing units that can be dismantled and reconfigured as required – as in a theatre, where the scenery changes regularly.

This is a shed on a dramatic scale, capable of handling 30,000,000 passengers annually. The vast majority of them arrive by public transport, using the Underground and bus services. One 85,000-square-metre satellite building was constructed in tandem with the terminal, and there is provision for a second when needed.

Architecturally, Terminal 5 provides a spectacular experience for passengers in the tradition of the great nineteenth-century train sheds: the departure area, under the elegant double-curve roof, is as dramatic as any comparable space in the world – a far remove from the cramped facilities found in some of the older Heathrow terminals (which face redevelopment). The terminal is designed to be easily navigated by outgoing and incoming passengers: it takes just two minutes to reach the check-in zone from the rail platforms.

There were moments when it appeared that Terminal 5 could be 'value-engineered' beyond recognition, with any exciting features dropped at the request of cost consultants, and the role of Richard Rogers Partnership (now Rogers Stirk Harbour + Partners) reduced to the provision of an external envelope. Indeed, four other architectural practices were involved with various aspects of the project. The completed terminal is, however, recognizably a Rogers building and forms an impressive gateway to London.

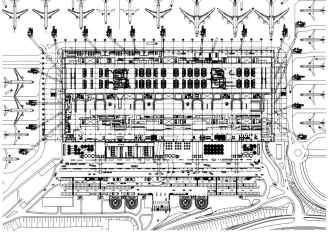

Opposite
The banks of escalators set amid the steel-and-concrete structure of the deep station activate one of the most exciting spaces on the Jubilee line extension.

Below
The District and Circle line platforms had to be accommodated between the Jubilee line platforms below and Portcullis House above.

Bottom
The Jubilee line platforms have the distinctive steel panels and glazed safety screen that are common throughout the Jubilee line extension.

Right
East–west section, demonstrating how the station provides the structure of Portcullis House above.

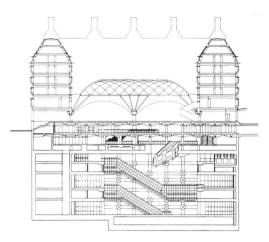

At first sight, the monumentally austere interior of Westminster station, completely rebuilt as part of the Jubilee line extension project, might appear to have little in common with Michael Hopkins's beautifully crafted Portcullis House, of which it forms a vast undercroft. Yet the two projects were designed and built in tandem and are structurally indivisible.

An interchange with the District line at Westminster was planned for the Jubilee line extension from the beginning. The existing station was part of London's first underground railway, opened in the 1860s, and had to be accommodated (and kept open) as the 40-metre-deep box for the extension was excavated around it. The proximity of Big Ben, which stands a street's width away from one of the biggest holes in London, further complicated the engineering of the station.

Lowering the level of the District line tracks by 300 millimetres – no mean operation in itself – secured headroom for a new ticket hall one level below the central courtyard of Portcullis House. The District line is a level below that. The Jubilee line extension is accessed via banks of escalators (seventeen in total) threading through the main structural columns, with the deep platforms stacked one above the other outside the edge of the station box.

The predominant impression of the station is one of constant movement. Trimmings are kept to a minimum. The aesthetic is formed by the raw materials of the structure: rough and polished concrete, and stainless steel. Architecture and engineering come together in a fine balance, fulfilling an ambition that lay at the very centre of the Jubilee line extension project.

CULTURE

6

CAMDEN

18

4

3

ISLINGTON

12

29
11 17

22

13

20

21

KENSINGTON
AND CHELSEA

2 15

19

WESTMINSTER

LAMBE

HACKNEY

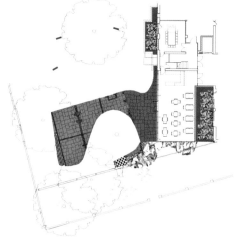

The building now housing Camden Arts Centre was designed by Arnold S. Tayler and opened in 1897 as the Hampstead Central Library. It is an attractive, if modest, building in an Arts and Crafts Tudor manner, although the original interiors were largely lost when it was gutted during the Second World War. The library closed after the new central library at Swiss Cottage, designed by Basil Spence, opened in the mid-1960s. The building was converted into an arts centre, a role it has fulfilled with considerable success for more than thirty years, attracting up to 45,000 visitors annually.

Tony Fretton's project provides additional facilities for users of the centre without changing the essential character of the place as an exhibition and education venue with close links to the local community. As a prelude to the project, the centre commissioned Muf to interview building users and staff, research the history of the site and include their findings in the brief. Muf was subsequently responsible for the new layout of the garden to the rear, which had previously not been accessible to the public.

The key element in Fretton's project is the provision of a new step-free, ground-floor public entrance area facing Finchley Road – the former entrance on Arkwright Road, up steep steps, has been closed – with direct access to the cafe and bookshop and views right into the building. This radical intervention involved cutting large openings into the existing façade. Upstairs, at gallery level, the project assumed a very different character, one of renovation of the fabric and renewal of the services, with the spaces remaining essentially unchanged. Work was completed in time for the centre's reopening early in 2004. The final phase of the £4,600,000 project – the installation of a wall comprising ten panels of glass 40 millimetres thick and 2.8 metres high, facing Finchley Road and forming an acoustic barrier – was completed in the autumn of 2005.

Muf's garden scheme refers to the history of the area, revealing the footprints of houses that once stood on the garden site, and using a mix of paving and planting to explore the interface between nature and architecture. A paved terrace extends from the cafe into the sloping garden.

At quite modest cost (funding came from the National Lottery, the local authority and private donors), this exemplary project has re-equipped an important local amenity not only to continue in its established role but also to expand its constituency and influence.

Opposite, left and bottom right
A glazed wall facing Finchley Road screens the refurbished Camden Arts Centre from the noise of traffic and forms a public marker for the project.

Opposite, top right
Previously disused garden space has been transformed to a design by Muf.

Right
The gallery spaces have been re-equipped and renovated, but are essentially unchanged.

The first phase of the Natural History Museum's Darwin Centre, designed by HOK, opened in 2002. The centre houses the museum's vast zoological archive – 22,000,000 specimens of animals, birds and fish preserved in alcohol, some of which were collected 250 years ago – and allows, for the first time, a degree of public access to this internationally renowned collection. The second phase of the project contains the entomological and botanical collections, as well as laboratories and offices. Danish practice C.F. Møller Architects won the commission in competition in 2001. Its new building, opened in 2009, replaces a utilitarian interwar block tacked on to Alfred Waterhouse's masterpiece, completed in 1881.

With a project cost of nearly £80,000,000 and covering 19,500 square metres, the new building forms an effective link between the original museum and HOK's block. Its transparency renders it a relatively neutral neighbour to the Waterhouse building. At the back is an eight-storey atrium overlooking the museum's Wildlife Garden. Through the all-glass, west-facing façade, the 'cocoon' that forms the core – indeed, the *raison d'être* – of the building is visible. A massive structure that cannot be seen in its entirety from any one point, it symbolizes the collections of insects it contains and dominates the surrounding public spaces. Inside is a series of environmentally controlled storage spaces for the precious specimens. A route for visitors winds up, over, around and through the archives, offering glimpses into the laboratories and allowing the public to see and experience spaces that were previously out of bounds, without disturbing the scholarly research work going on inside them. One of the benefits of the scheme is improved circulation within the museum.

The design of the cocoon involved intensive exploration of its geometry and structure. Its walls are 30 centimetres thick to ensure stable environmental conditions inside. The storage spaces are necessarily mechanically cooled and ventilated, but the emphasis in the project has been on a low-energy agenda, with a hierarchy of servicing solutions.

Following on from Richard MacCormac's addition to the Science Museum, and work by Norman Foster (pp. 180–83) and Kohn Pedersen Fox for Imperial College, not to mention HOK's first phase of the Darwin Centre, this building adds significantly to the sum of high-quality new architecture in 'Albertopolis', the group of cultural institutions in Kensington.

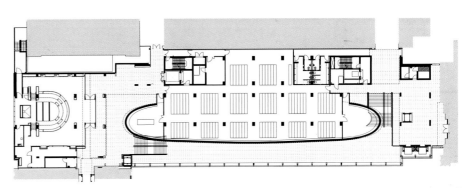

Burd Haward was approached in 2005 with an unusual brief: to design a mixed-use development combining a concert hall with a cafe-bar and a restaurant, shoehorned into a tight site at the heart of Camden Town. The clients particularly wanted to create a venue with an informal ethos that could attract new, younger audiences to classical music: the Forge's programme is freely leavened with jazz, folk and world music. The restaurant and bar, Sicilian-themed, along with a small number of flats, were to provide a degree of funding for the venture. (The same agenda, on a larger scale, underpinned Kings Place; see pp. 76–77.)

Having ruled out the idea of converting the existing buildings, which were undistinguished and dilapidated, Burd Haward produced designs for a new scheme. The existing central courtyard was glazed over to connect a three-storey building (containing cafe, restaurant and flats) on Delancey Street to the recital hall. The latter, a double-height space seating 120, has its own entrance

in Delancey Passage. The courtyard doubles as a foyer for the hall and an extension to the restaurant. The big idea is that the two work together: on occasions, an event will spread across the ground floor.

The internal spaces, generously day-lit and detailed to a standard that belies the modest (£2,500,000) budget, are a delight, and the courtyard, with its 'living wall', is the key to a low-energy services strategy. The brick-clad elevation to Delancey Street is an excellent piece of contemporary contextual design. The architect sees it as mediating between shabby Camden High Street and the elegant terraces of Regent's Park. In fact, it is a good example of the way in which the best contemporary architects – and Burd Haward is a young practice – work easily and unaffectedly in tune with the city.

Below
The Forge sits comfortably in the variegated context of Camden Town.

Opposite, top
The section shows the relationship between the cafe-bar (left) and the performance space (right).

Opposite, bottom
The two spaces can be used in tandem, with the removal of internal partitions.

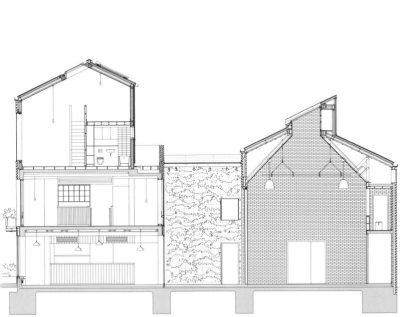

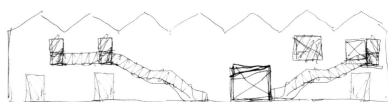

Opposite
The studio takes its cue from the simple industrial sheds found in this area of London, with saw-toothed roofs providing ample north light. The first-floor studios are accessed via external metal staircases.

Right
The main internal space is lofty and functional, a workshop for the fabrication of artworks in heavy-duty materials.

The continued paucity of built works by David Chipperfield in Britain – the BBC Scotland building in Glasgow (2006) is his largest completed to date, although several are under construction at the time of writing – is extraordinary, given the formidable international reputation of an architect whose work seems continually to scale new heights in terms of both refinement and inventiveness. Chipperfield's work has an apparently effortless appropriateness that reflects his intuitive feeling for materials and strong sense of place.

Antony Gormley is not only one of the most celebrated of living British sculptors, but also an artist with a remarkable facility for communicating with the public: his *Angel of the North* is a popular landmark in the north-east. Gormley's studio is located above the railway cutting that leads into King's Cross, in an area of industrial sheds, and its design was clearly strongly influenced by the no-nonsense character of the locality. The studio is a workplace – Gormley does not live on the site – and at first glance appears to be simply a highly functional container for the conception and production of works of art, although it is soon obvious that it is something altogether more sophisticated. Gormley's work is often very large in scale, so generous spaces were vital, but smaller, more intimate studios and offices were also specified in the brief. The work that goes on here ranges from sketching and discussion to the assembly of large pieces of sculpture. The galvanized-steel staircases that are the most distinctive feature of the exterior lead up from an enclosed entrance yard to upper-floor studios at both ends of the building, bookending the full-height main studio. All these spaces benefit from even light from the north, while the main façade of the building is punctuated by a series of window openings, irregularly but far from artlessly disposed.

The outcome of a close collaboration between architect and client – a relationship that was both fertile and, at times, tense – the studio can be read as Chipperfield's passionate counterblast against the fad for 'icons' that gripped the architectural world at the beginning of the twenty-first century. Chipperfield's first

instinct was for a flat-roofed structure, but it was the absolute need for perfect daylight that drove him back to the classic saw-toothed factory form. He has described the completed building as 'a pastiche of a nineteenth-century building, a kind of perfect version of a building that you should be able to find, but when you start looking it is actually very difficult'. But the studio is less pastiche than a fascinating commentary on London's neglected industrial vernacular.

London is full of lost theatres. The Hackney Empire in east London could have been one of them had it not been for the local community, which loved the place and did not want to lose it, and a cast of prominent outsiders who rallied to the cause of saving and reinvigorating it. The playwright and actor Harold Pinter, for example, who was born yards from the 'wonderful' theatre, recalled his parents taking him to see the comedian Max Miller on stage there. Comedian Paul Merton commented of the Empire: 'It's been an absolute joy and has reminded me of why I do what I do.' Famous performers from Marie Lloyd to Ralph Fiennes have trod its boards.

The Empire is a significant work of the great theatre architect Frank Matcham. It was constructed (in thirty-eight weeks) in 1901, with seats for 2800, and launched some of the greatest stars of music hall. By the 1980s, however, after years in use as a bingo hall, it faced demolition. Impresario Roland Muldoon started a rescue operation, with the building vested in a charitable trust. A mixed programme was presented, ranging from stand-up comedy and world music to traditional pantomime and opera. An architectural competition held in 1997 was won by Tim Ronalds, with Homa and Sima Farjadi. After it became apparent that the project was too costly to get National Lottery backing, Tim Ronalds Architects developed a somewhat reduced version (costing under £20,000,000), and the actor and comedian Griff Rhys Jones led a successful fund-raising campaign. The auditorium reopened early in 2004 and the scheme was fully completed in the autumn of that year.

The project combines restoration of the historic theatre with new build. Services needed total renewal, and facilities for both audience and performers were dire. Aspects that did not trouble Matcham, for example access for the disabled, had to be addressed. A key requirement was gaining more space on the cramped site in Mare Street. Fortunately it was possible to acquire the corner site next to the theatre; the undistinguished pub that stood there was demolished and a new block constructed, with a large bar on the ground floor and a hospitality/function room and small studio theatre on the upper levels. The new building also provides additional access to the auditorium, and its exterior

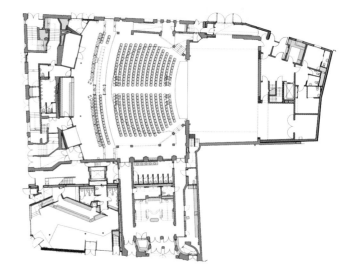

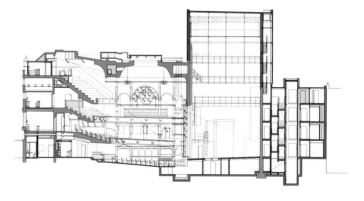

features the first use in London of large supergraphics in the style of American architect Robert Venturi. The 3.5-metre-high letters spelling out the name of the theatre are made of terracotta, in common with the external ornament on Matcham's building.

Although the Empire is listed Grade II*, English Heritage (the government's adviser on the historic environment) allowed a radical reconstruction of the entire backstage domain, with a big new flytower clad in fritted glass panels. A new get-in area gives lorries direct access to the stage for the installation and removal of scenery, and new dressing-rooms finally offer performers reasonably decent accommodation. The Matcham auditorium and front-of-house areas remain fundamentally unchanged. A restoration of the 1901 colour scheme was considered, but research revealed that the original hues were extremely pale and at odds with the current taste among the public for rich and warm theatre interiors, so a revised version of the scheme done in the 1960s was carried out. One of the great strengths of the project is the fact that the Empire appears to have been little altered, instead merely freshened up. This is a transformation operation that wears its colours lightly.

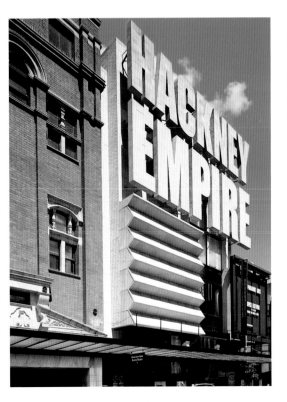

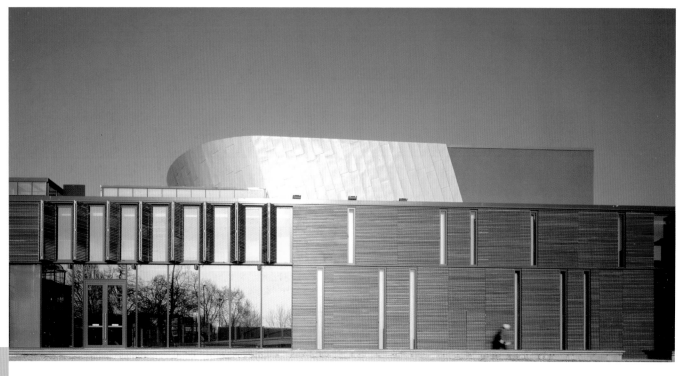

The Hampstead Theatre was the first entirely new theatre to be built in London since the completion of Denys Lasdun's National Theatre on the South Bank in 1975. It provides a well-equipped permanent home for an institution that has built up a striking artistic reputation over nearly forty years despite using distinctly makeshift premises.

By the 1990s the Hampstead Theatre's extended Portakabin next to the Swiss Cottage Baths and Library was in a poor state. Bennetts Associates was commissioned as early as 1994 to work on plans for a new theatre, initially on the same site, but it soon became clear that there were advantages in relocating it to the north, close to Eton Avenue, where it would replace an unsightly block of public conveniences. Bennetts subsequently produced a masterplan for the entire site, in line with Camden Council's aim to regenerate the area. In the 1960s Basil Spence had proposed a new town hall for Camden at Swiss Cottage, alongside the baths and library, but it was never realized. Much of the site therefore remained unresolved and rather unpleasant leftover open space, shut off from the street. The baths have now been demolished, while the library, a listed building, has been refurbished by John McAslan + Partners. A new swimming pool by Farrells has been built, together with housing (of very routine character), and the landscape plan for the site has been developed by Gustafson Porter.

The new theatre, which was finally built in 2000–2003 with the aid of National Lottery funding, contains a single elliptical auditorium with flexible seating for up to 330 people, aiming to retain the sense of intimacy that was the great strength of the old theatre while doubling seating capacity. The stage, adaptable for proscenium or open-plan productions, and workshop facilities are vastly improved, as are the dressing-rooms and offices. There is also a dedicated rehearsal space and education room, which can also be used as a small studio theatre.

The main entrance is directly from Eton Avenue. Inside, it becomes apparent to the visitor that the building has three storeys, two above ground and one below. Bridges and ramps channel audiences into the auditorium. Mechanical services are concentrated at basement level in a space that extends below the adjacent landscaped park. The aim was to provide access to the building at street level, removing the need for ramps or lifts. Achieving this meant securing consent from other building owners to move the car-park ramp serving an adjacent office block: it now runs through the basement of the theatre.

The auditorium reads as a strongly modelled solid mass, clad in matt zinc, clearly rising through a largely transparent pavilion (where areas of timber slatting punctuate the glazing), which contains the foyers and other public spaces. Finishes in the foyer areas are simple and durable – steel, concrete and timber – with lighting devised by Martin Richman dramatizing the space. The auditorium is lined in timber, with colour adding warmth and texture. The architect cites the rustic Georgian theatre at Richmond, North Yorkshire, as an exemplar for the comfortable but informal ambience they sought to create.

Bennetts Associates had no experience of theatre design when it tackled this project, and perhaps that was an advantage. The building reflects close collaboration between client and architect. The move to new premises has reinforced the position of this famously innovative theatre on London's drama scene, and Swiss Cottage has gained an impressive new public landmark.

Opposite, top
The zinc-clad mass of the auditorium emerges powerfully inside the building, where audience amenities are provided on two levels.

Opposite, bottom
The strongly modelled, elliptical form of the auditorium sits within the rectangular frame, which contains foyers and backstage facilities.

Below, left, and opposite,
top right
Allies and Morrison's carefully considered extension takes its cue in terms of scale and materials from Charles Harrison Townsend's original building of 1901.

Below, right, and opposite,
top left and bottom
The extension is arranged around a double-height space from which cafe, shop, education spaces and new galleries are accessed.

The Horniman, tucked away in the south London suburb of Forest Hill, is one of the most idiosyncratic of the capital's smaller museums in terms of both its architecture and its contents (a mix of ethnography, stuffed animals and musical instruments). It is a well-loved local institution, established for 'the recreation, instruction and enjoyment' of south Londoners, but it is not on the tourist trail. Its original building, however, opened in 1901, is a remarkable and – for Britain – unusual example of the Art Nouveau style, designed by Charles Harrison Townsend for philanthropist founder Frederick Horniman.

The museum stands next to a public park, also created by Horniman, but, until the completion of the new scheme, it turned its back to the park, and could be entered only from the busy London Road. Allies and Morrison was commissioned to develop expansion plans in 1995. The brief was to provide a new gallery for temporary exhibitions, an education centre, a cafe and a shop. Accessibility had to be addressed as part of a major development programme that also saw the repair and refurbishment of the original building. The decision

was made to reorientate the museum so that the main entrance is now from the park.

Allies and Morrison's extension, stone-fronted and with a metal-clad curved roof, takes its form and scale from Townsend's original: to the gardens, for example, it is faced in red brick. Inside, a day-lit, double-height space provides access to all parts of the building. The cafe, shop and education rooms are at ground level, with the new galleries, including a space specially designed for displaying musical instruments, below (actually at street level, since the slope on the site is dramatic). To the north, the building opens up to a paved court – where a restored Victorian conservatory provides a venue for social events – and to the park beyond.

This is a finely crafted, highly sensitive scheme that integrates old and new painlessly and brings light and air to the mysterious world of the Horniman. Not that the character of the original has been diluted: it is still possible to use Townsend's entrance, up steps from the street. The amenities of the museum, which is a real community asset, have been vastly improved, and a Victorian institution given a new lease of life.

The day-lit interior of Hothouse is animated by irregular window openings. The main elevation is clad in brick.

The site for this innovative community arts building is at the north-eastern edge of Hackney's London Fields: an oddly shaped slice of former industrial land, hard up against a busy railway line. The project was commissioned by Free Form Arts Trust, which was established in the 1980s to promote the visual arts as an aid to social cohesion and regeneration, and initially operated from a scattered collection of small buildings. The brief was to provide an integrated base for the trust, with offices, gallery space, studios and workshops, but budgetary restrictions meant that the project had to be phased (the first phase opening in 2003), and was completed only in 2007.

The building responds brilliantly to the awkward site with a boomerang-shaped plan. The elevation to London Fields is of brick, with randomly arranged window openings. A low ground-floor space houses offices and a reception area, but the first floor is double height and generously day-lit by a continuous band of glazing. To baffle noise from trains, the building's elevation to the railway viaduct has obliquely placed windows. Meeting rooms are on the flat roof, timber decked and open for community use, and there is a conservatory, roofed with photovoltaic panels. Vertical connections are provided by a central timber-clad stair. Detailing is of a high standard for a building that cost only £2,200,000.

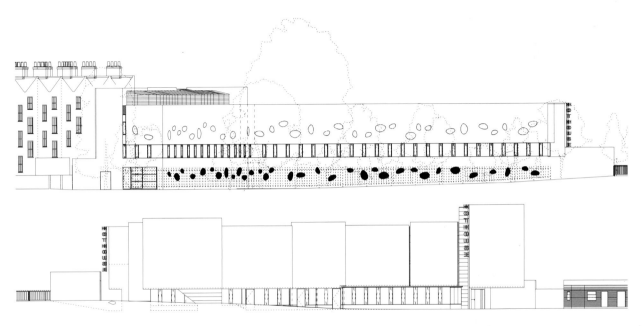

The Idea Store Whitechapel – actually a public library, designed for Tower Hamlets Council – is a significant landmark for David Adjaye. His rapid rise to prominence has been achieved through exhibition fit-outs – for example, at the Design Museum and Victoria Miro Gallery, now Victoria Miro 14 (pp. 106–107), both in London – and lavish domestic interiors. Then followed the sensational Elektra House and, more recently, the Dirty House (see pp. 232–33), also both in London. The important public commission for the Idea Store was a test of Adjaye's ability to work on a large scale and to a tight budget. (Early in 2003 Adjaye was shortlisted for the design of the new British Embassy in Warsaw – an achievement in itself for a young architect.)

The Idea Store concept clearly develops the philosophy of Will Alsop's Peckham Library in south London (pp. 84–85), updating the idea of the public library to fit contemporary attitudes and lifestyles. The aim is to demystify the form: the way to get people into libraries, it is argued, is to build them in shopping hubs and run them in the same way as shops. A library should be not just a repository of knowledge and information, but also an active presence in the community, linked to lifelong learning programmes, attracting people who would not usually visit such an institution.

The Idea Store Whitechapel forms part of the frontage of one of the East End's main thoroughfares. The five-storey building has shops at street level; the remainder of the 4500-square-metre floor space consists of flexible areas in which library and education spaces are mixed. The façade was envisaged as more than an enclosure: the curtain wall of coloured and clear glazing and glass-faced aluminium panels was designed as a medium for displaying information, although it has not in the event been used as such. (The idea is hardly new: Richard Rogers and Renzo Piano wanted to make the piazza frontage of the Centre Georges Pompidou, Paris, into an electronic noticeboard; they were inspired in turn by Oscar Nitschke's unbuilt Maison de la Publicité project of the 1930s.) Inside there is a full-height atrium extending over the pavement and containing stairs and escalators to draw people up the building. The top floor contains a cafe with spectacular views over the City and East End. If all this does not demystify the library, nothing ever will.

Transparent and colourful, David Adjaye's Idea Store offers a new image of the public library as an accessible and welcoming place. It is part of the ongoing regeneration of the eastern fringe of the City.

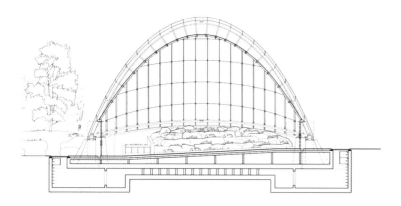

The Royal Botanic Gardens at Kew is a historic London institution that seems determined to keep up with the times. A well-known tourist attraction (with 2,000,000 visitors a year), it is even more significantly a major focus for scientific research and plant conservation. Scattered around the gardens are forty listed buildings, including such iconic landmarks as Sir William Chambers's Pagoda and the Palm House designed by Decimus Burton and Richard Turner. Since the turn of the new century Kew has commissioned a number of new buildings and structures from several contemporary practices, demonstrating a refreshingly broad taste.

The strongly expressionist Alpine House, designed by Wilkinson Eyre (which was also responsible for a masterplan for the Gardens) and completed in 2006, has been characterized as a twenty-first-century garden folly, but its striking form is designed to provide the particular environmental conditions required by the rare plants that grow in it. John Pawson's undemonstrative Sackler Bridge dates from 2008. In the same year, the more obviously spectacular Xstrata Tree Walk, designed by London Eye architect Marks Barfield and engineered by Jane Wernick, was opened, offering a treetop walk 18 metres above the ground. It is hugely popular with the young and energetic, and there is reportedly scope for extending the walkway.

Opposite
Striking in form and
resembling a bridge, the
structure of the alpine house
reflects a sophisticated
environmental strategy. Air
is drawn in from underneath
the building and cools the
interior, exiting through vents
at the top.

Right and below
Walters and Cohen's Shirley
Sherwood Gallery is an
elegant pavilion in the
Miesian tradition, a sensitive
addition to the Victorian
Marianne North Gallery.

Edward Cullinan's Herbarium and Library Wing is an important addition to Kew's resources. It includes a new home for the historic library of the Royal Botanic Gardens as well as a climate-controlled store for more than 8,000,000 plant specimens. The palette of materials – brick, cedar cladding and bronze curtain walling – was selected to respond to the context of the landscape and existing buildings.

Two further projects form extensions of existing buildings. Walters and Cohen's Shirley Sherwood Gallery of Botanical Art, completed in 2008 close to Kew's Victoria Gate, is connected to the Marianne North Gallery, a memorable building designed in 1882 by James Fergusson to contain nearly 900 paintings by the Victorian traveller and botanist Marianne North. Walters and Cohen has produced a pavilion in the Miesian tradition, carefully detailed and gimmick-free and sensitively linked to the North Gallery.

Edward Cullinan Architects' Herbarium and Library Wing, completed in 2009, is the latest addition to the botanical library of books and specimens founded in the former Hunter House, overlooking Kew Green, in 1853. Earlier phases of extension, ranging in date from 1902 to the 1980s, had produced a confused and increasingly inadequate agglomeration of buildings, ill-equipped to receive visitors and researchers. Cullinan's building reflects the strengths of the practice: it is radical and innovative but never pursues visual drama at the expense of practicality. A typical move was to place the offices on the top floor, where those working can enjoy the views and access to external terraces. The floors below are essentially for storage. The building, clad largely in timber on an energy-efficient concrete frame, is connected to the rest of the complex by a subsidiary new block, a circular drum that contains the main reading room.

'The room itself is to be the first exhibit': this was the brief given to HOK International by the British Museum when the practice began design work on the restoration and conversion of the King's Library. This noble space, some 91 metres long, was the first part of the British Museum to be constructed (in 1823–27), and it remains the most widely admired of the works of Sir Robert Smirke. Built to house King George III's collection of more than 60,000 volumes, and retaining the splendid original bookcases, the King's Library is a Neo-classical masterpiece, comparable with the work of Karl Friedrich Schinkel in Berlin. Administered in recent years by the British Library, the King's Library was passed back to the museum after the library moved to its new building in St Pancras in 1998, taking George III's books with it. The decision was made to refurbish the King's Library as a gallery of the Enlightenment – an intellectual revolution that, fittingly, led to the creation of the modern museum – and as an introduction to the museum's vast collections. The opening was scheduled for 2003, marking the 150th anniversary of the founding of the British Museum.

The project, which won a special conservation award from the RIBA in 2004, is a triumph of tactful restoration, in which modern technology has been seamlessly integrated into a highly sensitive historic ensemble. The fine book-presses and floor-mounted display cabinets have been reused (and supplemented by replicas) to display about 3000 objects from the collections, including scientific instruments, sculpture, archaeological and ethnographical items and specimens of natural history. The adaptation of the cabinets meant inserting air conditioning, fibre-optic lighting and modern security systems. Thousands of spare volumes from the House of Commons library fill some cases, and busts and antique vases are displayed on pedestals. The ambience is that of a great library of the Enlightenment era, where works of art and scientific specimens would commonly be displayed alongside books. The absence of interactive computer terminals and other electronic paraphernalia is particularly welcome: the room and its contents speak for themselves and lead the visitor to explore the collections spread around the museum.

As part of the project, the original Smirke decorative scheme was faithfully restored (with advice from Dr Ian Bristow, an architect and historic-building consultant) and the marble, granite, scagliola and plasterwork elements, as well as the finely crafted timber floor, painstakingly cleaned. Although the library may appear untouched by modern intervention, its restoration was a revelation to those who knew it in its previously shabby and crowded state, disfigured by ill-designed British Library displays. For many years the British Museum treated its Grade I-listed building with contempt, but under more inspired leadership it is now making amends. The restoration of the museum's front hall and the Queen Elizabeth II Great Court project (pp. 86–87), which forms a natural complement to the King's Library scheme, equally reflect the fact that Smirke's building is not just a container for objects, but also a magnificent artefact in its own right.

The King's Library, long recognized as one of the finest interiors in London, has been given a new dimension as a gallery of the Enlightenment. The project included the addition of new cases and the installation of air conditioning and modern lighting.

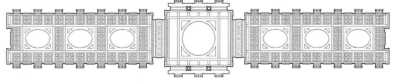

Dixon Jones's work shows a remarkable diversity, extending from the refurbishment of historic buildings to major infrastructure projects, such as that for Exhibition Road in Kensington (pp. 28–29), and large commercial buildings. The practice won the commission for Kings Place in competition in 2002, from a shortlist containing Porphyrios Associates and John McAslan + Partners, among others. The building was constructed in 2006–2008.

The highly unusual nature of the £96,000,000 project reflects the interest of the developer, Peter Millican of Parabola Land, in cultural regeneration. Alongside 28,000 square metres of office space, the building contains a 425-seat concert hall, teaching and practice rooms and a full-size rehearsal hall. These facilities are used by the Orchestra of the Age of Enlightenment and the London Sinfonietta, which previously lacked a permanent base. The ground floor and basement contain art galleries, restaurants and cafes open to the public, capitalizing on the building's location next to Battlebridge Basin on Regent's Canal.

The stone-clad rotunda on the north-eastern corner of the site provides a dramatic canalside landmark and helps to break down the building's large volume into distinctly separate elements. To the south, the masonry-framed Pavilion, with a generously scaled waterfront arcade, provides a point of transition to the surviving nineteenth-century warehouses, now converted to office use, along the western side of the basin.

The western edge of the development abuts York Way, a road with heavy traffic, and looks across the railway tracks into King's Cross station and the site of the forthcoming massive King's Cross Central scheme (pp. 32–33). The elevation here is triple-glazed, its outer layer an undulating, reflecting glass screen (a 'crinkle-crankle wall', as Edward Jones describes it) that forms the building's principal public face. This slick, if slightly bland, feature is an expression of the offices behind, which are accessed from an entrance foyer on the ground floor.

Office developments in Britain are customarily inaccessible to the public – more so than ever, in the light of the terrorist attacks on London in 2005 – so that the innovative approach of Kings Place is refreshing. Stealing a march on King's Cross Central, but part of an ongoing renaissance of the surrounding area, the scheme could before long form part of an enjoyable urban promenade linking Camden Town to the East End.

Below
Containing offices for two national newspapers, the building is innovative in also housing extensive public spaces, and a concert hall and rehearsal space for two leading orchestras.

Opposite
The external form of Kings Place responds both to the heavily trafficked York Way and to the more tranquil context of the canal behind.

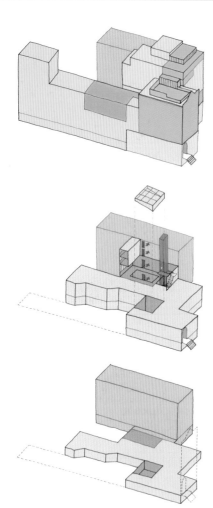

The London Library is Britain's pre-eminent private subscription library, and has been famous as the haunt of writers and scholars for 150 years. Founded by Thomas Carlyle, it moved to St James's Square in 1845. The present, Grade II-listed building by J. Osborne Smith was constructed in the 1890s – a pioneering example of steel-framed construction – with a series of extensions dating from the 1920s to the 1990s. By the beginning of the new millennium, however, the library was chronically short of space: it acquires more than 8000 books annually (requiring nearly a kilometre of new shelving), and accommodation for readers was in short supply, as was office and workshop space.

The £25,000,000 development project by Haworth Tompkins – perhaps best known for its work on theatres, including the Royal Court and the Young Vic (pp. 90–91 and 112–13) – involved the reconstruction of Eliot House, a 1930s block in Mason's Yard, just to the north of the library. This building, which was acquired in 2004, provides 30 per cent more shelf space, catering for at least a quarter of a century of future expansion, and creates a second entrance into the library from Mason's Yard (also the location of the new White Cube gallery). The existing book stacks, remarkable for their use of cast iron on an open-grilled grid, have been extended upwards by three storeys, with the existing structure replicated as far as possible. A new reading room has been constructed at roof level, with a members' room below and a terrace overlooking the square. All this involved emptying the library of books during 2007, decanting them into Eliot House, then moving them back during 2008. The recast Eliot House links at all levels to the 1890s building.

The project included not only new construction but also a complete overhaul of the library's historic premises, with the renewal of aged services and installation of new environmental controls, lifts and staircases, and the stripping out of unsightly accretions. The main staircase remains the principal route through the library, and the issue hall and reading room are now carefully restored.

Some members of the London Library may have been concerned that the unique ambience of the place would be affected by all these changes (although it is hard to see how the library could have survived in the long term without the alterations). But Haworth Tompkins has, on the strength of its Royal Court project, a sure touch when it comes to marrying old and new, and a particular feeling for materials and textures. Preserving the character of the library has been a key aim, since for the architect, a building of this calibre is a historical palimpsest: every layer counts. With the complex project complete, this aim appears to have been met.

Left
Haworth Tompkins' project provided for a phased programme of expansion for the library on its cramped West End site.

Opposite
New and old are skilfully welded together in the development, with greatly improved facilities for readers.

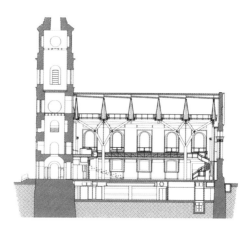

Left and opposite
The conversion of St Luke's to a concert and rehearsal venue has preserved the great internal volume of the building.

Below
The new structure, its roof supported on slender steel columns, is entirely contemporary in design, with no attempt at pastiche.

Nicholas Hawksmoor is reckoned to have been one of England's greatest architects, but his work has not always received the respect it deserves. His masterpiece, Christ Church Spitalfields, stood derelict for thirty years; and St George in the East was never fully restored after wartime bombing. The Church of St Luke, Old Street, designed by Hawksmoor in collaboration with John James and completed in 1733, was abandoned by the Diocese of London in 1960, unroofed and left to rot. Fortunately its external walls and remarkable obelisk steeple survived four decades of neglect, and today St Luke's – externally unchanged save for stonework repairs and cleaning, and standing in its well-preserved churchyard – has a new role as a concert hall, recording studio and rehearsal space, a conference and events venue, and the base for the London Symphony Orchestra (LSO).

Since the original interior was irretrievably lost and a literal reconstruction had been ruled out on grounds of cost, Levitt Bernstein's scheme introduced a flexible space, the Jerwood Hall, within the original walls. The new roof is supported on four steel columns, with a shallow balcony on three sides of the space and retractable seating, giving a capacity of up to 350 people. Below the hall, the former crypt has been reconstructed to house a cafe, offices, a library and an instrument store for the LSO. Further spaces excavated below the churchyard contain more rehearsal and meeting accommodation, while a modest extension above ground, on the site of the former vestry hall, houses the artists' entrance and provides full disabled access. Within the building, surfaces have been largely left as found, and the raw, unplastered walls of the hall provide a stark contrast to the elegance of the new interventions.

In 1998 the Victoria and Albert Museum (V&A) launched Daniel Libeskind's 'Spiral' extension project. It was finally abandoned in 2004 after it was denied National Lottery funding, but in retrospect its loss is hardly to be regretted. It had grown stale by 2001, when the museum launched Future Plan, a strategy for the development of its existing complex of buildings. Sir Aston Webb's magnificent frontage to Cromwell Road, completed in 1909, conceals an agglomeration of spaces constructed since the 1860s. Under Future Plan, large tracts of the V&A have been transformed, and the project is ongoing. A distinguished cast of architects and designers includes Casson Mann, Gareth Hoskins, Pringle Richards Sharratt, Wright & Wright, Softroom, Stanton Williams, Eva Jiricna and Wilkinson Eyre. Within the overall discipline of the plan, the various projects have shown a commendable degree of respect for the museum's historic fabric.

MUMA (McInnes Usher McKnight Architects) won the £32,000,000, 4500-square-metre Medieval and Renaissance Galleries project in competition in 2003, a major achievement for a young practice founded only in 2000. The results have been universally acclaimed in both museological and architectural terms. The galleries, ten in total, occupy space in the south-east corner of the museum campus, including two of the large courts designed by Aston Webb, used to show sculpture and large-scale architectural elements. By opening up a series of smaller rooms in the basement, the architect created spaces ideal for displaying smaller objects in more intimate surroundings.

In a building where many generations of visitors have, enjoyably or otherwise, become lost, it was crucial to create connections to the rest of the museum and, of course, to ensure accessibility for all. A former light well was roofed over (with a technically innovative glazed roof engineered by Dewhurst Macfarlane) to provide a new circulation hub, complete with lightweight stair and glass lift. A low-energy services strategy completes a ground-breaking package. But the project's greatest strength is the fact that it provides a perfect setting for 1800 wonderful objects – the real stars of the show.

Asked why the Peckham Library and Media Centre is raised 12 metres above Peckham Square, a new public space intended as a focus for community life and regeneration in this underprivileged area of south London, Will Alsop is apt to reply: 'Why not?' In fact, the logic behind the move becomes apparent to anyone who ascends to the library. There are views not only of the square and the surrounding area, but also, through the highly transparent, multicoloured northern elevation, of the public and commercial monuments of the City and West End a few miles away: Peckham's perceived isolation from central London is revealed as an illusion.

The overhang of the library shelters part of the square from the weather. Elevated above the streets, the library is part of the urban fabric and, at the same time, appealingly apart, a semi-secret world that has a particular attraction for young people. Public libraries were traditionally seen as places where the masses could be educated and 'improved'; a worthy ideal, but one too paternalistic and condescending for the twenty-first century. Peckham Library is unashamedly colourful, shapely and sensuous, a container for a new approach to education and information.

The library itself, clad in green patinated copper with a prominent red 'tongue' on the roof, cantilevers out from a five-storey vertical block containing the entrance lobby, offices and staff facilities, and a multimedia centre for IT training. Within the reading room, three timber pods set on stilts house a meeting room, a children's activity area and a specialist Afro-Caribbean library. The building has presence and glamour, but is far from extravagant; the naturally ventilated interior is made for low-cost running.

This is a building for the local community, wearing its serious purpose lightly and reflecting Alsop's conviction that architecture must be interesting, stimulating and unforgettable as well as functional. Peckham Library is all those things and more. It has a great deal to say about the city, the relationship between learning and enjoyment, and the place of art in architecture.

Below
The library's interior provides a new and stimulating environment at the heart of the community in which to read and learn.

Opposite
The south elevation shelters a new square, developed as a focus for this deprived inner-city community.

The Queen Elizabeth II Great Court starts with the simple idea of turning an underused open courtyard into a glazed covered space, a social and circulation focus for the British Museum. Rick Mather's revamps of the Wallace Collection and, with Building Design Partnership (BDP) engineers, the National Maritime Museum are variations on this theme. Modern structural engineering and glazing technology facilitate the operation, providing an economy of means that the Victorians (who invented the idea of the winter garden) lacked.

Where the Great Court scores above both these projects, however, is the fact that it is located in central London, at the heart of one of the most famous – and most visited and frequently overcrowded – cultural institutions in the world. It was conceived not just as an addition to the amenities of the British Museum but equally as a new public space for London, open late into the evening, a space where you can linger but that also forms the most convenient through route from the London University precinct to Great Russell Street. The huge mass of the museum has become permeable, part of the fabric of the city. For some, the monumental gravitas and cool – even icy – aesthetic of the space are a deterrent to relaxing in the cafe areas, which admittedly seem incidental and somewhat transient, crushed by the grandeur of their surroundings. The number of visitors thronging the Great Court on a typical day makes the scheme seem inevitable, however, and the only way in which the museum could sensibly develop for the future.

When the British Museum was built in 1823–47 to Greek Revival designs by Sir Robert Smirke, the enfilade of galleries was arranged around the central court, 'a dull, miserable looking space', as a contemporary critic described it. In 1854–55 Smirke's brother Sydney constructed the famous Round Reading Room in the middle of the court. Over the next century, all the space around the drum of the Reading Room was filled with book stacks, and the central court became a distant memory. The decision to remove the British Library to a new building at St Pancras (opened in 1998) freed the space around the Reading Room, which itself had to be retained, for museum use. Norman Foster was the winner of a competition held in 1994. Work started on site in spring 1998 and was completed in two and a half years – a considerable achievement in itself.

As part of the project, the much-damaged façades of the court were extensively repaired, and the demolished south portico rebuilt in replica. Foster, in collaboration with engineer Buro Happold, designed the lightweight roof structure with 3312 glass panels, each one a different size owing to the slightly off-centre placement of the Reading Room in the court. Its structure rests on the perimeter walls and on slender columns buried in the new cladding of the drum. The roof provides a calm, even light, regardless of external conditions, and its airy elegance contrasts with the solidity of the great staircases wrapped around the Reading Room, now a public reference library, its original decor carefully reinstated. Education facilities and lecture rooms are buried below the floor of the Great Court. A separate, but related, Foster project has located new ethnography galleries north of the space, finally breaking down the barrier to circulation imposed by Sir John Burnet's Edward VII Galleries of 1914.

Allowing visitors to 'read' the museum and its extraordinary collections in a new way – traditionally it was a wearying procession of didactic spaces – the Great Court begs comparison with I.M. Pei's ambitious reworking of the Louvre as an exercise in the modernization not only of museum spaces but also of the relationship between museum and urban community.

Below
Long section, showing how the Great Court forms part of a continuous route through the British Museum.

Opposite
The Great Court was conceived as a major public space, using areas of the museum previously inaccessible to the general public.

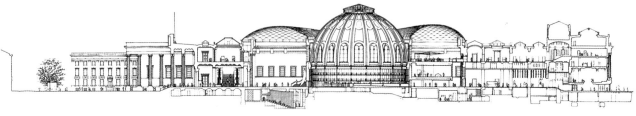

Left and opposite, top
Ancillary spaces are housed in a new block, which wraps around a section of the drum of the historic building and contains a full-height top-lit galleria.

Opposite, bottom
The remarkable iron structure of the Roundhouse, which was first constructed as an engine shed, has been immaculately restored as part of the conversion project.

John McAslan + Partners has a reputation for reviving the fortunes of neglected historic buildings: the restoration of the De La Warr Pavilion at Bexhill-on-Sea, East Sussex, for example, was a landmark project. The practice faced a real challenge, however, when commissioned by philanthropist Torquil Norman to convert the crumbling Roundhouse in north London into a state-of-the-art performance venue.

Built as an engine shed in 1846, and housing a rail turntable, the Roundhouse quickly became redundant and was used as a gin warehouse for nearly a century before its reincarnation as a focus of the 1960s rock and fringe-theatre scene. Facilities were, however, primitive, and by the 1980s alternative uses for the decaying building were being canvassed – one abortive proposal was its conversion into a store for the Royal Institute of British Architects' drawings collection.

Norman bought the Grade II*-listed building in 1996 with the aim of turning it into a performing-arts centre targeted at young people. His project, which was subsequently given additional funding by the National Lottery, had the enormous advantage of retaining intact, and restoring, the great internal space and its magnificent iron-and-timber roof structure. A new steel roof was ingeniously constructed above and around the existing structure, providing acoustic insulation and space for lighting and sound systems. The central glazed oculus, long obscured, was opened up and fitted with triple glazing and black-out facilities. A new gallery level

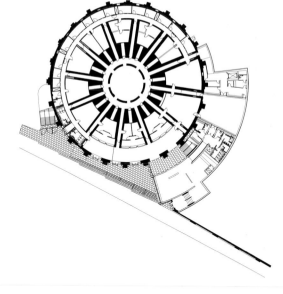

was inserted to provide additional accommodation for audiences of up to 3300 people, and WCs and a bar were slotted in below. The basement, which originally contained nothing more than ash pits for steam locomotives, was radically reconfigured beneath a new concrete floor slab, with rehearsal and recording studios around a central performance space seating 200 people.

From the start of the project it was obvious that not all the facilities required could be accommodated within the historic envelope without compromising its character, and so a new wing was constructed, wrapping around a section of the drum and facing Chalk Farm Road. It contains stairs and lifts, a cafe-bar, the box office and administrative spaces set off a top-lit galleria, which functions as an enjoyable, dynamic social hub.

The new architecture is polite and well-detailed, in a straightforward contemporary manner. It is the restored Victorian drum that is the star of the show, externally little changed but internally transformed to highlight the quality of its structure. The main performance space is highly flexible, with no fixed seating or stage.

Some feared that the familiar ethos of the Roundhouse would be lost in the process of repair and conversion, but miraculously it has survived the transformation. This is one of the best examples of adaptive reuse in recent years, and a model for what might be achieved elsewhere. The total cost of the project, excluding technical fit-out, was £19,000,000, which seems exceptional value for money.

ROYAL COURT THEATRE SW1

Left
The familiar frontage to Sloane Square remains unchanged.

Below and opposite, right
A characteristic of the refurbishment was the retention of many interior finishes and surfaces, as found, giving the building a rich and varied palette and texture.

Opposite, left
West–east section, showing the restaurant beneath Sloane Square, left, and the theatre, right.

The Royal Court Theatre has been famous since the 1950s as a venue for innovative, mould-breaking productions. (It was there that John Osborne's *Look Back in Anger* premiered.) The theatre itself, although listed Grade II, is not of outstanding architectural interest: its fussy 1880s façade makes little impression on Sloane Square and certainly does not challenge the sleekly elegant curve of Peter Jones (pp. 142–43) on the end of the King's Road.

Haworth Tompkins's reconstruction of the theatre confronted a number of problems, quite apart from the confined character of the site. The distressed, not to say scruffy, ambience of the interior was widely seen as part of its charm, and nobody wanted it sanitized. But facilities for English Stage Company staff, performers and audiences were very poor.

The scheme has added a new six-storey block of dressing rooms and offices alongside the main building, with more accommodation in a deep basement. The upstairs studio theatre has been totally rebuilt. A considerable slice of the budget went into the construction of a new bar and restaurant under Sloane Square (replacing an existing public convenience), with an entrance from the square's central paved area as well as from the theatre. The local authority's subsequent refusal to allow access from the square was, to say the least, perverse.

The main façade, cleaned and with new lighting, otherwise remains unchanged. Inside the theatre, the approach has been one of stripping back dilapidated and poor-quality finishes, leaving old brickwork and new concrete exposed, so that the interior is a place of rich and memorable texture. A new main staircase has been constructed of thin, stepped concrete spans, meticulously detailed. The effect recalls Carlo Scarpa's careful juxtaposition of materials, a contrast to the sleek look of many new/old schemes. Audiences and actors appear to like the rebuilt Court: the spirit of the place lives on.

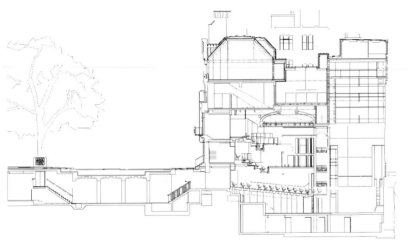

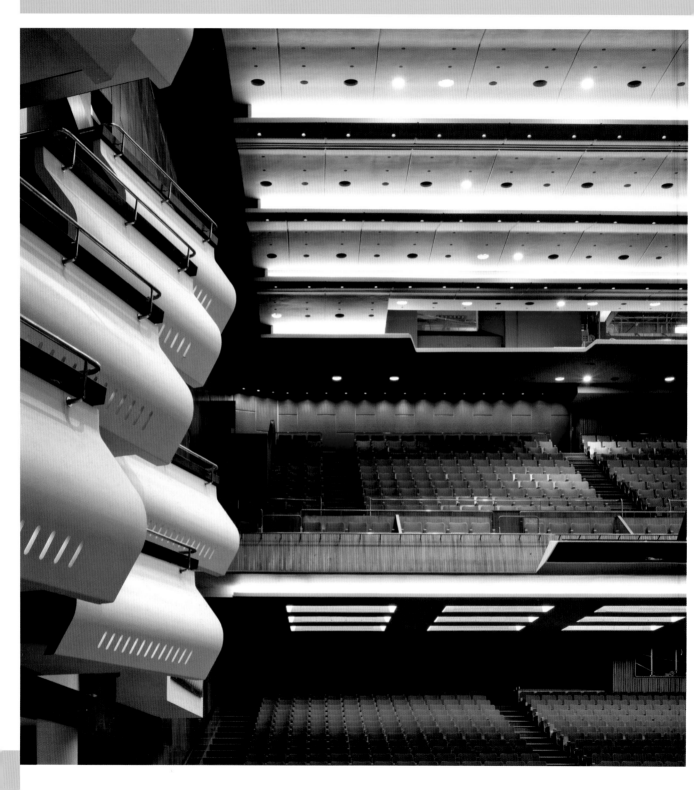

Opposite and below, left
Allies and Morrison's refurbishment project aimed to restore the interior of the Royal Festival Hall in line with the intentions of its original architects, and to reverse some of the detrimental changes made since 1951.

Below, right
The opening of the People's Palace restaurant, along the river front of the building, made good use of one of the spaces created as a result of the 1960s extension, but its style was a deliberate throwback to the lighter aesthetic of 1951.

Allies and Morrison was appointed as long ago as 1992 to work on a phased programme of repair and refurbishment for the Royal Festival Hall. The only surviving building from the 1951 Festival of Britain on the South Bank, this is one of the key British buildings of the post-war period – 'the prime monument of the Welfare State era', as historian Elain Harwood has described it. The Festival Hall is a beautifully made and highly subtle building that marries the optimism and drive of the post-war years, when the Modern Movement took centre stage in Britain, with the decorative and craft-orientated preoccupations of an older tradition, transmuted via the medium of Scandinavia. The form of the building, with its 'egg in a box' auditorium surrounded by open foyers, was the conception of Leslie Martin, while the interiors were designed by a London County Council (LCC) team led by Peter Moro. The two were able to offer encouragement and advice when Allies and Morrison began work there in the early 1990s.

The changes to the building and its context made under the Greater London Council (GLC) in 1963–65, including a bland new riverside frontage and a network of upper-level walkways around it, had compromised the original vision. The GLC's 'open foyers' policy of the 1980s allowed free access to all, not just concert-goers, from early morning until late at night, allowing many more people to enjoy the building but generating an uncontrolled invasion of the public spaces by poorly designed shops and cafes.

Allies and Morrison was an excellent choice for the task of updating and restoring the building: its roots are in the Cambridge school that Leslie Martin himself had run. Early phases of work reinstated the character of the original (west) entrance foyer and created an elegant new restaurant overlooking the river. A stretch of 1960s walkway masking the hall from Belvedere Road was removed and a new cafe opening on to a 'festival square' created on the south side of the building. Catering and retail outlets were reorganized and redesigned.

The context of Allies and Morrison's project was the masterplan for the South Bank drawn up for the South Bank Board (as successor to the GLC) by Rick Mather, winner of a competition in 1999. Implementation of the masterplan has been slow – the service roads and undercrofts around the Queen Elizabeth Hall and Hayward Gallery remain depressingly grim and the bleak Hungerford car park remains undeveloped – but one element that has been realized is the construction of a new administrative and retail block, designed by Allies and Morrison, along the edge of the Hungerford railway viaduct, providing space to decant administrative offices and shops from the Festival Hall. The removal of the offices allowed the upper floors of the building to be opened for public use.

The major phase of works on the hall took place between 2005 and 2007, closing the building for a lengthy period. Funded by a major National Lottery grant, the project was originally costed at around £50,000,000, but the eventual bill was more than £110,000,000. The result has generated some criticism. In particular, substantial changes to the stage area in the auditorium – part of an acoustic overhaul designed by Kirkegaard Associates – have been condemned as needlessly radical. (The famous organ has yet to be reinstated.) The loss of the sunken bar at the centre of the main public level – because it was inaccessible to the disabled – also seems an unnecessary change, when other bar areas are available to all. And the row of chain restaurants and cafes inserted at the riverside level of the building is a mundane addition, although it does offer facilities previously lacking on the South Bank. Yet the hall has been rejuvenated and there is plenty of evidence of money well spent, with historic interiors restored and the whole building made open and accessible.

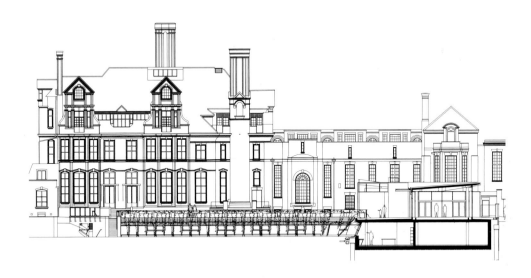

Craig Downie's discreet pavilion at the northern end of Exhibition Road is a short walk up the street from the more forceful intervention of Foster + Partners at Imperial College (pp. 180–81). Housing a new exhibition space, public reading room and reception area for the Royal Geographical Society (RGS), the pavilion is a modest but elegant addition to the townscape of 'Albertopolis', the collection of museums conceived by Prince Albert at South Kensington in the nineteenth century.

The new building is just one part of an overhaul of the society's premises to a masterplan by Studio Downie dating from 1997. The RGS, founded in 1830, came to Lowther Lodge, its splendid headquarters on Kensington Gore, in 1913. The building, designed by Richard Norman Shaw, had been completed forty years earlier as a private house. In 1930 a new wing was added on the corner of Exhibition Road, incorporating a 750-seat lecture theatre, to designs by Kennedy & Nightingale, which showed sympathy for Shaw's work. An upgrade of the heavily used theatre was an important element in the overall development plan, which also involved refurbishing the Shaw building to provide new educational facilities and greatly improved storage and study spaces for the society's huge archive (including 500,000 historic maps).

Creating a new building in the garden as the public face of the RGS was more of a challenge, particularly in Kensington and Chelsea, a borough not renowned for its sympathy to new architecture. Yet the new pavilion is both uncompromisingly modern in its vocabulary and uncommonly sensitive to its surroundings. By excavating part of the garden, Downie was able to secure space for the reading room and book stacks and for archives storage at lower-ground-floor level. Much of the new storage space is beneath an extended garden terrace that is an excellent place for summer parties. Angled glazing, inspired by Ahrends Burton Koralek's now iconic 1970s additions to Keble College, Oxford, provides controlled natural light for the reading room. The ground-floor exhibition space and reception area – the only parts of the £7,000,000 development visible from the street – are housed in the lightweight glazed pavilion of steel, glass, brick and concrete, with a silvered copper roof. This structure is beautifully detailed, with warm red bricks used to tie it visually to its Victorian neighbour. A helical stair connects the two levels. A 20-metre-long glass wall facing the street incorporates etched glass panels by artist Eleanor Long. This element is a delightful feature of a genteel, academic neighbourhood into which Downie has introduced, to quote the *Architectural Review*, 'an object lesson in modern urban etiquette'.

St Martin's is hard to miss: prominently located at one corner of Trafalgar Square and with a packed programme of services and concerts, it is a familiar part of tourist London (and the parish church of Buckingham Palace). It is also a church with a long-standing commitment to social service, ministering to the homeless and rough sleepers and providing facilities for the local Chinese community. These latter activities were squeezed into the cavernous former burial vaults below St Martin's, and into a former school founded by the church, part of a group of parish buildings just to the north.

The interior of the church, designed by James Gibbs, completed in 1726 and Grade I-listed, was, for all its inherent splendour, drably decorated and badly lit. In 2001 Eric Parry won a competition to design a radical transformation of the whole complex, to be funded by the National Lottery and a public appeal. The phased project, costing around £38,000,000, was completed in 2008.

The restoration of the church itself was a relatively straightforward matter, with a version of the original colour scheme restored in place of faded pastel hues; only the discordant new east window jars. The remainder of the project was logistically and structurally complex, involving the redevelopment of the vaults and the creation of new spaces linking the church and the school below ground, and providing a new cafe, a shop, a public hall and rehearsal rooms. All these areas, perhaps a little bland in feel, are accessed via a glazed entrance pavilion, containing lift and stairs, which is the focal point of an enlarged public space formed to the north of the church. Provision for the homeless is now concentrated in the refurbished school and the basement area below it. Given the hurdles this project faced, its completion represents a heroic achievement.

Above
Eric Parry restored the Georgian church, renovating and extending the crypt and creating new social and community spaces.

Opposite, left, top and bottom
A new entrance in a glazed pavilion gives access to the basement.

Opposite, right
The new work contrasts dramatically with the Classical bulk of James Gibbs's church.

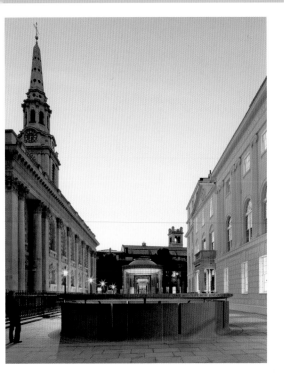

Siobhan Davies is one of the leading figures on the British dance scene and heads Britain's foremost independent dance company, as well as being heavily involved in professional training and broader educational initiatives. From its foundation in 1988, her company existed without a permanent home, but in the spring of 2006 it moved into its new base in Elephant & Castle in south London.

The building project involved the conversion and extension of a redundant three-storey school building of 1898 on St George's Road. Other buildings on the site remain in use by the Charlotte Sharman Primary School. The brief was to provide rehearsal spaces, changing and therapy rooms, offices and meeting rooms, as well as a main studio that could accommodate up to sixty people for public performances. Sarah Wigglesworth (who won the commission in competitive interview) had the advantage of an association with the company that extended over a decade; she understood and sympathized with its culture and responded strongly to its special needs.

The solid, decent but unremarkable old school building offered plenty of scope for continued use but equally for fairly radical adaptation. The decision was made to remove the staircase slot that connected the two classroom blocks and to insert a new double-height space. This forms a natural focus for the building, connecting offices and changing rooms in the western block with meeting rooms and the smaller rehearsal studio in the wing to the east. A 'sofa in space' – a balcony complete with oversized sofa – overhanging the void at first-floor level is an engaging place where dancers can relax between rehearsals.

Stairs, lifts, WCs and plant are in a new extension to the rear of the building, facing the school playground. It is a lightweight, partly glazed structure, suspended on steel beams, that contrasts agreeably with the solidity of Victorian brick. A smaller extension at the side of the building contains an escape stair.

The principal space, the main rehearsal and performance studio, sits on top of the building, replacing the existing second-floor rooms – a matter of 'making something of the roof', says Wigglesworth. Although modest in scale, it is a memorable and dramatic space where walls and ceiling, in a radical reinterpretation of the gothic tradition, are one. The studio can be blacked out or opened up to give dancers views over London. An all-timber structure using monocoque construction was considered, but was ruled out on the grounds of cost in favour of a composite of timber and steel. Elements of the old rooms were retained so that their memory has been preserved in the new space. Externally, the billowing roof structure, designed with engineers Price & Myers, reads as a tent or a boat, a new landmark on the busy road. The architect considers its overlapping shells to be 'gravity-defying forms that seem to swell above the plane the dancers work on'.

Sarah Wigglesworth is best known for the extraordinary Straw Bale House, completed in 2001 by the railway tracks out of King's Cross in north London, a challenging new-build project almost too full of ideas. This very different project, costing a modest £4,200,000, is an assured performance and an object lesson in the creative marriage of old and new.

Below, left
The main rehearsal and performance studio is placed on top of a converted school and has a dramatic roofscape that forms a landmark on the approach to Elephant & Castle.

Below, right
The services are in a new block next to the playground of the former school.

Opposite
Internally, the studio has an almost gothic quality, with controlled natural light providing an intense, enclosed but naturally lit space that responds to the needs of dancers.

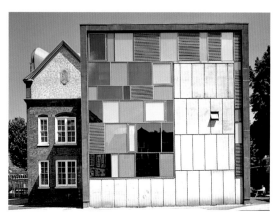

The Tate Gallery of Modern Art – now Tate Modern – which opened in 2000 in the former Bankside power station, has been a spectacular public success, with nearly 5,000,000 visitors a year, and is a major contributor to the regeneration of Southwark. The project provided a new use for Sir Giles Gilbert Scott's building (completed as recently as 1963), which faced likely demolition. The winner of the architectural competition for its conversion, Swiss practice Herzog & de Meuron, was as a result catapulted into the front ranks and won the coveted Pritzker Prize in 2001.

Since Tate Modern's opening in May 2000 the strengths and weaknesses of the scheme have steadily emerged: the galleries seem too small for the number of visitors they attract, and lack flexibility, while the lifts, escalators and top-floor restaurant are also hard pressed to cope with the crowds. The vast turbine hall, though – the venue for a series of spectacular installations by such artists as Doris Salcedo, Rachel Whiteread and Anish Kapoor – is genuinely popular and one of the most impressive public spaces in London. The defects of the project are outweighed by its sheer bravado and sophisticated and confident approach to the recycling of an industrial monument that could easily have vanished.

Tate, under Sir Nicholas Serota, returned to Herzog & de Meuron for a major extension, originally planned to open in 2012 and giving Tate Modern an additional 21,500 square metres of space. The initial proposal, for a glass-clad ziggurat at the rear of Scott's building, was given planning consent in 2007, despite criticism from many quarters. A year later Tate returned to Southwark's planning committee with revised proposals (given planning permission in 2009), which provided for a building of similar form but now clad in brick, a nod to Scott. Costed at £215,000,000, the scheme received a one-off grant of £50,000,000 from the government in 2007. Fund-raising continues, but the completion date is now set to be 2013 at the earliest.

The designs may be contextual on one level, but the bulk of the new building – as tall as the chimney of the former power station – shows little respect for Scott's work. The façades make use of a lattice of brickwork to filter light into the eleven-storey building, which will include a new restaurant, a members' room and a roof terrace as well as galleries. Perhaps the most welcome aspect of the project is the proposed conversion to subterranean galleries of the massive circular oil tanks to the south of the old power station. With their raw concrete left exposed, they could be some of the most impressive art spaces in Europe.

Below
Overlooking the River Thames in Southwark, the building's original turbine hall has been retained, although transformed into a vast public space, while the galleries and ancillary facilities are grouped over seven levels on the north side, accessed by prominent escalators and a discreet staircase.

Opposite
Herzog & de Meuron's major extension to Tate Modern takes the form of a vast brick-clad ziggurat rising to the level of the chimney of Giles Gilbert Scott's original building.

Opened in time for the Christmas season of 2005, the Unicorn Theatre is one of only three new theatres built in London in the last thirty years (the others are the Hampstead Theatre and the Young Vic; pp. 62–63 and 112–13). It is an outstandingly confident, competent and visually delightful work that firmly establishes Keith Williams (who won the job in competition in 2000) as a contender for other major cultural projects in Britain and beyond: in 2008 he completed a new opera house for Wexford, Ireland, and his Marlowe Theatre in Canterbury is under construction at the time of writing.

The Unicorn Theatre was founded in 1947 by Caryl Jenner, who used former Army trucks to bring performances by professional actors to children around London. Twenty years later, the company settled at the

Arts Theatre in Covent Garden, where it remained until 1999, but it always had aspirations for a home of its own. A site on Tooley Street, a short walk from London Bridge station, emerged as a possible location as a direct consequence of Norman Foster's masterplan for More London, the large riverside development on the south bank of the Thames that includes City Hall (pp. 318–19). Providing space for such an established cultural institution as the Unicorn bolstered the credibility of More London as a genuine mixed-use urban quarter, not simply an office ghetto. The £13,700,000 project was also in tune with Southwark Council's regeneration agenda, and it received generous support from the Arts Council Lottery Fund and other sources of public money.

The Unicorn's artistic director, Tony Graham, wanted a building that would be 'rough yet beautiful' and that did not patronize its youthful audience: 'children grow up, not down', he commented. The input of Graham and his colleagues, and also of local schoolchildren, was a significant influence on the development of Williams's proposals.

The building contains a main theatre (the Weston), which seats up to 340, a smaller studio theatre (the Clore) and a rehearsal studio, as well as a foyer, a cafe, education and meeting spaces, and the usual backstage facilities. Working with engineers from Arup to make the best use of a tight site, the architect devised a structural solution that places the main auditorium, free of columns, above the open, glazed, double-height foyer on the ground floor and the studio theatre set behind it. The staircase to the auditorium is in a corner tower, cantilevered over the foyer.

Externally, the solid box of the auditorium is clad in pre-weathered copper panels; elsewhere, brick, terracotta and stucco are used as facing materials. Projecting the theatre box over the narrow historic street – coincidentally named Unicorn Lane – that lies to the west of the building provides extra space in the auditorium. (The plan's skew was intended to relate the building to an adjacent new office development, but the designs for the latter changed, so the two structures remain out of alignment.) A projecting glass box slotted in below the raked auditorium seating punctuates the copper cladding. Behind is a multi-purpose space that serves variously as boardroom, function area or simply a place where school groups can consume their packed lunches. On the Tooley Street elevation the green room, traditionally an enclosed and often claustrophobic retreat, breaks through as a second glazed extrusion, allowing actors to see out and be seen.

The Unicorn has a powerful impact on its surroundings, its contrasting transparent and solid elevations reflecting, Williams says, not just the public and the private, backstage components of the building, but also ideas about 'a dynamic future as well as the architectural precedent of this part of London, the narrow streets and warehouses that once occupied the site'. There is in the building nothing that 'talks down' to its users, nor, it must be said, much evidence of the 'roughness' that the client envisaged. Details, at least those front of house, are remarkably refined, with nothing extraneous or wilful. The use of stone floors, walnut joinery and high-quality concrete gives no hint of the relatively tight budget for the project. The main auditorium is carefully scaled to the needs of its primary users, with a semicircular form that positively encourages a sense of intimacy.

The success of this building – for audiences, for performers and for the public who merely enjoy it as an incident in the cityscape – derives from the way in which Williams and his team conceived it as a series of dynamic interlocking volumes. These allow the Unicorn not only to enthral audiences but also to hold its own in a potentially overbearing context of commercial development.

Opposite

Providing an element of cultural activity in the huge More London development, the Unicorn Theatre manages to combine glamour with an appropriate durability and flexibility. Externally, the building features a range of materials, including distinctive copper cladding. Unusually in a theatre, there are extensive views to the surrounding streets. The range of attractive spaces includes the green room (top left) and the full-height main foyer (top right).

Below

The cross-section shows the theatre's organization, with lighter, transparent spaces below and the closed volume of the auditorium itself above. The studio is seen at the bottom right of the building.

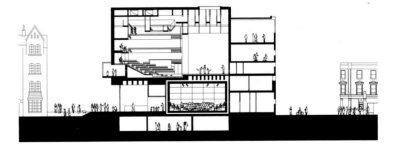

Opposite
Phase I of the project has revealed the graceful arch and iron structure of the dramatic central space. A cafe and shop are on the ground floor.

Below, left
A new ramped area leads to the entrance pavilion, which also contains further gallery space and a learning centre.

Below, right
The plan shows the original galleried structure, with the new addition to the left.

The Victoria and Albert Museum of Childhood in Bethnal Green began its existence as an institution dedicated purely to the local area. In 1865 a group of benefactors bought the iron sheds (nicknamed the 'Brompton boilers') that had temporarily housed the South Kensington Museum – later the Victoria and Albert Museum (V&A) – and re-erected them as a museum at Bethnal Green. It later became a branch of the V&A and in 1974 was relaunched as the Museum of Childhood, housing the V&A's collection of toys.

Externally, the building is extremely sober, the rich decoration planned in 1871 by architect James Wild having been omitted on grounds of cost. Inside, however, the iron structure is of exceptional quality, exhilarating in its lightness and grace. An architectural competition held in 2002 resulted in Caruso St John, best known at the time for the New Art Gallery Walsall in the West Midlands, being appointed to draw up a development strategy to remedy the building's shortcomings, principally an acute lack of space for storage, offices and visitor facilities. In addition, it was proposed to restore the historic interior and strip away the clutter accumulated over more than a century. Phase I of the project, with a modest budget of £1,500,000, was completed in 2003. It included the provision of new furniture – chunky but not inappropriate – and lighting, and the refurbishment of the existing structure and the surviving Victorian display cabinets. A shop, reception area and cafe were installed on the ground floor. A new colour scheme – as opposed to a reinstatement of the

original polychromatic designs – was developed by the architect in collaboration with artist Simon Moretti. As a temporary measure, a new entrance ramp and steps were built of timber, pending the construction of Phase II.

The second phase of the project, which required the museum to be closed for a year, was completed late in 2006. It provides a new entrance area, WCs and additional gallery space in a two-level pavilion attached to the front of the museum. A new learning centre, doubling the museum's capacity for school groups, was part of the project. The forecourt was completely remodelled to form a gently sloping approach, accessible to all.

Caruso St John has been experimenting in a number of recent projects with the revival of architectural decoration. At Bethnal Green, the façade of the new addition is clad with polished marble and granite panels incorporating intricate patterns inspired by the work of Victorian designers, notably Owen Jones. It is this aspect of the project, finally realizing something of Wild's vision for the building, that gives it special interest, hinting at the potential for an architecture of richness and referentiality that avoids the historicist clichés of the worst of postmodernism.

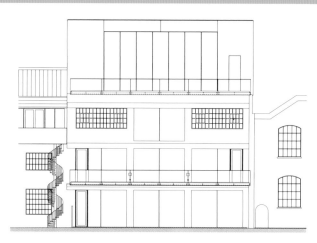

Victoria Miro, now one of the leading figures on the London contemporary art scene, launched her gallery in Cork Street in 1985. In 2000 it moved into a converted furniture factory on the fringes of Hoxton and Islington, a 'found' art space of the sort now familiar across the globe, beautifully reworked by Trevor Horne. In 2006 a major extension to the gallery, Victoria Miro 14, opened. Conceived by Claudio Silvestrin, with Michael Drain Architects overseeing the execution, the 835-square-metre extension is a private space showcasing Miro's own collection, and a place to receive privileged clients. It sits on top of the brick-built factory, a sculptural, white-rendered box that is a dramatic addition to the townscape, seen across the adjacent canal basin and forming a marker from nearby City Road.

But it is inside that the potent character of the project emerges most clearly. The new gallery is approached via a strikingly narrow staircase (with seventy-two steps, and a lift discreetly concealed) running along the edge of the building and terminating in a window, which floods the upper flights with natural light. The top-lit gallery itself is a generous 5.5 metres high, providing scope for the display of a wide variety of artworks, and is cantilevered over Wenlock Basin. A balcony provides excellent views over east London. Above the gallery is Miro's office and library. A series of further narrow staircases bisects the gallery space and connects to the lower floors and the top-floor study/library. The mix of materials includes timber floors, white-painted walls, and limestone for the main stair and external areas. As a carefully crafted new space tacked on to the converted factory, the project creates a stimulating juxtaposition between two distinct environments for the display of art.

Above and left
The new addition to the Victoria Miro Gallery is a sculptural white box sitting on a converted factory building.

Opposite, top left and right
Internally, the space features white walls, oblique views and dramatic stairs.

Opposite, bottom
The project adds a new dimension to the former industrial area that forms its context.

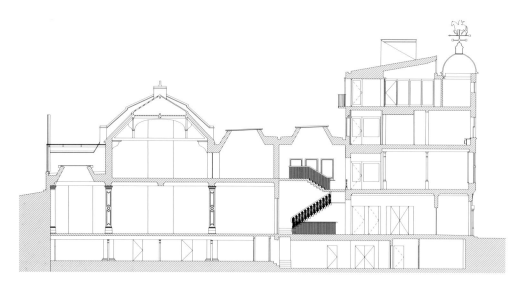

The Whitechapel Gallery, completed in 1901, was described by Nikolaus Pevsner as 'wonderfully original and quite an epoch-making building'. One of three striking London buildings designed by Charles Harrison Townsend (the others are the Bishopsgate Institute in the City and the Horniman Museum in Forest Hill; see pp. 64–65), the gallery was founded by social reformer Henrietta Barnett and largely funded by the progressive philanthropist J. Passmore Edwards. Despite the completion of an extension and refurbishment project by Colquhoun Miller in the 1980s, this internationally acclaimed centre for the display of contemporary and modern art was, by the 1990s, desperately short of space. Each time a new exhibition was installed, the whole gallery had to close as there was no storage space. Visitor facilities were poor, and educational programmes – heavily oversubscribed – lacked suitable accommodation. The building had ceased to meet the needs of the community it was intended to serve.

The decision by the borough of Tower Hamlets to vacate the public library adjacent to the gallery and replace it with a new Idea Store (see pp. 68–69) provided an obvious site for expansion. The 1890s library by Potts, Son & Henning (also funded by Passmore Edwards) was not of the calibre of its neighbour, but it was a listed building of some charm, more domestic than civic in character, perhaps, and could not be demolished. Following its acquisition in 2003, an international

competition in 2004 for its reuse was won by Ghent-based Robbrecht en Daem Architecten, whose portfolio includes a number of arts projects in Belgium and The Netherlands. The £10,000,000 project, developed with artist Rachel Whiteread as consultant and constructed with the young London practice Witherford Watson Mann as associate architect, reopened in April 2009.

Externally, the library remains unchanged, apart from the street façade being cleaned. Two new galleries were formed in existing spaces: the Commissions Gallery in the former ground-floor reading room, lit by newly inserted roof lights and designed to house site-specific installations; and the Collections Gallery on the first floor in a fine top-lit space that has proved excellent for displaying artworks. A new creative studio, designed for educational activities, is located on the third floor. Overall, display space at the Whitechapel has been increased by nearly 80 per cent. There is also a new space for the storage and study of the gallery's extensive archive – and a very attractive new restaurant.

The project is rooted in a renewed sense of commitment to the East End, in line with the aims of the Whitechapel's founders a century ago, but equally ensures the gallery's future as an international centre of artistic excellence. It is a model of intelligent and sensitive reuse.

Opposite and left
The redevelopment of the Whitechapel Art Gallery has connected the existing gallery with the former library immediately to the east. The 1890s library remains externally almost unchanged.

Below
Internal spaces are cool and minimal.

The practical arguments for a major extension to the British Museum are clear. The museum lacks a dedicated space for special exhibitions; it also needs additional accommodation for its conservation studios and laboratories, and is desperately short of storage space. However, Rogers Stirk Harbour + Partners' £135,000,000 project, while addressing these needs, has generated considerable controversy, and was rejected by Camden Council before finally gaining planning permission late in 2009.

The project, the first significant addition to the British Museum since the completion of Foster + Partners' Queen Elizabeth II Great Court in 2003 (pp. 86–87), is on Montague Place, at the north-east corner of the museum site and immediately west of the much-admired King Edward VII Galleries, designed by Sir John Burnet and completed in 1914. The objections to the new project from a number of amenity groups focused on the allegedly damaging impact of the scheme on Burnet's building and on the Great Court. In fact, much of the new accommodation is below ground, while the overall height of the development is lower than that of the King Edward VII Galleries.

The scheme calls for an existing building belonging to the museum, dating from the 1970s and cleverly disguised as a pair of Georgian houses, to be demolished, but it is hardly distinguished. The designs provide a series of linked four-storey pavilions, clad in textured glass and stone and intended to mediate between the scale of the museum and that of the fine Georgian terraced houses on Bedford Square. Significantly, the Commission for Architecture and Built Environment, while generally supportive of the project, felt that its external expression could have been bolder, and the public face of the new building shows a certain lack of confidence that contrasts with the ebullience of Burnet's work.

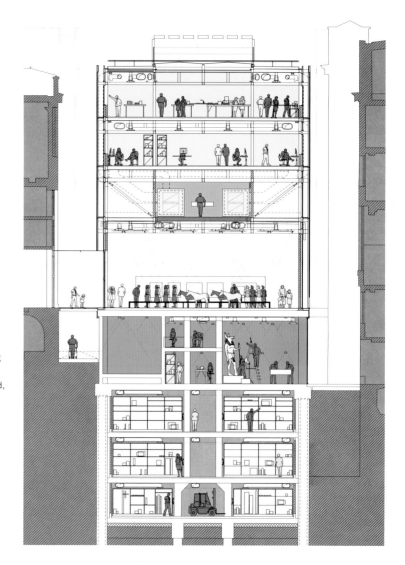

Opposite
Much of the accommodation in Rogers Stirk Harbour's addition to the British Museum is located below ground, reducing the impact of the building on its context.

Below
The very restrained exterior of the new building defers to its neighbour, the King Edward VII Galleries, designed by John Burnet.

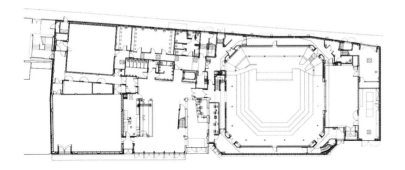

Opposite and above
The first-floor bar overlooks the new double-height foyer at the heart of the theatre complex.

Below
The updated frontage is an eye-catching addition to the street, especially at night, when the mesh façade of the auditorium is dramatically lit.

Located less than 150 metres east of the famous Old Vic Theatre, the Young Vic was founded by Frank Dunlop in 1970 as an offshoot of the National Theatre, but is now an independent institution. For the original building, set on a wartime bomb site, architect Bill Howell of Howell, Killick, Partridge & Amis provided a new auditorium with 450 seats, a studio and a cafe, within a shell of raw concrete blocks. An existing shop was converted to house the foyer. Intended as a temporary facility, Howell's building became a permanent fixture and was extended over the years in an ad hoc fashion. But under increasingly stringent health and safety regulations the theatre faced closure if no improvements were made, and in 2003 a major reconstruction was commissioned.

Haworth Tompkins, founded in 1991, is a youthful practice with a strongly urban agenda, reflected in its Coin Street housing not far from the Young Vic (pp. 244–45). Past projects include a major reconstruction of the Royal Court Theatre in Sloane Square (pp. 90–91), the Open-Air Theatre in Regent's Park and two incarnations of the Temporary Almeida. At the Young Vic, as at the Royal Court, the challenge was to preserve the essential character of a well-loved institution ('light-footed, critically engaged and classless') while equipping it with the facilities it badly needed: a more spacious foyer, an improved cafe and bar, enhanced technical provision, and expanded rehearsal and storage spaces as part of a complete back-of-house rebuild. Specialist theatre-design practice Studio Todd Lecat collaborated with the architect on the design of the performance and rehearsal spaces.

Haworth Tompkins's £12,500,000 scheme, completed in the autumn of 2006, has retained the Howell auditorium largely as it was, raising its roof to provide space for a new technical walkway. The entrance through a former butcher's shop is also almost unchanged, although there is now an additional double-height foyer space with a cafe and bar on two levels. To the west of the main auditorium are two new studios containing rehearsal space that can also be used for performances, with seats for up to 210 people. Adequate office space for the theatre's management has finally been provided.

The most obvious change has been to the exterior of the theatre. A new elevation to The Cut was hand-painted by artist Clem Crosby and encased behind industrial mesh. By night, it is lit from below, giving the Young Vic a new street presence.

Haworth Tompkins has a particular skill for working with old – often quite ordinary – buildings and responding to their spatial and material qualities. It is a talent that emerges powerfully in this project.

HEALTH AND LEISURE

1 DOON STREET DEVELOPMENT

2 EMIRATES STADIUM

3 EVELINA CHILDREN'S HOSPITAL,
 ST THOMAS'S HOSPITAL

4 HAMMERSMITH SURGERY

5 KALEIDOSCOPE

6 KENTISH TOWN HEALTH CENTRE

7 LABAN DANCE CENTRE

8 LONDON EYE

9 LUMEN UNITED REFORMED CHURCH

10 MAGGIE'S LONDON

11 MARGARET THATCHER INFIRMARY,
 CHELSEA ROYAL HOSPITAL

12 O2

13 PAUL O'GORMAN BUILDING,
 UNIVERSITY COLLEGE LONDON

14 PETER JONES

15 POTTER'S FIELDS PARK PAVILIONS

16 RICHARD DESMOND CHILDREN'S EYE CENTRE,
 MOORFIELDS EYE HOSPITAL

17 ST BARTHOLOMEW'S AND
 THE ROYAL LONDON HOSPITALS

18 ST PANCRAS CHAMBERS

19 WEMBLEY STADIUM

HACKNEY

TOWER
HAMLETS

SOUTHWARK

16

17

17

15

7

Lifschutz Davidson Sandilands' Broadwall housing on the South Bank, completed in the mid-1990s for Coin Street Community Builders (see pp. 244–45), has been widely admired as a model of urban regeneration, both physical and social. The practice's involvement with the area has continued: its reconstruction of the Hungerford footbridge was completed in 2002 (pp. 30–31), and it was also responsible for developing a comprehensive urban design strategy for the South Bank.

The Doon Street project again has Coin Street Community Builders as client, but has generated extended debate. Awarded planning consent by Lambeth Council, it was subjected to a public inquiry and finally given the go-ahead by the then Communities Secretary, Hazel Blears, in 2008 in the face of opposition from English Heritage (the government's adviser on the historic environment), the amenity societies and Westminster Council.

The controversial element of the scheme is a forty-three-storey, 140-metre-tall residential tower, which will affect views across the Grade I-listed Somerset House over the River Thames and also impact on those of the National Theatre, itself a listed building. Destined to be occupied by affluent private owners, the tower effectively funds the development of the remainder of the site, just south of the National Theatre and empty for half a century. Affordable low-rise housing, a swimming pool, a sports hall, dance studios and offices for the Rambert Dance Company, and a public square, all with clear public benefits, are planned.

Broken down into a series of distinct elements, the project responds to the traditional urban grid, which has been largely ignored in post-war redevelopment. The tower will be slender and, no doubt, elegantly detailed, but it is regrettable that the continuation of Coin Street's heroic regeneration programme depends on the creation of luxury housing and the intrusion of a forceful vertical element into an area where it is less than appropriate.

Opposite
The Doon Street tower
will form a dramatic, and
controversial, addition to the
skyline of the South Bank.

Below and bottom left
The tower, containing luxury
housing, contrasts with the
scale of exisiting buildings.

Bottom right
A new swimming pool for the
local community is one of
the benefits of the scheme.

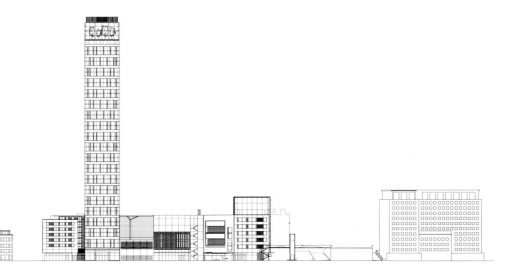

In the late 1990s Arsenal Football Club's decision to quit its historic ground at Avenell Road in Highbury, north London, was controversial. There was even the possibility that the club would move to another area of London – in fact, it had been founded in Woolwich, across the River Thames – but Islington Council was anxious to see it remain within the borough. Highbury Stadium is itself extraordinary, with two splendid Art Deco stands dating from the 1930s, and incorporating such facilities as bars and restaurants of a standard not found at any other British football ground. Now listed buildings, the east and west stands have been converted to housing as part of a sensitive redevelopment of Highbury by Allies and Morrison.

The new Emirates Stadium, 500 metres from the old ground, on former industrial land next to the east-coast railway line, reflects the huge ambitions of one of London's 'super-clubs'. It was intended to be a landmark structure, with greatly increased capacity (seating 60,000) and state-of-the-art spectator facilities, including ample provision of private boxes. HOK Sport Architecture (now Populous) won the commission in 1999. On the basis of the designs, Arsenal was able to secure £100,000,000 from the Dubai-based Emirates airline in return for putting the latter's name on the stadium for up to fifteen years.

HOK Sport Architecture's Rod Sheard argues that sport is 'the world's first truly global culture. Consequently, the stadium will become the most important building any community can own.' Costing a total of £170,000,000, the project is linked to a regeneration campaign for the surrounding Lower Holloway Road area, to include the construction of 2000 new homes, healthcare and nursery facilities, and a waste-recycling depot. The stadium is surrounded by a new urban park, a valuable amenity.

The roof structure of the elliptical building is conceived as a 'floating' dish, seamless in appearance, suspended over the 'saddle' of the seating bowl and supported on two huge steel trusses, each 220 metres long. The slick glazed cladding of the landmark stadium bowl gives it the look more of an airport terminal than of the traditional football ground. Impressive claims are also made for the low-energy credentials of the project.

Left and opposite, top right and bottom
Seating up to 60,000 people, the stadium sets a new standard for club grounds in Britain. An important agenda for the project is the advocacy of sport as a regenerative force in the city.

Opposite, top left
A cutaway diagram shows the levels of seating up to the canopy.

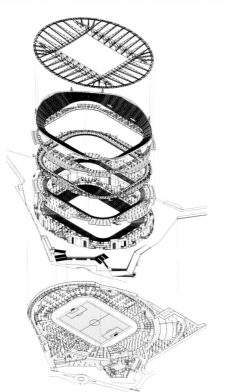

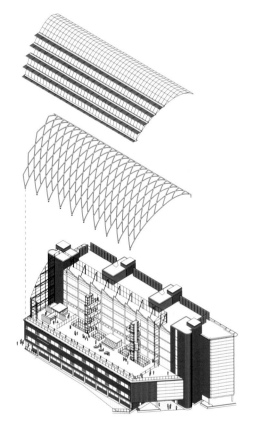

Opposite, top left and bottom, and right
The top four floors of wards in the Evelina Children's Hospital are backed by a conservatory with a spectacular glazed and shaded roof. It encloses an enjoyable day-lit public space and provides impressive views. The building is clad externally in terracotta tiles.

Opposite, top right
The wards are welcoming spaces, enlivened by decorated floors and bright colours. Sinuous walkways, rather than the more traditional corridors, lead through them and separate bed areas from nurses' offices and private bedrooms.

Michael Hopkins's architecture is notable for its extraordinary diversity. London buildings of the last few years by the practice include the rather mannered Portcullis House at Westminster, with the remarkable Jubilee line Underground station beneath it (pp. 48–49); Haberdashers' Hall at Smithfield in the City and a nearby housing scheme at Charterhouse, both making extensive use of brick; and the sleek steel-and-glass headquarters for the Wellcome Trust on Euston Road (pp. 344–45). Shortlisted for the Stirling Prize in 2006, the Evelina Children's Hospital, just across the River Thames from the Palace of Westminster, is certainly another outstanding work by Hopkins.

Won in competition in 1999, the project was intended to create 'a real children's hospital, not an adult hospital with cartoons on the walls': a light-filled, colourful environment with a distinctly non-institutional ethos. The site is on the south-west corner of the St Thomas's Hospital campus, with the park of Lambeth Palace on the opposite side of Lambeth Palace Road.

The 16,000-square-metre, £60,000,000 building, which opened late in 2005, accommodates up to 140 inpatients, plus outpatients' departments, operating theatres, consultants' offices, a cafe, a pharmacy and other facilities, on seven floors.

The field of hospital design is dominated by specialist practices adept at working within the parameters of the Private Finance Initiative (PFI) procurement strategy. Hopkins Architects had never designed a hospital when it embarked on this project, so there was a great deal of learning to be done. This progressive work in many respects provides a vivid contrast to much new hospital architecture developed under PFI; the recent new block for University College Hospital, just across the road from the Wellcome Trust, is a particularly dire example. As the *Architectural Review* commented, design for the National Health Service too often produces 'hospitals resembling rambling horizontal oilrigs rather than places of peace and healing'.

The focus of the new Evelina Children's Hospital (a Victorian institution in origin) is a great glazed conservatory, largely naturally ventilated, which rises beside the inpatient wards on the top four floors – a spectacular design in a tradition familiar from other Hopkins projects. The wards are served by snaking routes in place of conventional corridors, another move intended to counter the usual institutional ambience. There are excellent views from the four uppermost levels to the historic heart of Westminster and the gardens of Lambeth Palace.

Lower floors house outpatients' clinics, operating theatres, and the reception and other support spaces. Externally, terracotta tile cladding is used extensively. The internal aesthetic of the building is one of steel and glass, animated by the use of vivid colour, for example in the bright-red lift towers. Extensive use of artworks is another prominent feature of the building, featuring even in the rubber floor coverings.

Opposite, top
From inside the building there are only oblique views of a busy road, while a highly glazed façade overlooks an enclosed inner courtyard.

Opposite, bottom
The interior is characterized by a skilful use of natural and artificial light and cool colouring.

Above
Situated at the Hammersmith roundabout, and facing a flyover, the building presents a deliberately defensive if elegant façade that defers to the imagery of sailing and the nearby river.

The centre of Hammersmith has never recovered from two disasters: the construction of the monstrous, polluting flyover and associated road links in the 1960s (would it have happened in Belgravia?) and the abandonment of Norman Foster's visionary transport interchange project (1977–80). It is now dominated by a dreary postmodernist shopping and office centre, some packing-case hotels and, of course, the flyover. The large, dull Victorian church of St Paul makes little impact in this context, although its immediate setting has been much improved in recent years by the creation of a small but pleasant park, and some efforts have been made, very belatedly, to tame the traffic and give pedestrians some rights. For all that, it is a dire spot.

Guy Greenfield's surgery, white and curvy, and with real value for the local community, is therefore a tonic for Hammersmith. The architect was appointed in 1996 by the local health authority, and the building houses a large and busy medical group practice. It stands close to the church, on a busy roundabout, hence the lack of windows on the street front.

The eye-catching form of the centre is not arbitrary, but is designed to respond to the landscape of the new park and to baffle noise from the road. Inside, a corridor forms an additional barrier between the exterior and the medical consulting rooms, giving passers-by an oblique glimpse into the building across planted areas. A generous entrance area, further filtering the grime of the streets, leads to the reception lobby. A strong emphasis has been laid on clarity and legibility. Views out to the internal courtyard, with its Japanese-style garden, have a calming effect. The use of colour and natural materials – slate floors, for example, in public areas – is equally cheering. The project is rooted in a belief that surroundings matter to patients, and it is in a large part to this that it owes its success.

Van Heyningen & Haward is a practice with a strong track record in education, health and community projects, and a reputation for producing high-quality buildings that manage to be both practical and stylish. The firm was a sound choice – as winner of a competition organized in 2003 by the Commission for Architecture and the Built Environment – for Kaleidoscope, Lewisham Children and Young People's Centre.

The concept of Kaleidoscope was highly innovative: to provide on one site in Catford a base for the children's and young people's health, social and educational services that were previously scattered across the borough. This was not just a building project but also a symbol of a new integrated approach by the various agencies involved; there are now 260 staff in twenty-three teams working in or (in outreach work) from the centre.

Consultation with the local community – there was a competition for the name of the centre – was a key feature of the procurement process for the building, which contains five floors of accommodation on a C-shaped plan with a central courtyard. The ground and first floors house consultation and treatment space; above are three floors of mostly open-plan offices for healthcare, social services and education staff. The desire for openness and natural light and the need to provide privacy are skilfully reconciled with a mix of clear and opaque glazing and a complete absence of internal corridors. Glazed pods allow staff to conduct telephone conversations with clients in private. Colour is used to good effect throughout the building. The project was built in twenty months on the basis of a traditional contract, ensuring the faithful realization of the designs and producing a building that is, for its cost (£8,450,000, or less than £2000 per square metre), extremely well detailed.

Scandalous cases of child abuse and neglect, generating public criticism of childcare agencies, have shocked the public in recent years. Perhaps the integrated approach that produced this building will provide a more effective system of support for the vulnerable young.

Opposite
Kaleidoscope's rational
form and excellent detail
provide a model for quality
public architecture.

Right
The interiors are colourful
and welcoming.

Below
The building has a civic
character that enhances
its context.

KENTISH TOWN HEALTH CENTRE NW5

Left, below, and opposite, top
AHMM's health centre in
Kentish Town uses colour
internally to good effect.

Below, left
The internal focus of this
high-quality community
facility is a central 'street'.

Opposite, bottom
The exterior of the building,
mostly white-rendered, has
echoes of the pioneering
health centres of the 1930s.

Described as 'a Finsbury Health Centre for the twenty-first century' (referring to Berthold Lubetkin's pioneering north London building of 1938), Allford Hall Monaghan Morris's Kentish Town Health Centre realizes the vision, which emerged some decades ago but has all too rarely come to fruition, of integrated community health facilities. It includes GP and dental surgeries, screening and diagnostic services and children's healthcare, all on one site. The prime mover behind the project was Dr Roy MacGregor, who developed the detailed brief for the building and saw it through the planning and construction phases, financed by a public/private partnership, with only 40 per cent of the funding coming from the National Health Service.

In common with other projects by this phenomenally successful practice, the centre combines clear planning with decisive form and a bold use of colour; there is none of the blandness often associated with health-sector buildings. The plan is organized around a central 'street', and views out and access to natural light are key elements of the design. Reusing – and completely filling – the constrained site of an existing clinic, the architect has cantilevered rooms out on the first and second floors to make the best use of space. Small areas of garden, including mature trees retained on the site, provide break-out points, while staff enjoy the use of a rooftop terrace. The white render used on the exterior, with a ground-floor plinth clad in brick, may be an all-too-familiar feature of recent London buildings, but it has a purity that looks back to the ground-breaking healthcare buildings of the 1930s. As usual, the details are crisp and, together with good-quality furnishings, suggest a budget rather larger than the quoted contract value of £10,100,000.

LABAN DANCE CENTRE SE8

Herzog & de Meuron's Laban Centre is a unique building housing a unique institution. Named after Rudolf Laban (1879–1958), 'the father of modern dance', the centre operated for nearly thirty years from a sprawl of converted buildings in New Cross, a few miles from its new Thameside site at Deptford Creek (formerly a refuse tip). Its removal to Deptford is a component in the strategy to regenerate the area, which was once a centre of shipbuilding – and boasts an outstanding Baroque church, St Paul's, designed by Thomas Archer – but is now one of London's poorest districts.

Herzog & de Meuron's victory in the competition of 1997 (Peter Zumthor, Enric Miralles, David Chipperfield and Tony Fretton were among the contenders) came at a time when its Tate Modern project in London was moving from design to construction (pp. 100–101). Following delays in securing National Lottery funding, the centre was built in 2000–2002 and opened formally early in 2003.

On a superficial level, the centre can be read as a shed in the local tradition, raised above the mundane by its bold use of external colour in the form of polycarbonate sheets fixed in front of the glazed façade panels. The revelatory qualities of the building, however, are to be found beyond the façades. The interior is planned around three 'wedges' of circulation space, internal streets intended to encourage creative interaction and a memory of the rambling (but well-loved) collection of buildings that the centre formerly inhabited. Internal courts bring natural light deep into the building and allow views across it. Studios (a total of thirteen, none strictly rectangular) are arranged on the perimeter, while a 300-seat theatre – a facility the centre hitherto lacked – fills the centre of the building. A cafeteria and library are placed along its creekside edge. Two hefty spiral staircases, painted black, provide the principal means of vertical circulation and are seen as places for social encounters.

The centre is big-boned, generous and tough, designed to take hard wear from a teaching and learning community that is used to hard work and long hours. This is a creative 'village', intended to reinforce the Laban's established sense of community. The client, led by the centre's director, Marion North, had a strong input in the development of the scheme.

Colour was a vital ingredient from the beginning. Artist Michael Craig-Martin, whom the architect first encountered as a trustee of the Tate, was brought in at an early stage and the strong hues he chose give a sense of orientation and identity to the internal spaces.

Herzog & de Meuron has never been the 'minimalist' practice that some imagine, but the Laban reflects an increasingly expressive element in its architecture that recalls, in some respects, the work of the German architect Hans Scharoun. The full impact of the centre was realized when a remarkable landscape scheme by Günther Vogt was completed in 2004. The Laban Centre can be regarded as one of the few really significant projects generated by the cultural building boom of the 1990s.

Despite its monumental scale, the British Airways London Eye has a delicate presence on the London skyline.

The idea of the London Eye, perhaps the most popular of all London's millennium projects, emerged late in 1993 when David Marks and Julia Barfield produced proposals for a giant wheel in response to an ideas competition launched by a Sunday newspaper. During 1994 the idea turned into a feasible project as the architects worked on the scheme with engineer Jane Wernick of Arup, forming their own company to build it. A site was found close to County Hall, across the River Thames from the Palace of Westminster.

The Millennium Wheel, as it was initially described, was controversial: the chairman of the Royal Fine Art Commission, for example, became a vociferous opponent. Nonetheless, Marks Barfield pressed on, enrolling British Airways as a development partner in 1995. Planning consent was given in October 1996, and the search for specialist collaborators began. Work began on site in January 1999, and the plan was to open on New Year's Eve, just under a year later. By the summer, the 335-tonne structure was complete, cantilevered off the South Bank and awaiting the final lift. Subsequent delays in lifting the wheel led to the formal opening being postponed until March 2000.

Spanning 135 metres – the height of the spire of Salisbury Cathedral – and carrying thirty-two capsules, each holding twenty-five passengers, the Eye is a large object. Yet its impact on the London skyline – it can be seen from Kensington Gardens – is ethereal. Moving at a steady half a mile per hour, it provides staggering views across London from the Thames Estuary to Windsor. Some early criticisms of the project focused on the fact that big wheels were nothing new: George Ferris set his 120-metre-high wheel spinning in 1893. That turned out to be irrelevant. It was not so much the originality of the idea or the quality of the technology that mattered – and the London Eye is as far removed from a Ferris wheel as a TGV from Puffing Billy – as the piquancy of the siting. Within six months of its opening the Eye had attracted 6,000,000 visitors. The idea of having pure fun on the South Bank, forgotten since the closure of the Festival of Britain in 1951, and peering down on the homes of the Prime Minister and the Queen proved irresistible.

The Eye is not quite, as some have claimed, the Eiffel Tower of the twenty-first century. It may not be around in a hundred years, but for the moment it is a London sight that everyone wants to see and experience.

LUMEN UNITED REFORMED CHURCH WC1

The Lumen United Reformed Church (previously Regent Square Presbyterian Church) was a decent if unremarkable 1960s replacement for a much larger church, designed as a reduced version of York Minster but badly damaged in 1945 by bombing. Theis & Khan's £1,800,000 remodelling was driven by the (tiny) congregation's wish to make the building more accessible and useful to the local community while retaining and expanding its primary role as a place of worship: in short, to give it a new lease of life and save it from likely redundancy. A church hall was sold off to fund the scheme.

The building – which did not even merit a mention in Nikolaus Pevsner's *Buildings of England* – has been transformed. The greater part of the 1960s church has been retained as a worship space that can also be used as a meeting hall; indeed, clearing the concrete-framed structure of furniture makes its basic dignity all the more apparent. The focus of the space is an enigmatic tapered cone, constructed of rendered polystyrene, enclosing a top-lit 'sacred space' that can be used for private prayer or small gatherings. A new font has been designed by the sculptor Alison Wilding. The rest of the church space has been turned into a cafe, clearly visible from the street. The original church building is enclosed by new low-rise structures containing a mix of community spaces and offices. At the rear of the site, a small cloistered garden provides a calm retreat from the city streets.

The imagination and courage of the congregation and the clear commitment of its architect have given a new sense of purpose to a building that could easily have been sold for redevelopment and lost to the community.

Below
The 1960s church building has been cleared of furnishings and transformed into a community space and cafe.

Opposite
A 'sacred space' is contained in a free-standing cone, a sculptural form that reasserts the essentially spiritual nature of the building, which has found a new role.

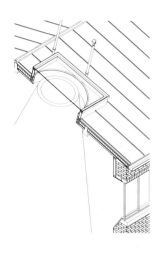

Below
The section of the building shows how the roof forms a protective umbrella, filtering light into the interior.

Opposite
Low-rise, domestic in scale, and intended to provide a home from home for cancer patients and their families and friends, the centre shelters under a lightweight roof, which brings daylight to the heart of the building. A high wall encloses landscaped courtyards and buffers the centre against noise from the street.

Maggie Keswick Jencks, garden designer and wife of the architecture critic Charles Jencks, died of cancer in 1995. During her long illness she came to realize the desperate need of cancer sufferers (and their families and friends) for counselling, encouragement and practical support, as well as medical treatment. So the idea of Maggie's Centres emerged, and they are being developed in a number of cities around Britain. Located close to major hospitals, they contain counselling, therapy and meeting rooms and generous social spaces with an ambience unlike that of the hospital itself. The first opened in Edinburgh (reflecting Maggie Jencks's Scottish roots) in 1996, and subsequent projects in Scotland have involved architects of the stature of Frank Gehry and Zaha Hadid. Each centre is developed as a result of local fund-raising so that local communities are involved from the start.

London's Maggie's Centre, attached to Charing Cross Hospital, was designed for no fee by Richard Rogers Partnership (now Rogers Stirk Harbour + Partners). The site, a short distance from the practice's riverside offices, is on a prominent corner adjacent to Ralph Tubbs's hospital complex of the 1960s. It is conceived as an 'open house', 370 square metres in area, all on one storey, except for a small office area at mezzanine level. A bright-red wall encloses the building, blocking out noise from the street, and the internal spaces, arranged around two open courtyards landscaped by Dan Pearson, are top-lit. The focus is the kitchen and eating area, a place for meeting, socializing and relaxing. In the Rogers tradition, the building has been designed in such a way that it can be adapted in the future, with folding external and internal doors that allow spaces to be reconfigured, and 'plug-in', modular furniture that can be moved freely. Timber is used extensively, reinforcing the comfortable, domestic feel of the internal spaces, and Alvar Aalto furniture and bright rugs add to its warmth and intimacy. From the street, the building has an elusive presence, as it is wrapped in trees that buffer it further against noise and pollution and shade the interior in the summer. A lightweight 'floating' roof over the mezzanine floor filters daylight into the heart of the centre.

This is a modest project for the practice, but one into which a great deal of energy and thought has been channelled. The ethos is essentially domestic: a 'home from home' that contains memories of a series of Rogers houses, from Creek Vean in Cornwall to the architect's own residence in Chelsea.

The infirmary is essentially a modern building but with an external envelope in classical style, using traditional materials and high-quality craftsmanship. The only interior designed by the Terrys is the chapel (opposite, bottom left).

'Harshly functional' was the verdict of Nikolaus Pevsner on the 1960s infirmary block at Chelsea's Royal Hospital. There were certainly no objections to the proposed demolition of this structure (designed by Ministry of Works architects under Eric Bedford), which offered substandard accommodation for its aged residents. Its replacement, in contrast, became the subject of a brief but intense battle between architectural traditionalists and those, led by Richard Rogers (whose home overlooks the Royal Hospital), who felt that the scheme was a timid exercise in pastiche and an inadequate response to the context of Sir Christopher Wren's hospital.

The competition for a new infirmary was first won by American healthcare specialists Steffian Bradley Architects. Criticism by the Royal Borough of Kensington and Chelsea's planners of the designs for the exterior of the building led to a direct commission in 2004 to Quinlan & Francis Terry to design its external envelope in a Classical manner. But the Terry designs, in turn, sparked disapproval not only from Rogers and his allies but also from others who could hardly be seen as part of a modernist lobby. Following comments from the Georgian Group and others, who feared that the new building would challenge the dominance of Wren, changes were made to the designs: the columns of the proposed portico became engaged pilasters and the idea of a cupola was dropped.

The client brief demanded a very traditional plan of small rooms for 125 residents, along central corridors, with staff accommodation, placed in the attic storey, a chapel, a medical centre and a physiotherapy suite. Load-bearing brick façades combined with concrete floors form a rational structure. A south-facing colonnade overlooking a landscaped courtyard echoes that on Wren's main building.

Quinlan Terry rejects the suggestion that his building 'competes' with that of Wren. Using a yellow brick, in contrast to the warm red brick of the Royal Hospital, was, he says, part of a strategy to give the new block a clear identity of its own. The classical order used for the portico is Tuscan, while Wren used the grander Doric order on his north elevation. As usual with Terry's architecture, the craftsmanship, including the work of bricklayers and stonemasons, is of high quality throughout.

The infirmary is a remarkably quiet and respectful piece of work, suitably modest or slightly dull depending on your tastes. Looking at it, one wonders what all the fuss was about.

Opposite
The structure has become a
prominent East End landmark.

Below
The interior has been refitted
completely, and now seats
more than 20,000 people.

The Millennium Dome, as the O2 was known before its transformation into one of the most spectacular music and events venues in the world, excited more media coverage and public debate than any British building of the last century. It is necessary to look back to the Crystal Palace of 1851 to find a parallel. The Crystal Palace was widely derided and the 1951 Festival of Britain was disowned and then demolished by an incoming Tory government, yet both have gone down in history as triumphs. The Dome, too, was ridiculed and seen as a disastrous waste of money before its recent reincarnation. In fact, only £40,000,000 of the total cost of the Millennium Experience (total: £760,000,000) was spent on the building, and since the latter provided 80,000 square metres of space capable of seating 35,000 spectators, it could have been seen as excellent value for money.

The Dome originated in the early 1990s, when John Major's government set up the Millennium Commission as a recipient of funds from the new National Lottery. The Commission was charged with funding landmark projects to mark the millennium. In selecting the former gasworks site on the Greenwich Peninsula as the site for the Millennium Festival, it was continuing the campaign of regeneration in the former London Docklands begun by Michael Heseltine in the 1980s. The design and communications company Imagination was given the task of planning the project, and Richard Rogers (then working on a masterplan for the whole peninsula) was brought in to design the architectural setting. The idea of a masted, cable-stayed, fabric-covered structure was developed by Rogers's partner, Mike Davies, and engineers Buro Happold were enlisted to provide a structural agenda. Following endorsement of the project by the new Blair government, work began on site in 1997 and the Dome was ready for an official opening on New Year's Eve, 1999 – an event marred by bad management, generating more adverse publicity for the project.

Following the closure of the Millennium Experience – which attracted more than 6,500,000 visitors during 2000 – the 'zones' inside the Dome, including structures by Nigel Coates, Zaha Hadid and Eva Jiricna, were demolished. This left a magnificent – but empty – space with no obvious use, although connected to central London by the recent Jubilee line extension. In 2001 the Dome was sold to Meridian Delta for conversion to an entertainment venue and was developed, in partnership with Anschutz Entertainment Group, to plans by HOK Sport Venue Event (now Populous) and Buro Happold at a cost of £600,000,000. The O2, named as part of a deal with a major communications company, opened in 2007 and is now one of London's most important attractions.

The demolition of a former nurses' home on Huntley Street provided the site for this Cancer Institute, named in memory of a child who died of leukaemia, and housing 350 research scientists, with 4500 square metres of laboratory space on five floors. The entrance to the new building adjoins the reinstated flank wall of an adjacent listed building (refurbished as part of the project), and its sheer glazed wall reveals a strikingly engineered staircase. The client wanted a transparent and accessible building, and this typical Grimshaw tour de force is, in visual terms, the focal point of the institute. Beyond the entrance area a top-lit atrium, covered by a roof of ETFE (ethylene tetrafluoroethylene) cushions, is formed in the light well of the listed building.

The diagram combines laboratory spaces in the core, enclosed and highly serviced, with 'write-up' areas facing west on to Huntley Street. Service areas are set along the eastern elevation, facing Chenies Mews.

It was also important to the client that the building should show some regard for its context, since Huntley Street contains, along with grim hospital blocks (still in use but meriting replacement), a run of listed houses. The fixed terracotta louvres that shade the street façade recall the extensive use of terracotta on the former University College Hospital building on Gower Street, designed by Alfred Waterhouse. As usual with Grimshaw, the detailing is meticulous throughout.

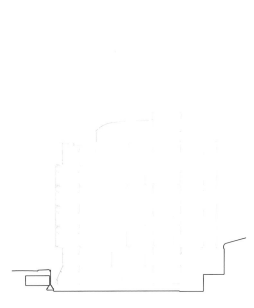

Opposite and bottom
The interior reconstruction provides a new full-height atrium with escalators serving all floors, and addresses the shortcomings of an awkwardly planned interior completed to a compromised plan in the 1960s.

Below
The exterior of Peter Jones is a 1930s classic of the Modern Movement.

Right
The plan of the building as reconstructed provides for large retail areas around an atrium.

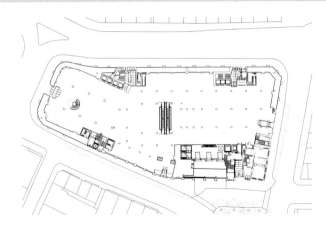

The Peter Jones store is one of the few modern buildings in London that has been almost universally popular throughout its life. The first phase of William Crabtree's scheme, with its great curving curtain wall on to Sloane Square, was constructed in 1935–37 as a replacement for an existing department store. The Second World War brought work to a standstill, and elements of the Victorian building were retained when the project was eventually completed in the 1960s to a compromised version of the original scheme. Inside, some awkward spaces were created, with poor connections between departments, although the progressive outlook of the John Lewis Partnership ensured that staff facilities, which included a theatre and squash courts, were a priority.

John McAslan's phased £100,000,000 reconstruction aimed to address the failings of the existing building and finally realize the promise of Crabtree's extraordinary vision. Floor levels were rationalized, the disjunctions within the building addressed, and new servicing and storage areas created. At the heart of the store, a spectacular new central light well rises seven storeys to the roof, with escalators serving all floors. Services have been entirely renewed, with a progressive energy strategy that makes use of chilled beams – for the first time in a British retail development – to cool the spaces. Existing façades have been seamlessly upgraded in line with modern environmental standards.

Externally Peter Jones remains the Modern landmark it has always been, but it has been re-equipped to retain its position as one of London's best-loved shops. This project has set a new benchmark for the sympathetic rehabilitation of classic Modern Movement buildings, all carried out with the store open to customers and within the context of a site tightly surrounded by busy streets.

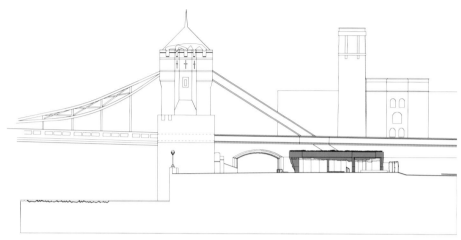

Deborah Saunt and David Hills of DSDHA have shared an interest in gardens and landscape since student days. The two pavilions they created at Potters Fields on the South Bank, close to the More London office complex and Tower Bridge, are essentially modern reinterpretations of the pavilions and grottoes found in the great landscaped parks of the eighteenth century.

Potters Fields Park, designed by landscape architect Gross Max, is part of a heavily used tourist trail along the South Bank, passing Foster + Partners' City Hall (pp. 318–19) and HMS *Belfast*. The park and More London occupy a large tract of land that was once a dense area of warehouses, destroyed by wartime bombing. The pavilions provide much-needed facilities for tourists and for the many Londoners who now work in the vicinity.

Each pavilion has a distinct identity. Parkside Pavilion, adjacent to City Hall, contains a cafe, public conveniences and cash machines. It is constructed of charred timber – allegedly the first use of the material in Britain – which is presented as a reference to the firebombs that fell on the area during the Second World War. Blossom Square Pavilion, close to Tower Bridge, houses shops, kiosks and sheltered public space. In contrast, it is made of white bleached timber. Both structures, designed in collaboration with engineer Jane Wernick, have a hand-hewn, rustic look that contrasts with the sleek, glassy aesthetic of the nearby office buildings and City Hall; few public buildings can compete with the latter for anonymity and inaccessibility. Costing less than £1,000,000, the pavilions are a modest gesture in favour of a friendly, human-scaled environment.

Opposite and left
DSDHA's two pavilions are
located close to Tower Bridge
and City Hall.

Below
Both pavilions are constructed
of timber: charred in the case
of Parkside Pavilion (left),
and unbleached for Blossom
Square Pavilion (right).

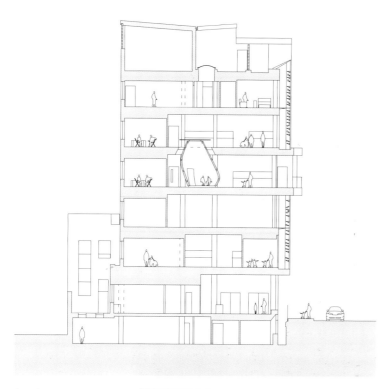

Opposite, above and right
An outpatient waiting area on the third floor is expressed as a bright red box emerging through the façade of the building.

Far right
The aim was to provide a light, open, colourful and legible interior.

Penoyre & Prasad's addition to Moorfields Eye Hospital – a world-class institution housed in a complex of buildings ranging in date from the 1890s to the 1930s, with indifferent later additions – is given a clear external identity by its striking main (southern) elevation, a tour de force both visually and structurally. The glazed façade is screened from solar gain by a series of folded aluminium louvres suspended on tensioned cables. Twinkling in the sun or illuminated by night, they give the eight-storey building a distinctive presence and a certain glamour.

The client's brief was to provide 'the best-functioning children's eye hospital in the world, without its looking like a hospital'. This agenda is equally clearly expressed inside the building, where transparency, natural light and vivid colour create an ethos far removed from the enclosed, institutional spaces so typical of hospitals. (Each floor is colour-coded to make direction-finding around the building simpler.) A full-height light well channels natural light into the internal spaces.

The emphasis throughout is on creating a welcoming, informal atmosphere. A cafe and shops are provided on the ground floor, where the building appears to float on a largely glazed entrance area. The third-floor outpatient waiting area is expressed externally by a bright-red box, emerging through the façade as a look-out point – a wilful but appealing gesture. Patient clinics enjoy good views out to a pleasant park.

Designing for sick children is a challenge. Powell & Moya rose to that challenge well at Great Ormond Street, as did Michael Hopkins at St Thomas's Evelina Children's Hospital (pp. 120–21). Penoyre & Prasad, a practice with a strong social commitment, has equally succeeded in creating an outstanding clinical facility that manages to be unintimidating and 'child-focused'.

One of Europe's largest public building projects involves two historic London hospitals, a few miles apart. Its schedule will extend over more than a decade and it will cost around £1,000,000,000.

St Bartholomew's Hospital (known as Barts) was founded in 1123 and until the Reformation was associated with the nearby Augustinian priory, the church of which survives in part as St Bartholomew the Great, Smithfield. Its buildings include the gateway to West Smithfield of 1702 and the early eighteenth-century ranges around the main courtyard, designed by James Gibbs, including the splendid main staircase and great hall, all Grade I-listed. The hospital's later additions are of considerably less architectural interest. In the 1990s a proposal to close Barts generated intense opposition, and it was eventually decided to retain the site in use as a hospital.

The Royal London Hospital in Whitechapel, east London, was founded in 1740, and the Georgian hospital survives, much altered, on Whitechapel Road. It fronts a large campus with a mix of buildings, a number of them listed, ranging in date from the late Victorian period to the early twenty-first century (for example SMC Alsop's Blizard Building; pp. 158–59).

Over several decades indecision about the future of both the Royal London and Barts led to a lack of investment and increasingly unsatisfactory conditions for patients and staff. In late 2003 the Barts and The London NHS Trust, which runs both sites, appointed Skanska Innisfree as preferred bidder for a redevelopment project embracing the two hospitals, with HOK as architect. Following a period of political indecision, when the entire project seemed threatened by growing doubts on the part of government about the Private Finance Initiative procurement route, work started on site in the summer of 2006. Completion is

scheduled for 2016, with major components opening in 2010–12. Up to 1250 inpatient beds will be provided, along with specialist emergency care and cancer and cardiac treatment facilities.

The Barts/Royal London project comes at a time when the value of the 'super-hospital' is increasingly the subject of debate, and attention is turning back to devolved, community-based healthcare provision. The architect has sought to address some of the most common criticisms of large hospitals of the recent past, including the suggestion that such institutions ignore the role of the environment as an agent of healing. On both sites the majority of existing buildings will be demolished: 60 per cent at the Royal London and just over 50 per cent at Barts. Listed buildings will be retained and refurbished. Barts will benefit enormously from the pedestrianization of the central square and its landscaping as the focal point of the hospital. A new hospital building will rise behind the retained façade of the 1930s King George V block on the south-east corner of the triangular site. Internally, a dramatic atrium forms

Below and opposite, right
At the Royal London, two eighteen-storey towers are clad in coloured glazing, a more innovative aesthetic than Barts, and one that was encouraged by local planners. The towers and a lower block sit on a three-storey brick plinth. In common with Barts, the building offers generous covered public spaces, top-lit and containing facilities for patients and visitors.

Bottom and opposite, left
The new Barts building is faced in stone and simple in form, in deference to its integration with the neighbouring Victorian buildings. It rises towards the back from an initial height of five storeys, avoiding an overpowering street presence.

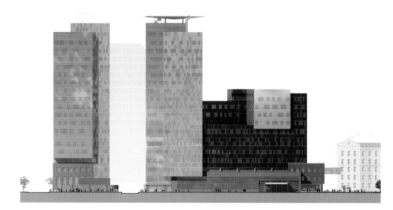

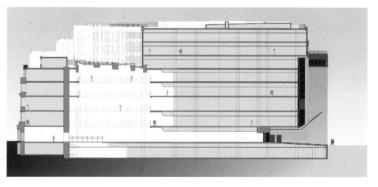

the heart of the new building. Externally, it is clad in brick and stone; the adjacent, widely admired Merrill Lynch development (2001) provided a precedent for such a contextual approach.

At the Royal London a more adventurous aesthetic was encouraged by planners in the borough of Tower Hamlets and by the Greater London Authority, with major input also from the Commission for Architecture and the Built Environment. Most of the new accommodation is provided in two eighteen-storey towers to the south of the site, complete with a rooftop landing pad for Air Ambulance helicopters. These massive new buildings, inevitably dominating the surrounding area, are clad in clear, opaque and translucent glazing in a range of colours, above a brick-clad base. Only 25 per cent of the total façade is transparent glazing, and on the south side the buildings are clad in metal filigree (even hospitals are subject to revised building-regulation requirements on the control of solar heat gain, although the new buildings are necessarily air-conditioned and sealed). A new civic space is created behind the restored main building dating from the 1750s, with a glazed 'health mall' providing access to all principal departments and giving the hospital a benign public face. Perhaps the last of its kind in London, the Royal London development responds to east Londoners' demands for major investment in local facilities. It remains to be seen whether this investment has been spent to best effect.

The flats in the former Midland Grand Hotel include an impressive penthouse in the clock tower (opposite, top right and bottom). The Grade I-listed building remains externally unchanged, but the flats are fitted out in tune with contemporary taste.

The inauguration of the Channel Tunnel Rail Link (CTRL) from the spendidly restored St Pancras International station (pp. 40–41) late in 2007 was a landmark event in the ongoing regeneration of the King's Cross area. It seems ironic now that St Pancras was once judged operationally redundant and faced demolition. The former Midland Grand Hotel, now St Pancras Chambers, designed in 1873 by Sir George Gilbert Scott and forming a frontispiece to W.H. Barlow's great train shed, was, however, not part of the CTRL project, save for a limited number of spaces at platform level. Closed as long ago as 1935 and thereafter in use until the mid-1980s as railway offices, it formed the subject of a developer competition in 1996. As a result, Manhattan Loft Corporation undertook the development of the Grade I-listed building as a mix of flats and hotel, the latter to operate under the Renaissance Hotels banner. The success of the project was inevitably linked to the rebirth of the station as an international travel hub, and

work on the hotel and flats (on the two upper floors) did not begin until 2006. By 2010 the sixty-seven flats were occupied, all having been sold off-plan, and the hotel was scheduled to open early in 2011.

The 245-bed hotel retains virtually all the most significant interiors in Scott's building, and the finest of these, including the magnificent grand staircase, have been faithfully restored to authentic decorative schemes. A striking new reception area has been created by glazing in the former carriage road, latterly used by taxis. Basements – formerly kitchens and storerooms – house services and a health spa. Most of the bedrooms are in a newly built west wing, designed by Richard Griffiths Architects to blend comfortably with Scott's architecture without being mere pastiche. The forecourt of the hotel, with a greatly expanded Underground concourse below (see pp. 34–35), has been restored to its original state and forms a worthy preface to the Gothic splendours inside the building.

'The most advanced stadium in the world, a benchmark for future stadium construction': that was the promise at the beginning of the Wembley Stadium project, and the completed building lives up to it. It was not without its problems, though: a series of construction setbacks and technical difficulties delayed its completion, and the 2006 Cup Final, scheduled to take place there, had to be moved to Cardiff.

The original stadium on the site, built for the British Empire Exhibition in 1924 and used for the 1948 Olympic Games, was widely loved. The World Cup Final in 1966 was one of its most inspirational moments. But the demolition of the 'twin towers' was surprisingly uncontroversial: it was generally realized that the building had had its day, could not compete on the international scene and was outclassed by the venues being constructed in Britain by such teams as Arsenal (pp. 118–19). In 1998, the World Stadium Team, a coalition of Foster + Partners and HOK Sport Architecture (now Populous), subsequently joined by engineering practice Mott MacDonald, won the competition to design the new English National Stadium. It was not until the autumn of 2002, however, that construction began, with £100,000,000 of National Lottery money funding the acquisition of the site.

The £352,000,000 new stadium seats 90,000 – nearly a third more than its predecessor – with vastly increased circulation space, escalator links to the upper tiers and 2600 toilets (more than any stadium in the world, it is claimed). Steeply raked seating provides unobstructed views for all spectators. There is full disabled access, including 300 viewing positions for wheelchair users. Catering facilities are of another order to those provided in the old stadium. Football is the focus of the new Wembley, but the stadium is also designed to cater for athletics events. Reduced seating and an elevated running track and field can be installed above the pitch, although the operation takes ten weeks using a modular prefabricated steel system.

The key feature of the new stadium is its partly retractable roof, which can be closed in bad weather to provide cover for all seats. The roof is supported on a great arch, visible from many parts of London, which replaces the twin towers as the symbol of British football. Some 133 metres high, spanning 315 metres and weighing 1750 tonnes, the arch, which was hoisted into position in the summer of 2004, is illuminated dramatically by night. With the staging of the Cup Final at Wembley in May 2007, the stadium took its place as one of the great sporting venues of the world.

Opposite, right and below
An important benefit of the new Wembley Stadium is a retractable roof, supported by the landmark arch, a dramatic symbol of regeneration.

Far right
The stadium can be reconfigured for musical and other events.

EDUCATION

CAMDEN

ISLINGTO

26

25

29

24

12

11

20

KENSINGTON
AND CHELSEA

15 14

WESTMINSTER

LAMB

5

22

1 BEN PIMLOTT BUILDING,
  GOLDSMITHS, UNIVERSITY OF LONDON

2 BLIZARD BUILDING, INSTITUTE OF CELL
  AND MOLECULAR SCIENCE,
  QUEEN MARY, UNIVERSITY OF LONDON

3 BRIDGE ACADEMY

4 BUSINESS ACADEMY

5 CHELSEA COLLEGE OF ART AND DESIGN

6 CITY ACADEMY, HACKNEY

7 CLAPHAM MANOR PRIMARY SCHOOL EXTENSION

8 EVELYN GRACE ACADEMY

9 FAWOOD CHILDREN'S CENTRE

10 GRADUATE CENTRE,
   QUEEN MARY, UNIVERSITY OF LONDON

11 HALLFIELD SCHOOL

12 HAMPDEN GURNEY CHURCH OF ENGLAND
   PRIMARY SCHOOL

13 HAVERSTOCK SCHOOL

14 IMPERIAL COLLEGE BUSINESS SCHOOL

15 IMPERIAL COLLEGE FACULTY BUILDING

16 JOHN PERRY NURSERY

17 KRISHNA-AVANTI SCHOOL

18 LAW DEPARTMENT,
   LONDON METROPOLITAN UNIVERSITY

19 MOSSBOURNE COMMUNITY ACADEMY

20 NEW ACADEMIC BUILDING AND
   NEW STUDENTS' CENTRE,
   LONDON SCHOOL OF ECONOMICS
   AND POLITICAL SCIENCE

21 RAVENSBOURNE

22 SACKLER BUILDING AND FINE AND APPLIED ART
   CAMPUS, ROYAL COLLEGE OF ART

23 ST MARY MAGDALENE ACADEMY

24 ST MARYLEBONE CHURCH OF ENGLAND SCHOOL

25 SCHOOL OF SLAVONIC AND EAST EUROPEAN
   STUDIES, UNIVERSITY COLLEGE LONDON

26 SURE START KILBURN

27 SURE START LAVENDER

28 WESTFIELD STUDENT VILLAGE,
   QUEEN MARY, UNIVERSITY OF LONDON

29 WESTMINSTER ACADEMY

HACKNEY

Surprisingly simple in appearance compared with Will Alsop's other recent work – the rooftop sculptural feature notwithstanding – the Ben Pimlott Building attracted some criticism on its completion. Ellis Woodman of *Building Design* complained about its 'shed-like gaucheness' and 'distinctly anaemic façades', and disliked the 'scribble' sculpture (Alsop's own creation).

Alsop was appointed in January 2002, following a high-profile competition, to design the first part of a two-phase development for Goldsmiths. The Ben Pimlott Building is named after a distinguished warden of the college who died suddenly in 2004; next to it, the second phase, designed by Stride Treglown and housing further facilities for the college, is nearly complete. The Ben Pimlott Building contains four floors of visual-arts studios above lecture and conference rooms on the ground floor, laboratories and offices for the department of psychology on the first floor, and digital media laboratories, including film-editing and sound-recording studios, on the second floor. The mix of activities reflects the range of teaching and research at Goldsmiths, which is well known as the breeding ground of a new generation of British artists.

Located in a relatively obscure part of south London, Goldsmiths wanted to make a splash with its new buildings. Its core is the former Royal Naval School of the 1850s, from which it has expanded over the last century into a variety of converted premises, including the former Deptford Town Hall. A new library by Allies and Morrison, completed in 1997, is its only other recent purpose-built facility.

Alsop's building occupies a gateway site, giving Goldsmiths a serious presence on the street and a connection to the local community. Its elevated position makes it a prominent feature of the local skyline, but it eschews the colourful display of the practice's Peckham Library (pp. 84–85) in favour of a purposeful industrial aesthetic not inappropriate to the activities contained within. Three elevations are clad in aluminium, with relatively minimal fenestration, the south elevation animated by a dramatic escape stair. The north elevation, in contrast, is entirely glazed, enabling daylight to flood the interior and spaces inside to be opened up to public view. The interiors are highly flexible, with tough finishes and the potential for reconfiguration in line with users' needs. At the top of the building a two-storey section is cut away to provide a terrace for outdoor displays.

Costing less than £7,000,000, the building seems to be good value for money, and the use of a design-and-build contract does not appear to have undermined the architect's intentions. This is not one of Alsop's greatest works, perhaps, but it is a highly serviceable and discreetly glamorous building that responds strongly to the brief on many levels.

Elevated above the surrounding houses, the new building with its many sculptural elements is a striking addition to the skyline of south-east London. Will Alsop's twisted metal artwork enlivens the cut-away terrace (opposite, top right).

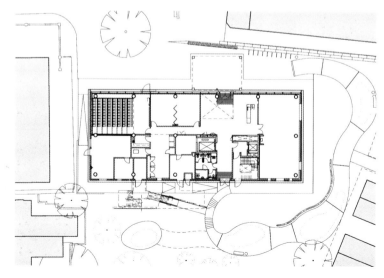

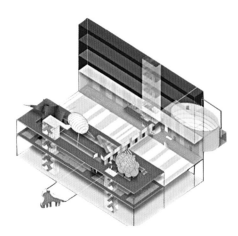

Will Alsop's Peckham Library (pp. 84–85), winner of the Stirling Prize in 2000, remains one of the modern architectural landmarks of London, a popular, colourful building that makes a strong case for iconic structures – as long as they are in the right place. His £45,000,000 medical school for Queen Mary, the subject of a prestigious competition in 2001, is in an equally unfashionable corner of London, tucked away behind the decaying Victorian blocks of the Royal London Hospital, to which the school is attached. (The hospital is being comprehensively rebuilt, under a Private Finance Initiative agreement, to plans by HOK; see pp. 148–49.) In this instance Alsop's taste for the expressive, colourful and even outrageous was tempered by a highly practical brief. The result is a building that is hugely stimulating as a place to work and study, and that makes a strong contribution to the public realm.

The brief provided for laboratory and research space for 400 people, lecture and seminar rooms, a lecture theatre seating 400, and a cafeteria. In addition, a highly novel feature is a public exhibition space intended to foster interest in science and medicine among young people. Occupying the full width of the site at basement level, above ground the building is divided into two parts on either side of a paved plaza, connected by a glazed link bridge on the first floor. The lecture theatre and cafeteria are in the smaller of the two blocks and are connected to an existing medical school building. The long spine of this smaller block forms the point of entry for members of the public.

The laboratories extend across the basement, while the upper floors of the main block contain offices, areas for writing up experiments and meeting rooms, set around a central atrium that extends down to the basement, providing the laboratories with natural light. (They are also lit by roof lights set into the plaza.) Within the atrium three sculptural pods – a familiar feature of Alsop's buildings – accommodate seminar and meeting spaces accessed at ground-, first- and second-floor levels. A fourth pod, bright red and two storeys high, known as the Centre of the Cell, contains 195 square metres of public exhibition space, with controlled views into the laboratories, and is entered via the bridge.

The most remarkable feature of this building, however, is its transparency, as the public square provides intriguing views into and through it. (The glazed façade of the main block is punctuated by painted glass artworks by Bruce McLean, with whom Alsop collaborates regularly.) Medical schools have traditionally been private, secure places. Alsop's building seeks to demystify the process of medical education, to open up spaces, where practical, in order to engage the public in what goes on inside.

Opposite, left and top right, and below right
The Queen Mary medical school consists of two blocks separated by a pedestrian route and connected by a glazed bridge.

Opposite, bottom right, and below, left
Externally and internally, the building is highly colourful, with sculptural pods, one of which (opposite) contains a public exhibition space. Others contain seminar and meeting rooms.

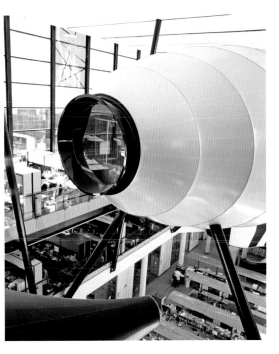

BRIDGE ACADEMY E2

The physical context of BDP's Bridge Academy contrasts vividly with that of the practice's earlier Hampden Gurney Primary School in Marylebone (pp. 176–77), but in both cases the architect faced the challenge of squeezing a lot of accommodation on to a very constrained site. In this case, the location was a derelict brownfield site next to Regent's Canal in a far from affluent quarter of the East End. As at Hampden Gurney, the only option was to design a largely vertical school, producing what has been described as 'a piece of architectural origami' in which roof areas are used for learning and social activities to compensate for the scarcity of space at ground level. The concept, developed by BDP, is already being applied elsewhere; in some respects, it is a return to the diagram of the classic London Board school and a move away from the typically 'horizontal' schools of the twentieth century, many of which made poor use of their sites.

Serving 1150 pupils, largely drawn from nearby parts of Hackney, the academy, which specializes in music and mathematics, was equally conceived as a facility for the wider local community and a conscious marker of regeneration. The multi-level landscape connects and unifies the three principal elements in the complex: teaching spaces, a sports hall and a 'music box', which can be adapted into a 450-seat concert hall.

A central square is the social heart of the school, and includes a dining area with views to the canal. The library is suspended on a curved beam above the square, leaving the ground unobstructed: the aim was to create 'a school without columns' (and without the corridors that provide spaces ideal for bullying), producing an open and flexible environment adaptable to changing educational needs. Materials, including cedar cladding and ETFE (ethylene tetrafluoroethylene) cushions, which form much of the canalside elevation, are part of a low-energy design strategy, continued in the natural ventilation of most of the building and in its form, conceived to maximize the use of natural light.

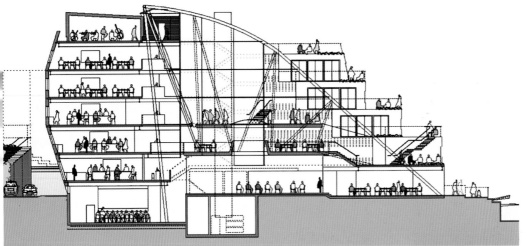

Opposite
Cedar cladding is part of the palette of materials applied to the Bridge Academy.

This page
The academy makes skilful use of a very tight site next to Regent's Canal by arranging teaching and social spaces on a stepped multi-level diagram. A central square forms the heart of the building.

BUSINESS ACADEMY DA18

Although the Bexley Business Academy presents a closed exterior, its interior is light-filled and open, encouraging integration and interaction. Photographs of pupils are displayed, promoting a sense of ownership.

Described as 'the first purpose-built, part-privately funded independent state school in Europe', the Business Academy at Thamesmead in the London Borough of Bexley is the product of the last Labour government's drive to tackle under-achievement in the state education system and to create centres of real excellence in areas where that system is seen to be deficient. In this instance, developer and property magnate Sir David Garrard assumed the role of project sponsor and worked closely with Foster + Partners on the development of the designs for the new building. Of about fifty academies planned around Britain, half of them in London, Foster + Partners has designed a further four. The emphasis throughout is on equipping young people to succeed in business and the professions.

For Norman Foster, the project provided the opportunity to develop ideas about school design that he had nurtured over some years. He envisaged a school that was 'open-planned, filled with light, democratic and flexible – with no corridors, no institutional barriers and with a philosophy of integration'. Opened in two phases in 2002–2003 and catering for 1300 pupils aged eleven to eighteen, the academy clearly reflects these ideals.

The predominant theme of the three-storey, 11,800-square-metre building is its open planning, with teaching and technical areas arranged around three courtyards for socializing and interaction: recent thinking about the workplace was clearly an influence here. The business courtyard, which is the academy's principal hub, incorporates a 'trading pit', complete with large plasma screens, where students can get a taste of City-style trading, as well as a cafe, a theatre and a television studio. While the teaching and technical areas are highly flexible, divided by moveable partitions, even spaces that must be enclosed for safety, such as science laboratories, have fully glazed partitions, ensuring that the theme of transparency and openness is not compromised.

Architecturally, the academy has been described as 'a ruthlessly simple box'. Its setting is far from glamorous, and the area has had serious problems with vandalism. By night, closing shutters turn the building into a relatively impregnable box; during working hours it is a beacon of progress for the local community, which makes extensive use of the facilities outside school hours. The double-skin façades, with shading louvres to baffle solar gain, are part of a low-energy services agenda to cut running costs and improve the overall sustainability rating of the building.

Given the aims of the academy, it is entirely appropriate that the building draws on Foster + Partners' wide experience of office design: why should a school be a place divorced from the world of work? Disciplined, quietly elegant and purposeful, this is a building with a mission.

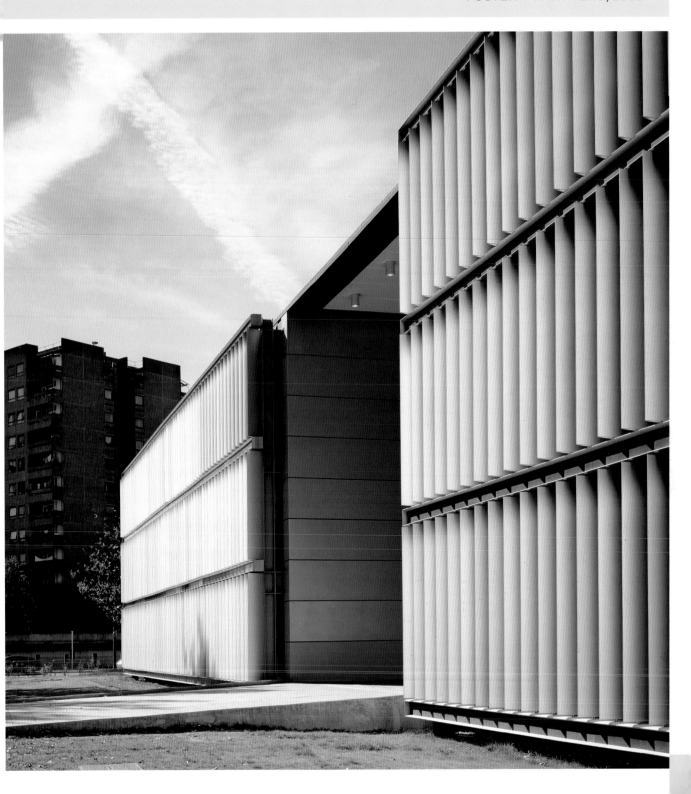

The new home of Chelsea College of Art and Design (now part of the University of the Arts London) formerly housed the Royal Army Medical College. The attractive, buildings of red brick and Portland stone, neatly detailed in a neo-Baroque manner, were constructed between 1898 and 1907. The site, across the road from Tate Britain – the two buildings replaced the notorious Millbank Penitentiary – was vacated by the Army during the 1990s, and was the subject of a number of bids from prospective users. It could easily have been sold to a developer and the listed buildings converted to upmarket flats. However, the government, unexpectedly perhaps, resolved to accept Chelsea College's bid.

The buildings, which include barrack and married-quarter blocks and a more formal officers' mess, are arranged on three sides of a central parade ground (latterly used for parking). They were well suited to the college's requirements, offering a range of spaces ideal for adaptation as studios, offices and workshops. There were proposals to landscape the parade ground as a formal square, with an underground gallery below it – possibly linked to the basement of Tate Britain. This aspect of the scheme has been temporarily shelved on cost grounds, but the central courtyard is often used by students for building large-scale artworks.

Allies and Morrison was an ideal choice for the £37,000,000 project, since the practice has a sympathetic approach to old buildings and is adept at new design in historic contexts. A number of later accretions were

demolished and new structures sensitively inserted. On John Islip Street brick pavilions have been added to the rear of the married-quarter block, making a new connection to the street. An entrance to the complex was formed between the mess block, which fronts the river, and the adjacent laboratory building, forming a light-filled atrium, crossed by walkways and containing a bar, cafe and shop. A small triangular plot at the end of the atrium has been filled by a new studio/workshop building, with large spaces that could not be carved out of the existing structures (the shape of the site is defined by a surviving fragment of the great wall that enclosed the long-vanished gaol).

The new work is well detailed, robust and elegant throughout, although never at odds with the context. The subtle transformation of this neglected site has reinforced the idea of developing an arts quarter around Tate Britain, which has long been an isolated cultural presence in an otherwise inert quarter of London.

Opposite
The development is a mix of refurbishment, conversion and sensitive new build, with a new atrium (bottom right) forming the principal point of entry to the complex. The contrast between old and new is deliberately exploited as a feature of the interiors (top right).

Below
The former Royal Army Medical College on Millbank provided a ready-made campus for the college.

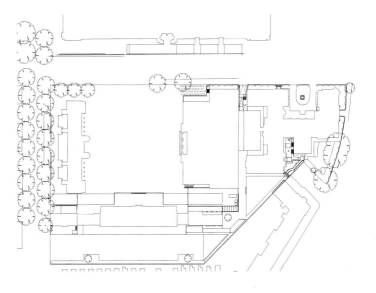

City academies remain controversial institutions, but they have generated innovative approaches to school design comparable with those that accompanied the educational revolution of the 1950s and 1960s. The site for Studio E's academy in Hackney was formerly occupied by Homerton College (which closed in 2007), and the academy had initially been allocated another site near by. Construction began in January 2008, and the school took in its first students in the autumn of 2009.

The academy is close to the ancient heart of the area – the National Trust's Sutton House is across the road, part of a group of listed buildings – and the site is bisected by a heavily used public footpath. The scheme bridges the latter, with external play areas either side of it. The architecture is colourful and expressive, with an emphasis on transparency and openness internally: fully glazed elevations to classrooms facing circulation spaces provide a vivid impression of a 'school without walls'.

There was a clear wish to root the building in the local community from the start. An unusual feature of the brief was the involvement of children from local primary schools – the future users of the building – in the evolution of the designs, extending beyond such ephemeral issues as the use of colour to the nature and use of the spaces in the building. The philosophy of the academy, structured and disciplined, draws on that which has made the nearby Mossbourne Community Academy (pp. 192–93) such a success. But the architectural expression of this philosophy is anything but oppressive: the interior is planned around creative subject 'clusters', with the cafeteria and other communal facilities in a top-lit concourse. In a far from affluent area of London, this building is already recognized as a symbol of regeneration of which local people can be proud.

Opposite
The City Academy is planned
as a series of clusters, making
the best use of scarce open
space in its inner-city location.

Right and below
Inside, the top-lit atrium gives
the school a social hub with a
cafeteria and other facilities.

De Rijke Marsh Morgan Architects (dRMM) is a young practice with a growing reputation for school design. At the 1950s Kingsdale School in Dulwich, south London, the firm added a pillowed membrane roof over the existing playground and a new assembly hall in a lightweight pod. That project was completed in 2004. For Clapham Manor Primary School, originally built in the nineteenth century, the brief from Lambeth Council was to replace the caretaker's house and an extension dating from the 1960s with new accommodation, in line with the school's enhanced status as a Department for Education and Skills 'beacon'.

The school is located in a conservation area and has the Grade II-listed Oddfellows' Hall as its neighbour. The new four-storey building, providing a relocated main entrance, offices and classrooms with full access for the disabled, was completed in 2007. The project involved the remodelling of spaces within the existing school

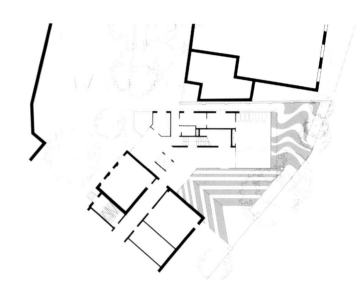

building to accommodate present-day educational practice, including the provision of enlarged classrooms.

The new building (total cost: £2,000,000) relates in scale to the existing school, but stands free of its brick façades; a glazed stairwell and double-aspect lift connect the two. It makes no concessions to the style of the older structure but is clad in polychromatic, patterned glazing over a curtain-wall system, 'a graduated loop of colour that shifts as it moves around the building, picking up the vernacular hues of its neighbours ... and the greens of the soft landscape towards the rear', according to the architect. The detailed treatment of the elevations was developed in close consultation with the school community and local residents. Clear, translucent and solid panels overlay the façade to allow daylight in while controlling solar heat gain. Their arrangement appears to be random, but is a response to the internal organization, maximizing light, fresh air (through opening windows) and views where needed. The colourful box is elevated on a recessed plinth of butt-jointed glazing, providing the requisite transparency for the main entrance area and school offices.

With its brilliant reworking of the traditional curtain wall, this project inserts a contemporary, jewel-like object into an austere Victorian townscape, offering local children a new and highly stimulating learning environment.

Contrasting stylistically and in materials with its Victorian neighbour, dRMM's addition to Clapham Manor Primary School in fact provides an infusion of sensitive modern design in a conservation area, with strong use of colour to lift the spirits of both users and passers-by. It is skilfully slotted into a tight site.

The first completed building in Britain by global star
Zaha Hadid, the Evelyn Grace Academy is the eighth in
a series of schools founded by the charity ARK (Absolute
Return for Kids). In fact, Hadid's role in the project was
circumscribed by the design-and-build procurement
strategy, which left her practice as 'executive architect and
concept guardian'. Detailed design was entrusted to B + R
Architects, which was charged with delivering the building
to a £36,500,000 budget and with construction completed
within eighteen months of the start on site. There was no
scope for extraneous frills, and some of the details jar –
faceted glazing, for example, in areas of the building
where more expensive bespoke curved panels would
have looked far better. In general, however, Hadid's
distinctive language emerges strongly in a building that is
certainly a striking landmark in a classic 'deprived' area of
London with associated problems of crime and delinquency.

The Academy consists of two quite separate schools,
Evelyn and Grace, which share dining, science, sports
and other facilities. The aim was to avoid the anonymity
of large schools and to create in each a real sense of
community (backed up by a rigorous disciplinary code), as
well as a competitive spirit. The site is typically constrained,
so that the classrooms are stacked vertically and
accessed via broad corridors. The planning is conventional
enough – in tune with the ethos of the schools – but
makes effective use of the site. The architecture makes
a clear statement about the mission of the academy as
an engine of regeneration and social advancement.

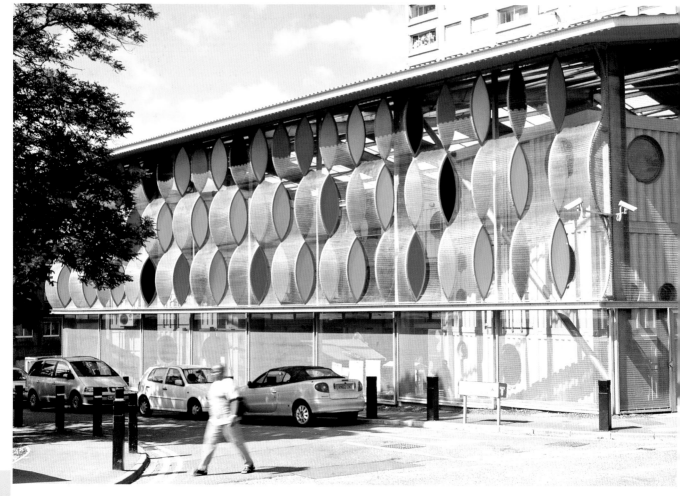

In common with educational projects by DSDHA, Greenhill Jenner, John McAslan + Partners and others, Will Alsop's Fawood Children's Centre represents a new approach to nursery-school design that responds to the real needs of children and their parents. Such buildings were underwritten by a government commitment to funding new nursery schools in disadvantaged areas of Britain.

The Stonebridge Estate in north London certainly falls into that category. It was developed between the wars, initially with two-storey houses, which gave way in the 1960s to brutally ugly slabs of local-authority flats. By the 1990s it had become a typical 'sink' estate, plagued by unemployment, poverty and rising crime. The transfer of the estate's management to a Housing Action Trust (HAT), however, signalled the start of a campaign to regenerate the area physically and socially, with much of the existing housing scheduled for clearance.

An existing nursery built in the 1960s, the Evan Davies School, had provided good facilities in difficult circumstances, but, after consultation with local residents, it was decided to create a new nursery on a new site on the north side of the estate. Alsop was appointed by the Stonebridge HAT in 2001 to develop proposals. The new centre was to be larger than its predecessor, open for longer hours – thus catering for working parents – serve an extended age range (six months to four years) and offer dedicated facilities for children with autism or special needs. The client wanted a building that was a symbol of regeneration as well as a practical resource for the community. In SMC Alsop it chose the ideal architect to realize that vision.

Instead of a compartmentalized building in the traditional mould, Alsop gave Stonebridge a huge, flexible, economical space. The building is a light-filled portal-frame shed, with a partly translucent pitched roof, containing a series of smaller free-standing structures – a design approach Alsop pioneered at Peckham Library in south London (located in another underprivileged area of the capital; pp. 84–85). The detailed brief for the building evolved gradually in discussion with the client and the future users. The internal landscape – essentially an 'inside/outside' space – contains a sandpit, water garden, cycle track and other delights for children. Free-standing pavilions are formed from recycled shipping containers (a commodity of which there is a permanent glut) piled up to three storeys high. There are no extraneous trimmings, and the industrial character of the building is mitigated only by the free use of vivid colour. Externally, the centre is clad in stainless-steel mesh with brightly coloured lozenges at the upper level. It feels reassuringly secure but never defensive or intimidating.

The centre was shortlisted for the Stirling Prize in 2005, the judges being initially 'bemused' but ultimately 'having been won over by its sheer bravado, carrying away with them an impression of amusement and delight'. This is surely one of Alsop's best buildings to date – as well as one of his cheapest, at a cost of £2,400,000 – and a classic instance of a happy marriage of architect and users, who seem to love the place.

Opposite, top left, top middle, and bottom
Cheap and cheerful but a visible symbol of regeneration, Alsop Architects' Fawood Children's Centre is part of the ongoing renewal of the Stonebridge Estate in north-west London. The use of vivid colour is an important part of the project.

Opposite, top right
Internally, recycled shipping containers are used to form rooms in the open space.

Right
Services, such as toilets, private offices and the kitchen, are contained in rectangular heated units. Play areas include a water garden, a cycle track and a yurt (bottom left). The entrance deck is on the right-hand side of the plan.

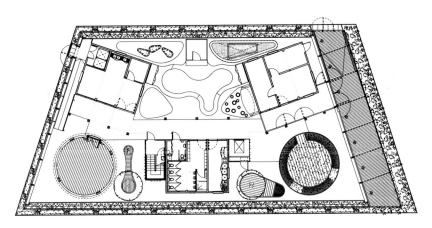

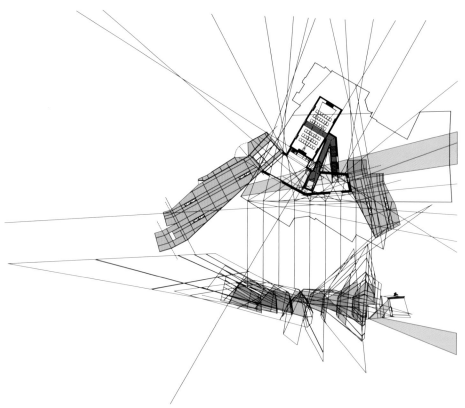

Left
The form of the Graduate Centre was developed with reference to pedestrian routes leading around the cottage and from a proposed new square behind the building to Regent's Canal.

Below and opposite, right
The new Graduate Centre includes both a converted lock-keeper's cottage and the new extension by Surface Architects, linked by a double-height foyer. With its vivid colour and strong form, the building is a stimulating addition to an essentially nineteenth-century context.

Opposite, left
Seminar rooms offer intriguing views over Regent's Canal.

Led by two former assistants of Will Alsop, Andy MacFee and Richard Scott, Surface Architects is one of the more off-beat young practices in London, eschewing the deadpan objectivity of such architects as Caruso St John and Sergison Bates in favour of determinedly expressive and colourful design. An earlier project by Surface for Queen Mary was the insertion of toilets and a lift for the disabled into the library, in a strikingly sculptural intervention that made a virtue of necessity.

The £650,000 graduate centre provides workspaces, seminar rooms and a common room for postgraduate students in the arts and social sciences. The new block, a series of interlocking forms in the best Deconstructivist mould, wraps around the north and west sides of a converted early nineteenth-century lock-keeper's cottage that had long been derelict. A boldly projecting extrusion on the canalside incorporates a huge picture window for the common room. To the rear, the building is clad in smooth aluminium. A double-height foyer connecting old and new buildings contains a stair and bridge link (facilitating full access for the disabled) that the architect describes as a 'tendril'. Strong colour is used freely inside.

Is this project an example of 1980s revival (as one critic implied) or the forward-looking work proclaimed by the architect? Such a question may be irrelevant, as the building is an enjoyable addition to the campus and a pleasant place in which to work.

Not so long ago, Queen Mary, of all the major colleges of the University of London, seemed to have the most disadvantages in terms of its site, which is a long way down Mile End Road in east London, next to Regent's Canal. Today, with the East End newly fashionable, Queen Mary is capitalizing on the huge potential of its locale and commissioning some high-quality buildings for its expanding campus: MJP Architects, Hawkins\Brown, Sheppard Robson and Feilden Clegg Bradley Studios (pp. 210–11) have all built there in recent years, and SMC Alsop's Institute of Cell and Molecular Science for Queen Mary, next to the site of the Royal London Hospital, is already an icon of east London (pp. 158–59).

The Hallfield Estate was the first major work by Denys Lasdun (in collaboration with Lindsay Drake) after the disbandment of Tecton, the partnership founded in the 1930s by Berthold Lubetkin, of which Lasdun was a member. The housing is very much in the Tecton tradition, but the school, completed in 1955 and now listed Grade II*, is unmistakably a Lasdun building. It anticipates, on a small scale, the drama of his later works (such as the National Theatre) and reflects the influence of Le Corbusier, in particular the Pavilion Suisse.

A competition in the late 1990s for an extension to the school, with Lasdun as one of the judges, resulted in a victory for Future Systems (which disbanded in 2008). The practice's flowing, organic approach to design was both sympathetic to the existing building and yet emphatically of a new era. Funding was, however, not forthcoming and the scheme was abandoned. In 2001 Caruso St John was appointed to develop fresh proposals. By this time the need for additional accommodation was becoming urgent, as the school had been using temporary huts spread across part of the playground for nearly twenty-five years. The brief to the architect provided for six new classrooms for juniors and three for infants. The new buildings were completed and occupied in 2005.

Even for a practice as thoughtful and history-conscious as Caruso St John, the challenge of building in the context of a Modern Movement icon was considerable. The scheme was subjected to intense scrutiny by planners in Westminster City Council, English Heritage and other heritage groups. Caruso St John's initial idea of constructing the new buildings in hard black engineering brick was vetoed, depriving the additions of a subversive element of drama. (Lasdun had used black brick for the infants' classrooms, but regrettably it was painted off-white in the 1970s.) Instead, a light-cream brick, not far removed in hue from London stock, was used.

The other key planning problem, apart from material, was the position of the new buildings in relation to the existing school. Lasdun's composition, with its sweeping contours and profusion of mature trees – survivors of both wartime bombing and subsequent redevelopment – is an essentially romantic response to the site. The two new blocks read as a natural extension of the earlier school, echoing Lasdun's engagement with the setting and taking advantage of a variety of views: classrooms are at the corners of the blocks with views out in two directions. In Peter St John's words, they read 'as if they are the last pieces of a complicated jigsaw'. Inside, exposed red-brick walls and black floors provide a powerful contrast to the more neutral internal palette of the original building. This project has all the subtlety and controlled drama expected of Caruso St John: it respects the icon to which it forms an addition but is not unduly reverential.

Opposite and right
The two new blocks are set either side of the original buildings and surrounded by trees, which provide an attractive and calming setting from inside and outside.

Below
The school is pleasantly small in scale in comparison with the surrounding blocks of the Hallfield Estate.

Opposite, top
The vertical form of BDP's
Hampden Gurney Primary
School marks a return to
tradition, with playing areas
high above the streets.

Opposite, bottom, and right
The school occupies a tight,
irregular site in central London.
The adjacent housing, also by
BDP, was crucial in providing
funding for the scheme.

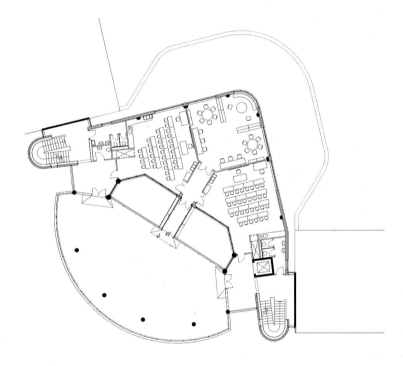

Sir Arthur Conan Doyle's fictional detective Sherlock Holmes famously referred to the Board schools of Victorian London as 'beacons of the future'. Towering above the humble terraced streets and often with playgrounds on the roof, these citadels of learning, according to Holmes, presaged a more civilized society.

Hampden Gurney Primary School by BDP (Building Design Partnership) marks, in one sense, a return to tradition. Post-war schools, even in inner London, have tended to be low-rise, but Hampden Gurney is a multi-level school and has playing areas set high above the streets. Yet in other respects – in its transparency, lightness and flexibility – it is a radical design, far removed from the rigidly compartmented academies of the nineteenth century.

The site was formerly occupied by a typical low-rise school of the 1950s, built inexpensively on land cleared by wartime bombing – a gash in the densely built-up area. Plans for a new school came to fruition in 1995, when BDP was appointed to design it after competitive interviews. The school itself is now framed by two housing blocks, also designed by BDP, which help to cement it into its context and were vital to the funding package.

The diagram of the building is clear and practical. The ground floor contains a nursery area, plus offices and a staff room. From there, pupils progress literally 'up the school': the top floor has a technology garden for those in Year Six. An assembly hall and a chapel (since this is a Church of England school) are located in the basement,

together with a playground for ball games. Other play areas, which can be used for open-air teaching in fine weather, are provided on the street front at each level. They are connected to the classrooms by bridges across the void that extends through the centre of the building and is a source of natural ventilation. A tensile fabric canopy extends above the atrium and provides some shelter for the rooftop play area. The openness of the steel-framed building reflects some skilful structural engineering (also by BDP), with a rooftop bow arch picking up the floor loadings.

Directly commissioned by the user, this school shows that Private Finance Initiatives are not the only, or the best, way to procure new education buildings. It is a revelation: the best new school in the capital for some years. This makes the delays imposed by the local authority, Westminster City Council (planning permission took three years to secure), all the more lamentable.

Haverstock School, which replaces a comprehensive school, occupies a very constricted site close to Chalk Farm Underground station. The street elevation is clad in perforated copper.

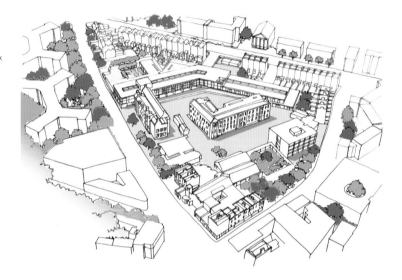

This 1250-place secondary school replaced a comprehensive school with a distinguished list of alumni, including David and Ed Miliband, and was, appropriately, the first school building in the London Borough of Camden to be procured under the Private Finance Initiative so actively promoted by New Labour. The school specializes in business and enterprise studies and seems to be building on the illustrious reputation of its predecessor. Construction was phased, to allow decanting from the old buildings.

In architectural terms, Haverstock School benefits from an extremely efficient plan form. In contrast to many earlier city schools, in which buildings were islanded in seas of asphalt, Haverstock's buildings, mainly three storeys high, fill the constricted site, enclosing a central courtyard, which includes areas for games as well as more intimate social spaces. The main circulation routes are on the ground floor, with corridors adjoining the central court, which itself provides a convenient route across the site. A bold frontage – a street elevation marked by a perforated copper screen – gives the school a civic presence on Haverstock Hill, close to Chalk Farm Underground station. In environmental terms, the school benefits from the use of natural light and cross-ventilation, reducing its use of energy. A 5-metre-tall sculpture by Kisa Kawakami in the three-storey entrance atrium commemorates Feilden Clegg Bradley Studios partner Richard Feilden: the school was his last project before his untimely death in 2005.

IMPERIAL COLLEGE BUSINESS SCHOOL SW7

Left, below and opposite, top
The Business School gives
Imperial College an imposing
'front door'. Inside, a striking
steel drum houses banks of
lecture theatres.

Opposite, bottom
The Sir Alexander Fleming
Building, one of a number
of other projects by Foster
+ Partners on the college
campus.

Imperial College – effectively the British equivalent of Massachusetts Institute of Technology – occupies a crowded site in South Kensington, between the Royal Albert Hall and the Science and Natural History museums. During the 1960s Thomas Collcutt's magnificent Imperial Institute, except for its landmark tower, was demolished to allow for the expansion of the college. Some fine town houses by the late nineteenth-century architect Richard Norman Shaw were also flattened. Unfortunately, most of the new buildings subsequently developed by Imperial were of mediocre quality, but in more recent years the college has raised its sights: John McAslan has refurbished and extended the library, for example.

Foster + Partners' involvement with the college developed from the practice's work early in the 1990s on Albertopolis, a masterplan for the entire South Kensington museum and education quarter. As part of a subsequent development plan for Imperial College, the firm designed the Sir Alexander Fleming Building (1994–98), a structure of outstanding quality housing medical research and teaching facilities. The next Foster addition was the Flowers Building, containing multi-disciplinary research space and slotted into a tight backland site next to the Science Museum's Wellcome Wing.

The Business School, in contrast, is prominently located on Exhibition Road: the project is linked to a radical reconstruction of the college's main entrance. Part of the accommodation is contained within a refurbished 1920s block, while, behind the glass walls of a new building, a stainless-steel drum, housing banks of lecture rooms, makes an arresting addition to the streetscape.

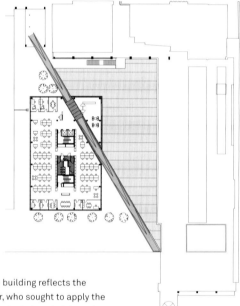

For all its academic excellence, Imperial College had, until quite recently, a poor record of architectural patronage. Apart from its residential blocks by Sheppard Robson – recently demolished to make way for new buildings by Kohn Pedersen Fox – the college's rapid expansion during the 1960s produced nothing beyond the routinely functional. At that time, some fine Victorian buildings on the South Kensington site, including Thomas Collcutt's magnificent Imperial Institute, were flattened to facilitate the expansion.

The four buildings completed since the 1990s by Foster + Partners for Imperial, along with several commissions to other practices, have helped to remedy the situation. The excellent Sir Alexander Fleming Building (1994–98), housing medical research and teaching accommodation, was the first, and the unashamedly showy Business School, incorporating a new main entrance to the college on Exhibition Road, the largest and most prominent (pp. 180–81). The Faculty Building is immediately behind the Business School, in Dalby Court, an internal square that contains, at lower level, the college's massive heat and power plant, which could not be moved. The new building forms part of Foster + Partners' wider masterplan to improve Dalby Court and pedestrian routes across the campus. By constructing a deck across the court, with a ramped route that cuts through the Faculty Building, Foster formed a new link between Exhibition Road and Queen's Lawn, the formal heart of the college. Basement levels provide a small parking area for cars and space for 600 bicycles.

The rationale behind the building reflects the agenda of the college's rector, who sought to apply the lessons of the commercial sector to its administration. All heads of department, plus key managerial staff, have offices in the building, and there is plenty of space for meetings and other 'interaction'.

The fit-out of the interior is elegant and practical, and the building is designed for low-energy operation. What makes it distinctive is its external cladding, featuring solid panels in three shades of blue, selected by Danish designer and perennial Foster collaborator Per Arnoldi. Forming a pattern on the glazed façade, the panels appear to be randomly placed but are in fact calculated to shade offices from solar gain. Columns painted deep orange, set along the edge of the ramp and visible through the façade, provide another element of strong colour. The days when Foster's palette was confined to grey and silver have gone.

Opposite
The plan shows the way in which a new route across the campus cuts through the Faculty Building. Storage space for bicycles is provided at basement level.

Right
The building sits in a previously sterile internal court containing the college's main power plant, which had to be accommodated in the scheme.

Below, left and right
The strong use of colour is an important element of the scheme, with solid panels on the glazed façade additionally helping to baffle solar gain.

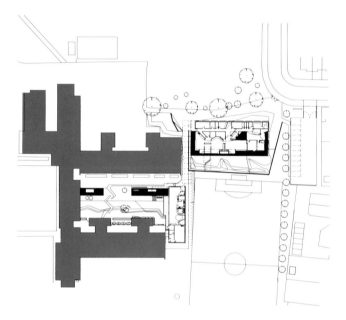

This precise and elegant but highly practical little building, constructed in ten months and costing less than £500,000, is one of a number of 'neighbourhood nurseries' – some new, others adaptations of existing buildings – that have opened as part of a pioneering initiative by the London Borough of Barking & Dagenham. This strategy focuses on the more deprived areas of the borough, which, although a crucial part of the Thames Gateway, is far from affluent. Three projects have been commissioned from DSDHA, the practice formed by Deborah Saunt and David Hills in 1998. At the time of the commission, DSDHA had yet to complete a free-standing building, although it had won a Commission for Architecture and the Built Environment-sponsored competition for nursery-school design.

The brief in this instance was initially for a building accommodating twenty-six children within the curtilage of the existing John Perry Primary School. (As Phase 2 of the project, a fifty-place day-care facility was constructed on adjacent land.) The architect conceived the new building as 'a studio for children', closing one end of a courtyard surrounded by low-rise school buildings dating from the 1950s, and partly inspired by the idyllic studio and garden created by Barbara Hepworth in St Ives. Instead of a conventional enclosed environment, the client wanted open, light spaces that connect with the outside world (the typical family home in this part of London is a local-authority flat). The use of polycarbonate sheet, a cheap but tough material, to form the western elevation of the building, facing the existing courtyard,

was a response to this requirement, its aluminium-framed windows set at child height. This elevation incorporates the most dramatic feature of the building: a boldly projecting canopy, cantilevering 10 metres over the courtyard. Elsewhere, walls are constructed of insulated timber stud clad in brick – a hard Dutch engineering brick with an iridescent surface – with high bands of clear glazing, offering a defensive front to the outside world.

Inside the building, and in the revamped courtyard, the idea of a landscape for children has been realized with joy and imagination in spaces that are colourful and stimulating but never contrived or condescending. This is a building that invites discovery. It embodies DSDHA's quest for architecture that is comfortable but inspirational, both complex and simple, and strongly rooted in an exploration of the possibilities of materials. The firm is one of a number of young practices forging a new London vernacular.

DSDHA's additions to the John Perry Nursery include an extension to the existing school with a revamped internal landscaped courtyard (opposite, top left), and a free-standing day-care facility clad in Dutch engineering brick (opposite, top right and bottom).

The London boroughs of Brent and Harrow have the highest concentration of Hindus found anywhere in Britain. Brent has the magnificent Shri Swaminarayan Mandir, a glittering and beautifully crafted temple completed in 1995. A more modest version of this exotic landmark forms part of the Krishna-Avanti School in Harrow, a school reflecting the teachings of the Hare Krishna movement – and the first Hindu faith school in the United Kingdom. The marble-faced temple forms a small part of an essentially modern building that makes no attempt to ape the Indian vernacular, even though the commission stipulated that the design should use the traditional principles of Vastu Shastra, a system of construction rooted in the Hindu religion. It required, for example, that the building be placed on a strict north–south grid and on a level platform, which has been created in the middle of the sloping playing-field site.

The school is a single-storey structure, with classrooms arranged around a courtyard of which the temple – attached to the assembly hall and dining area – is the focus. Another requirement of Vastu Shastra is that metal be kept to a minumum, and the aesthetic here is instead one of timber construction with planted roofs.

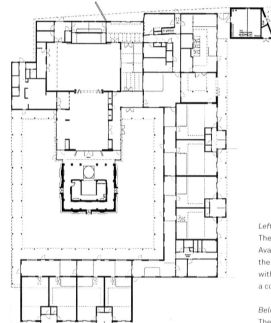

Left
The plan of the Krishna-Avanti School focuses on the *mandir* (or temple), with classrooms around a courtyard.

Below and opposite
The building is of timber, dictated by religious beliefs but producing a harmonious environment for learning.

The Law Department at London Guildhall University stands adjacent to Wright and Wright's Women's Library (2002) for the same university. Since its completion, London Guildhall University has merged with the University of North London to form the new London Metropolitan University, with its principal campuses in Whitechapel, on the edge of the City, and on Holloway Road in north London. The two buildings share an architectural vocabulary that is rational and pragmatic, responding strongly to practical issues and eschewing empty gestures. The use of red brick clearly defers to the adjacent Calcutta House, a converted tea warehouse now used by the university.

The site for the Law Department on Goulston Street was created by the demolition of a redundant swimming baths, although the basements from that building were reused. Commissioned as long ago as 1995 but constructed in 2001–2003, the building contains a conventional mix of lecture and seminar rooms and cellular offices for staff, all arranged on a longitudinal plan that reflects the narrowness of the site. A double-height, top-lit atrium extends the length of the building at the rear. All the main seminar rooms open off this space, which functions as much more than a corridor, providing a place for social and academic discourse. There is a large lecture theatre in the basement. Externally, the rear elevation is largely blank, since it faces a block of inter-war flats built by London County Council; this is, in every sense, a diverse quarter of London.

The building looks solid and immoveable, sober and dignified. It is faced in masonry and constructed on a concrete frame that is left exposed at various points inside the building. There is, however, a strong element of flexibility in the project: the seminar rooms can be reconfigured by means of moveable partitions, and the cellular offices could readily be stripped out if another spatial arrangement were needed. An unusual planning requirement was the provision of a barrow store for nearby Petticoat Lane Market.

The project uses ordinary, robust materials in a tough but polite manner – no gimmicks here, just a building that is thoroughly considered and well detailed. Oak furniture designed by the architect adds to the quality of the interior. This is a building that is easily ignored, but deserves respect for its response to the urban context and close attention to the needs of users.

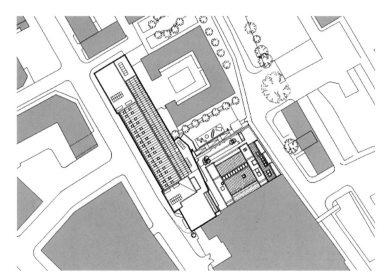

Opposite
Within a stone's throw of the City, Wright and Wright's Law Department, in common with the practice's earlier Women's Library, defers to the urban context in its use of severe red brick.

Right
Internally, the building provides a variety of dignified and enjoyable spaces, including the double-height, top-lit atrium.

Mossbourne Academy is a new sort of school in several respects. One of a new breed of city academies, designed to provide a shot in the arm for the state sector, it aims to equip pupils for careers in business and industry and, like other academies, is partly financed by a private sponsor. In the case of Mossbourne, backing came from Clive Bourne, a highly successful businessman born in Hackney, who made it a condition of his donation that Richard Rogers be commissioned to design the £23,000,000 new school, and also stipulated that it specialize in communications and information technology. Places at the school are heavily oversubscribed.

Designed to accommodate some 900 students aged from eleven to sixteen, the academy replaces a failed school on the same triangular site, which faces the green parkland of Hackney Downs to the north but is enclosed on two sides by busy railway lines. The V-shaped plan opens to the Downs, with two wings of accommodation pressed hard against the rail tracks; the simply rendered rear elevations are virtually windowless, and services and support areas buffer the teaching spaces against noise. Classrooms and other teaching areas are accessed from the north via staircases and galleries/cloisters. The aim was to minimize circulation space: there is nothing here of the central 'street' that is a feature of the academy in Bexley designed by Foster + Partners (pp. 162–63). The building is conceived as a series of vertical units, comparable to terraced houses, which provide pupils and staff with a home base; there is, for example, no central staff room.

This is the first timber-framed building (using mostly laminated softwood) designed by Richard Rogers Partnership (now Rogers Stirk Harbour + Partners). The lightweight structure sits on the rubble from the 1960s buildings that formerly stood on the site. The project is intended as an exemplar of sustainable design. Most spaces are entirely naturally ventilated, with rooftop wind towers drawing in fresh air. Solar shading and the use of concrete floors as thermal reservoirs reinforce the low-energy services strategy.

The academy is intended to be a resource for the whole community, accessible outside school hours, and the sports hall and flexible performance space are heavily used. With school uniforms designed by Paul Smith and a cafeteria menu supervised by the River Cafe, pupils at Mossbourne might appear to be a privileged elite, yet Hackney is London's most deprived borough and the Mossbourne experiment is a bold attempt to address social inequality. This is a project that the Rogers team addressed with evident relish, producing a building that wears its earnestness lightly and is much enjoyed by those who work and study there.

Left
The academy occupies a constricted site hemmed in by railway tracks.

Opposite, top and bottom right
A rare example of a timber-framed structure, the building stands on the rubble of the previous 1960s school.

Opposite, bottom left
Internally, the stress is on flexibility and openness, with a bold use of colour.

NEW ACADEMIC BUILDING AND NEW STUDENTS' CENTRE, LONDON SCHOOL OF ECONOMICS AND POLITICAL SCIENCE WC2

London School of Economics and Political Science (LSE), for all its internationally renowned academic excellence, has inhabited a lacklustre collection of buildings for the last century. Recent additions to the Aldwych campus in central London, however, include a new library (a radical warehouse conversion by Foster + Partners), a students' centre by Kohn Pedersen Fox, and a piazza and coffee bar by MJP Architects, as well as the conversion of former commercial buildings on Kingsway.

Grimshaw's new academic building is another exercise in reuse, in this instance involving an imposing commercial block, 24 Kingsway. The project, which doubled LSE's teaching space, was completed late in 2008. Grimshaw won the £71,000,000 commission in a high-profile competition in 2005. It envisaged the building as a key urban conduit, linking the existing campus to Kingsway and Sardinia Street (on the corner of which it stands), and to Lincoln's Inn Fields, which it faces to the east. The existing forecourt to Lincoln's Inn Fields was remodelled to form an external amphitheatre to the north and, to the south, a paved terrace, with a cafe that is open to the public as well as to the academic community. By opening up the corner to Sardinia Street, Grimshaw visually connected the project to LSE's existing buildings to the south.

The interior of the building was radically recast, with suspended floors creating a new central atrium – a light-filled, triple-height space with galleries on all sides, forming the focus of the building. The lecture and function spaces on the lower ground floor are accessed from the atrium; the largest lecture theatre seats 400. The new glazed roof is extremely lightweight, supported on bowstring trusses to minimize the structure. A roof pavilion accommodates executive meeting rooms and a function suite with splendid views over Lincoln's Inn Fields to the City. A sculpture by Richard Wilson acts as a marker on Kingsway, London's version of a Parisian boulevard.

The existing building's environmental failings were addressed by replacing the original windows with new double-glazed units. Natural light and ventilation are maximized, and pre-cooled water, extracted from a borehole reaching 100 metres below ground, is used for cooling. Solar collectors and photovoltaic panels are positioned on the roof.

In 2009 the Irish practice O'Donnell + Tuomey won an international competition to design a new £35,000,000 students' centre, replacing former hospital buildings colonized by LSE on a tight site behind Lincoln's Inn Fields. A new public space will be created as part of the project (which is due to be completed in 2012), inviting passers-by into the building. Inside, the scheme provides open stairs spiralling around a central lift shaft, forming 'a flowing, continuous ribbon of movement from street to roof garden, a vertical building working as a single organism', according to O'Donnell + Tuomey. The architect compares the designs to a Japanese puzzle, 'carefully assembled to make one coherent volume from a complex set of interdependent component parts'. Externally the building is to be clad in recycled bricks from the old hospital buildings, the façades folded and faceted to optimize vistas along adjacent streets. It will be naturally lit and ventilated throughout.

Below
Grimshaw's conversion of a large commercial block on Kingsway has doubled the LSE's teaching space.

Opposite, top and bottom right
LSE's new students' centre has been designed by O'Donnell + Tuomey for a constricted site. The form of the building is a response to the context.

Opposite, bottom left
The Grimshaw building has been radically reconfigured around a central day-lit atrium.

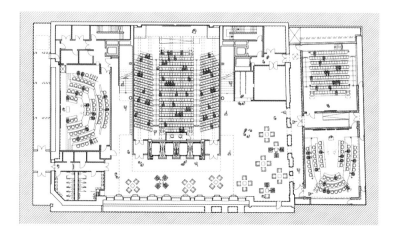

Alejandro Zaera-Polo, partner at Foreign Office Architects (FOA), has argued that architects' 'traditional role as visionaries ... has become redundant as the sheer speed of change overtakes their capacity to represent politics ideologically. We have been consumed in the means of production and in simply making buildings.' In this context, FOA's designs for the façade of the new Ravensbourne building on the Greenwich Peninsula, next to the O2 arena (pp. 138–39), constitute a determinedly anti-modernist, pluralist statement about the value of decoration in a postmodern world.

Ravensbourne College of Design and Communication (renamed Ravensbourne in early 2010) was founded in Chislehurst in the 1960s. Its decision to move to Greenwich was a bold one, as was its choice of architect: this is FOA's first completed building in London. The agenda for the Ravensbourne project concerned bringing together departments previously housed in a number of buildings and creating highly flexible working spaces with generous head-heights. This was facilitated by a structural strategy designed by engineers Adams Kara Taylor. Internally, the building focuses on two linked atria that are ideal for public events, such as fashion shows. The façade design, with clear memories of classic Islamic art, is a tour de force, executed in anodized aluminium (rather than the ceramic tiles initially proposed). Two lines of circular windows provide controlled daylight to each floor of the building.

This is a distinctive but practical building that reflects the impact of the O2 on Greenwich Peninsula. (Sadly, late in 2009, Zaera-Polo and his wife and professional partner, Farshid Moussavi, announced their intention of closing FOA.)

Opposite
The façade of Ravensbourne, clad in anodized aluminium, makes a bold statement about the continued relevance of decoration in architecture.

This page
The building injects a new element into the developing urban quarter on the Greenwich Peninsula.

SACKLER BUILDING AND FINE AND APPLIED ART CAMPUS, ROYAL COLLEGE OF ART SW11

The Royal College of Art's sculpture department and foundry have for some years occupied a former industrial building on Battersea Bridge Road. The continuing need of the college for further space – and the abandonment of a Grimshaw-designed extension project, which would have involved the demolition of part of the college's listed premises in South Kensington – has generated major expansion plans for the Battersea site. In the autumn of 2009 the Sackler Building opened as the new base for the college's painting department, which had previously occupied cramped accommodation in the main college building.

Architect Haworth Tompkins, known for its expertise in the imaginative reuse of old (but not necessarily 'historic') buildings, has here transformed another mundane industrial structure. The existing brick enclosure of the building on Howie Street was retained and a new independent steel structure inserted within it, providing 7-metre-high painting studios typically measuring 8 by 7.5 metres, with a new roof that allows north light to penetrate the spaces while baffling solar glare. A central corridor connects the studios; the building is essentially open-plan, with only a few cellular offices and workshops. A mezzanine provides an upper level of studios. The aim, explains the architect, was to retain the industrial feel of the building as 'a factory appropriated for painting use', to retain as much

Below, left, and right, top and centre
A major new multi-purpose building will occupy a site close to Battersea Bridge.

Below, right
The site plan shows the existing sculpture department (red), the Sackler Building (light blue) and the new building (dark blue).

Opposite
The Sackler Building is a modest but elegant conversion of a routine industrial building into painting studios for the Royal College of Art.

of the original fabric as possible in an 'as found' condition, and to create spaces made for hard wear. To this end, there are sealed concrete floors and steel handrails and balustrades. The £3,000,000 project has doubled the area of space within the existing envelope for a modest cost.

Haworth Tompkins is also the architect for the college's major new building project in Battersea, which will include a gallery, a lecture theatre, exhibition space and a social area as well as teaching accommodation for a number of departments. Retail units will animate the frontage to Battersea Bridge Road, and the entrance to the new building – which is scheduled to go on site in 2010 – will address Battersea Bridge.

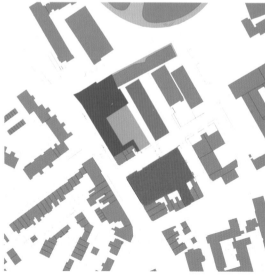

As at Haverstock School (pp. 178–79), Feilden Clegg Bradley Studios (FCB) faced a challenge with this project in terms of squeezing accommodation for a large number of pupils (in this case nearly 1400) into a very tight site. This faith school developed by the Diocese of London is an 'all through' institution, with early years, primary and secondary departments, so that it is possible for a child to spend up to fifteen years at St Mary Magdalene.

The winner of an RIBA Award in 2009, the £27,000,000 school is certainly one of the more distinguished products of the education boom of the New Labour years. It has a notable presence on Liverpool Road, from where views into the assembly hall and playground reflect the aim to engage with the wider local community. FCB defines the character of the interior as one of 'autonomy with coherence', and the relationship between the internal spaces is based on careful study. The nature of the site meant placing the sports hall on the first floor, with a football pitch above, clad externally and internally in timber. Other external elevations are mostly clad in ceramic tiles. Detailing is of a high quality throughout. In environmental terms, the performance of the school is everything one would expect of FCB: virtually all spaces are naturally ventilated, and heating is by means of a biomass boiler.

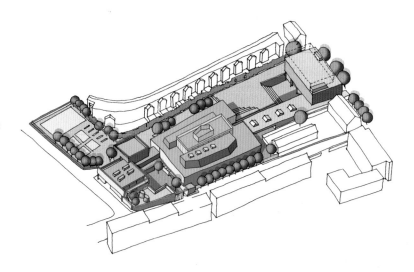

Opposite, top left and bottom
The academy's sports hall is located on the first floor, and is clad externally in timber.

Opposite, top right
Interiors are simultaneously vibrant and rational, providing a stimulating environment for pupils.

Above and left
The site was extremely tight, so the buildings had to be carefully disposed to provide open space for a school that caters for children of all ages.

The creation of a basement courtyard allowed new gymnasium and studio spaces at this level to be naturally lit.

The idea of the 'vertical school' has driven a number of recent school projects in London, often faced with the challenge of working on very constrained sites. The expansion of this school, a highly rated Church of England comprehensive with 900 pupils, meant going down, rather than up, and excavating new spaces below ground. The site, in a conservation area, is surrounded by listed buildings and public open space.

The school's specialisms in sport, dance, drama, art and music drove the project, which aimed to provide new accommodation for the art and music departments, a large new gymnasium and a dance studio. Gumuchdjian Architects' strategy was to place the latter two elements below ground, but there were significant problems in pursuing this option. For a start, beneath the existing playground was an eighteenth-century burial ground containing up to 3000 bodies, which had to be removed and reinterred: not only planning consent but also an ecclesiastical faculty for the works had to be given. Another major consideration was the need to channel natural light into the new spaces and to avoid their having an oppressively subterranean character or requiring artificial ventilation.

The solution was to create a large, open courtyard in the basement, to channel daylight and fresh air into the gymnasium and studios (which are accommodated in a mezzanine in the main volume of the new structure). The new art and music building sits on top. As part of the £5,000,000 project, the playground was given a rubber surface. Highly tactile materials – exposed concrete, painted steel and Cor-ten steel – and excellent detailing add to the delights of this ingenious development.

Below and right, bottom
A lightweight aesthetic and
the use of colour complement
a sense of openness.

Right, top and centre
Sections show the ingenious
solution that allowed the
school to grow on its highly
constrained city-centre site.

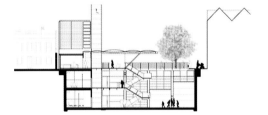

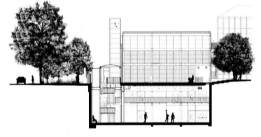

The School of Slavonic and East European Studies (SSEES), now part of University College London (UCL), was founded in 1915 and until recently was housed in a wing of the University of London's Senate House, off Russell Square. Its new building, which opened in the autumn of 2005, is located a few blocks to the north, close to the main UCL site, on land previously occupied by a delivery yard for the college's chemistry department. Vehicular access for that department had to be provided as part of the scheme and maintained throughout the construction process. Existing foundations, laid for a possible extension of the chemistry block in the 1970s, were reused.

The client brief called for about 3500 square metres of accommodation for 450 students and academic and administrative staff, including space for the outstanding specialist library, the seminar rooms and offices. The seven-storey building is radially planned, with upper floors extending over a street-level delivery route. In the 1960s the University of London was allowed to demolish large chunks of Georgian Bloomsbury and replace them with new buildings that paid little regard to historic context. In contrast, the street elevation of Short's building is made of load-bearing brick, the basic material of the surrounding terraced streets. It is, however, an extraordinary presence in a side street just off Gordon Square. The architect refers to it as 'a small urban palace', its style making reference to the brick churches of the Baltic. A heftily sculptured parapet supports a steep zinc-clad roof topped by prominent exhaust stacks.

Alan Short of Short and Associates has played a pioneering role in the evolution of an environmentally benign, low-energy architecture, of which his engineering block for Leicester's De Montfort University (1993) is a striking expression. The SSEES building is naturally ventilated, using passive downdraught cooling for the first time, it is claimed, in a city-centre public building anywhere in the world. The key to the ventilation strategy is the central atrium or light well, which draws air through the interior; a mechanical chiller cools the air in hot weather. One of the challenges of the project was dealing with the implications of this feature in terms of fire safety, as fire officers favour rigidly compartmentalized buildings. This building is treated as one sealed compartment. The street façade is actually an outer screen; the real façade lies behind it, and there is a dramatic entrance space between the two. The metal- and glass-clad internal structure provides a memorable contrast to the solidity of the street elevation. But the latter is a delight, bucking most current trends to create a highly individual, even eccentric, addition to the variegated public domain of London's central academic quarter.

Opposite, top left, bottom left and middle right, and right
The central atrium is the key to a low-energy servicing strategy. Fresh air is drawn through the building and extracted through rooftop stacks.

Opposite, top right and bottom right
The building is faced in brick but remains stylistically a radical intrusion into Georgian Bloomsbury. The curving lines of windows indicate the presence of staircases.

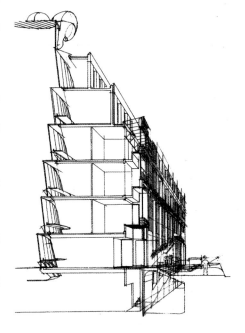

This project provides a neighbourhood nursery for thirty-six children and support facilities for parents. The site, close to Kilburn Grange Park in the borough of Camden, was formerly the playground of a Victorian school – now converted to flats – and was given back to Camden Council under an agreement with the developer. (Known as Section 106 agreements, such arrangements involve the release of land to councils for projects that will benefit the community.)

The project is rooted in the architect's conviction that 'children need a space of their own in which to thrive and to flourish'. In this area of London, the inadequacy of much local housing exacerbates the problems faced by young families, and most children will probably not have space to themselves at home. Meadowcroft Griffin's understated but carefully detailed and well-crafted architecture reflects a long process of research into the needs of the centre's future users.

The old playground's enclosing wall was retained and formed a starting point for the design concept of a perimeter brick wall with a garden interior. Another point of reference was the idea of the tree house, beloved of children over the centuries, which is expressed in first-floor activity rooms with exposed timber joists, timber-lined window reveals and window seats that allow views into surrounding mature trees. (The constraints of the site meant that part of the building had to have a second storey.) The relationship between external and internal space is crucial, and the two are linked by big double doors that open on to the courtyard.

Inside, the emphasis is on creating child-scaled areas, including 'secret' spaces they can make their own. The stress is on flexibility, with moveable screens that allow the interior to be reconfigured. Colour is used judiciously: relatively neutral shades inside the building encourage the children to cover the walls in their own paintings and drawings. Natural light infuses the building, and is controlled by the users with louvres, roller blinds and curtains.

This carefully considered nursery gives new meaning to the oft-abused term 'community architecture'. Designed in consultation with the community, it has real humanity as well as architectural quality rooted in a sure feel for materials, light and space.

Sure Start Kilburn sits within the curtilage of a Victorian school (now flats). A broad palette of materials, including exposed concrete, timber and render, embodies the urban contextual ambitions of one of a new generation of architects working on buildings for the community.

Opposite
Rigorous, rational and
practical, making use of
modular construction for
economy and speed of
construction, McAslan's
nursery draws inspiration
from classic Modern
Movement sources, but
equally responds to its
parkland setting.

Right
The plan includes enclosed
external play spaces. Its
spirit is similar to that of
the pioneering schools
of the 1950s.

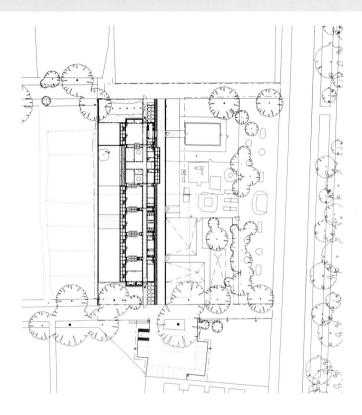

Another of the centres for children and their parents set up in underprivileged city areas under New Labour's Sure Start scheme (see also pp. 206–207), this project sits on an uninspiring site in open land, bordered by allotments, alongside the busy London Road in the south London borough of Merton. The community centre that formerly stood there was badly vandalized and eventually burned down. The nursery provides space for about ninety children and babies, in a building conceived as a 'pavilion in the park', or rather a series of interconnected pavilions.

The project had to be economical and rapidly constructed, so a modular 'kit-of-parts' strategy, with components fabricated off-site and applied to a primary steel frame, seemed a logical outcome. The linear plan is characteristic of McAslan and shows the influence of Louis Kahn that is pervasive in this practice's work. Services and support spaces face the main road, behind a relatively solid eastern elevation, and the activity rooms lie at the rear, with glazed façades opening on to a timber deck and enclosed external play spaces. The 1000-square-metre building also includes a cafe and

rooms for training and counselling (somewhat redundant since the abandonment of the Sure Start programme). Colour is used effectively but with restraint, and the use of timber cladding as a rain screen gives the building added texture. The design strategy is highly rational, but the outcome is a 'simple but inspired building' (as the *RIBA Journal* commented), child-centred and with the straightforward charm of the best examples of the golden age of school-building in the 1950s.

This was a small building by the practice's standards (the total cost was £1,420,000), but justified itself as a research project and test bed for new ideas, which have been developed in other educational projects. The involvement of Arup as engineer was highly significant in developing (in the words of Jo da Silva of Arup) 'an interdisciplinary approach that recognized and understood the interdependencies between building elements and systems, and how these are layered one on top of the other, reflecting both the order in which construction might take place and the interfaces between contractors'.

The dramatic expansion of higher education in Britain in recent years has had a huge impact on the housing market in a number of cities. In London, students have to cope with an overpriced and highly competitive housing scene, so most institutions have made efforts to increase residential accommodation within easy reach of their campuses. Queen Mary College – or Queen Mary, as it is now known – is no exception. The college, part of the University of London, has at its core the late Victorian People's Palace, designed by E.R. Robson (best known for his work as chief architect for the London Schools Board between 1872 and 1889). Post-war buildings include work by Feilden + Mawson, RMJM, Sheppard Robson, Colin St John Wilson and MJP Architects.

Feilden Clegg Bradley Studios' £29,500,000 project aims to provide not just housing but also a 'village': a tangible academic community, complete with shop, cafe-bar and laundry to supplement facilities available on the main campus. The student village occupies a long site, previously derelict, adjoining the Grand Union Canal to the east of the main campus. It provides nearly 1000 beds in flats and maisonettes for students, visiting academics and (that vital element of any higher-education budget) conference use. The new Mile End Park is across the canal to the east, and the main railway line from Liverpool Street station borders the site to the north.

The scheme includes six buildings, constructed in two phases from 2003 onwards. The first phase, at the core of the site and completed at the end of 2003, consists of three four-storey brick buildings set around landscaped courtyards, essentially inward-looking and secluded, with an appropriately restrained architectural language. In contrast, two more buildings, forming the second phase and completed in the autumn of 2004, give the project a potent public presence at the edges of the site. At the north end is an eight-storey block, Pooley Hall, which screens the village from the railway tracks and is clad in oxidized copper with a series of triangular bays punctuating its long northern façade. Sir Christopher France House extends along the canalside, and is also clad in copper, standing on a timber-clad plinth with a full-height, cut-out section allowing views in and out of the campus. The final phase of the student village was completed in 2006.

The scheme is remarkable in many respects. At a time when private developers, catering for a ready market, are providing new student housing of generally banal character, Queen Mary has opted for quality. There is nothing institutional or standardized about this housing: it provides no fewer than seventeen different room layouts, for example, and flats for between four and nine students. A great deal of care has been taken to create attractive spaces between buildings. The use of prefabrication (for bathroom pods, for example) and a tunnel-form, *in situ* concrete frame allowed the scheme to be constructed in less than two years, under a design-and-build contract that did not sacrifice design quality, thanks to the continuing involvement of the architect during construction. The project contributes to the ongoing renaissance of the East End and reflects Queen Mary's commitment to commissioning excellent new buildings, which also include the Graduate Centre by Surface Architects (pp. 172–73) and the Institute of Cell and Molecular Science by SMC Alsop (pp. 158–59).

Opposite
The project provides varied accommodation and pleasant outdoor space for students.

Right
Pooley Hall and Sir Christopher France House are the latest additions to a site comprising three-sided courtyards of brick buildings.

Below
The oxidized copper façade of Sir Christopher France House is the product of the biggest copper contract in England to date.

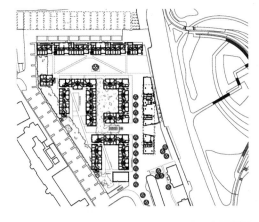

Westminster Academy caters for nearly 1200 pupils aged eleven to eighteen, with a special emphasis on business training. It is one of a number of recent city academies (specialist secondary schools part-funded by the private sector) in London designed by prestigious architectural practices, some of them with no previous experience of school design. Allford Hall Monaghan Morris, however, has a track record in educational architecture – for example, Great Notley School, Essex, completed in 1999, and the acclaimed Jubilee Primary School in Tulse Hill, south London (2002) – but this £25,000,000 project is its largest built school commission to date.

The site, in a far from affluent sector of the City of Westminster, was previously occupied by a local-authority office and health centre. These facilities were relocated elsewhere in the area, along with sports pitches, which have been reconfigured as part of the academy project. The Westway road is a pervasive source of noise and pollution, so it was accepted from the start that the building should be sealed and mechanically ventilated (using underfloor ducts).

At the heart of the school is a four-storey atrium orientated east–west and conceived as a social space – a 'town square' for the school community – as well as a circulation route. Classrooms line the atrium: a single row on the south side and a double row along the northern edge of the building, divided by a central corridor. The rectilinear plan is workmanlike and highly efficient. A separate sports hall, intended for use by the local community as well as by the school, contains indoor sports pitches and a dance studio.

The architect sought to create a colourful and visually appealing new landmark in this unprepossessing quarter of west London. The exterior is clad in alternating bands of glass and glazed terracotta, ranging in hue from dark green at ground level to yellow at the top. A sleek, smooth effect is obtained by setting the glazing in sheer curtain-wall framing. The sports hall is timber-clad, with large glass walls at each end. Colour is used freely inside the buildings, and internal finishes are tough and durable, requiring minimal maintenance.

Less of an architectural showpiece than earlier city academies designed by, for instance, Rogers Stirk Harbour + Partners and Foster + Partners (see pp. 162–63 and 192–93), Westminster Academy offers excellent value for money in a highly practical design that addresses the needs of students and community. It is the twenty-first-century equivalent of the late Victorian London Board schools, many of which remain in educational use today.

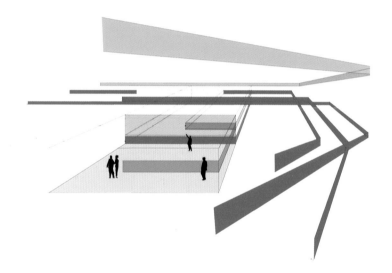

Above
The façade concept diagram shows the division of the space by colour according to age group.

Opposite
Located close to London's Westway, Westminster Academy inevitably has an internal focus, with a four-storey atrium acting as the central community space. Clad in hard-wearing terracotta and glass, the building is sealed against the noise of the busy road.

HOUSES AND HOUSING

CAMDEN

ISLINGTON

17

23

33

6

12

30 14

24

16

2

32

18 19

26

22

WESTMINSTER

LAMB

3

HACKNEY

TOWER HAMLETS

1   ABERDEEN LANE
2   BARKING CENTRAL
3   BEDZED
4   BLUE HOUSE
5   BOWZED
6   BRICK HOUSE
7   CARGO FLEET
8   COLONY MEWS
9   DIRTY HOUSE
10 DONNYBROOK QUARTER
11 FRAME HOUSE
12 GAP HOUSE
13 GAZZANO HOUSE
14 HOUSE IN HIGHGATE CEMETERY
15 IROKO HOUSING COOPERATIVE AND
    COIN STREET NEIGHBOURHOOD CENTRE
16 ISOKON FLATS
17 LONG HOUSE

18 LOW-COST HOUSING
    ASH SAKULA ARCHITECTS
19 LOW-COST HOUSING
    NIALL MCLAUGHLIN ARCHITECTS
20 NEWINGTON GREEN HOUSE
21 NEWINGTON GREEN STUDENT HOUSING
22 ONE CENTAUR STREET
23 OXFORD GARDENS
24 PARKSIDE HOUSING
25 ROOF GARDEN APARTMENT
26 STEALTH HOUSE
27 STRATA
28 STUDIO HOUSE
29 VASSALL ROAD HOUSING
    AND HEALTHCARE CENTRE
30 VXO HOUSE
31 WANSEY STREET HOUSING
32 WRAP HOUSE
33 YOUNG HOUSE

The house turns its back on the street to create a west-facing courtyard. All the main living spaces have generously glazed walls, which overlook the exceptionally private outdoor area.

Aberdeen Lane is a sparse, angular house beautifully cast out of *in situ* concrete. Its occupants, a well-known journalist and economist and their four children, had originally intended to commission Ferhan Azman and Joyce Owens of Azman Owens Architects to expand their Victorian town house. When they were shown a piece of scrubby land close to Highbury Fields in north London, however, the idea of an ultra-modern new-build house began to germinate.

The site, formerly a vegetable patch, is hemmed in by a detached house to the west, terraced mews houses to the east and a garden wall to the north. Planning consent had already been granted for a house with a north-facing garden, but permission was sought for a reorientated house with a west-facing garden – a much more desirable prospect – and granted by the council on condition that the building be of architectural interest.

The north and south walls of the brave, unashamedly modern house address the lane and the house to the rear, and are treated as solid façades with minimal openings. Instead, the house opens inwards to create a courtyard. This maintains a definite edge to the lane and prevents the property from being overlooked. Concrete was an obvious choice for these fortress-like walls, and

its extensive use became the defining feature of the project. Its structure of two interlocking cubes consists of horizontal slabs with double cantilevers, so that the top cube can overhang the bottom one without support. External cavity walls of reinforced concrete were left exposed both externally and internally. Their thickness was calculated so that the concrete could be poured and properly compacted using standard materials, to keep costs down. The concrete was moulded in birch-faced plywood shutters and the resulting smooth, blemish-free and surprisingly attractive surfaces are testimony to the skill of the contractor and the great care taken over each wall.

In contrast, the west elevation consists entirely of timber-framed glazing. The ground-floor living room and kitchen both have sliding doors to the courtyard garden, while the windows of the bedrooms above are veiled by vast wooden shutters.

AHMM's housing (this page) is one element in a project that has given Barking a new civic heart. The project includes the provision of a new public square (opposite) flanked by a covered arcade and dominated by a remarkable 'ruin' designed by Muf.

Town Square, Barking, is the civic heart of the London Borough of Barking & Dagenham, with the Town Hall (designed in the 1930s by Jackson & Edmonds but not completed until 1958), the Broadway Theatre (revamped by Tim Foster in 2004) and the undistinguished 1970s Central Library. In 1999 the local authority held a competition for the redevelopment of under-used land around the Town Hall. An ambitious scheme by Avery Associates was the winner, but it was subsequently abandoned in favour of AHMM's more pragmatic proposals, which included the retention and refurbishment of the library. The latter was incorporated into the first phase of AHMM's project (completed in 2007), which provided 200 flats in two parallel blocks, linked by the library. The second phase of the project, with 270 more flats, includes an eighteen-storey tower and two other blocks of housing. These buildings frame a square, one of only a handful of the 100 new public spaces planned by former London Mayor Ken Livingstone to have been realized.

AHMM's buildings are colourful and serviceable, well above the average for recent 'social' housing in London and comparing favourably with much private-sector residential development. The double-height arcade extending along the side of the revamped library is a pleasant gesture in the direction of civic space. But it is the square itself, designed by Muf, that has captured critical interest. Irregularly placed clumps of mature trees break down the formality of the space, providing a visual link to nearby parkland. At the north end of the square is a structure that is certainly unique in the recent architectural history of London, a fake ruin in the best tradition of the eighteenth-century Picturesque, built of brick and adorned with various sculptural fragments. It has no function but is purely a folly, there to be enjoyed.

On the southern edge of Greater London, BedZED – Beddington zero-energy development – occupies part of the site of a former sewage works. The context is of low-rise suburbia, although at a density of 100 units per hectare it provides a persuasive model for new housing on inner-city brownfield sites.

BedZED was effectively a test bed for radical ideas about sustainability in mass housing, with the ever-pioneering Peabody as developer and Bill Dunster (now ZEDfactory – see also pp. 224–25) as architect. It was designed as a socially mixed development for about 700 residents, with units for both sale and rent, one-third of the total being 'affordable'. An element of 'live/work' spaces was included, together with such community facilities as a nursery and a health centre.

Built of locally sourced and partly recycled components, this development is set in a traffic-free landscape. Colourful wind cowls, designed to catch the wind and push it through the buildings, form a marker for this innovative housing development.

The basic module is that of a three-storey town-house terrace, capable of being sliced up vertically into individual houses or cut up into flats and maisonettes. Every unit has access to a garden space, although many of these are formed as planted balconies or roof gardens and some are accessible only via bridge links. Residential units face south to benefit from sunlight, workspaces north.

BedZED is visually arresting. With brightly coloured wind cowls to catch the eye and a pleasing mix of brick and untreated oak boarding, it stands out a mile from the routine speculative housing schemes in the vicinity. Internally, it offers generous spaces a cut above the typical developer product. But the point of the place is not how it looks but the way it performs in environmental terms. The agenda was determinedly eco-friendly, beginning with the choice of site, continuing with the commitment to use recycled and low-energy materials for construction, and culminating in a services programme that reduces energy consumption by 60 per cent in comparison to the typical family home; it is claimed there are virtually zero carbon emissions. These results are obtained by common-sense solutions that, alas, have been largely ignored by volume house builders: good insulation (thick walls and concrete floor slabs), the controlled use of the sun's light and warmth (with glazed sun-spaces to act as environmental buffers), natural ventilation (hence the rooftop cowls, which incorporate heat exchangers) and, serving the whole complex, a combined heat and power plant that can burn waste materials. Rainwater and waste water are recycled for reuse on site. The development attracted keen interest from prospective residents long before completion, and has generated a community that appears to love the lifestyle it supports.

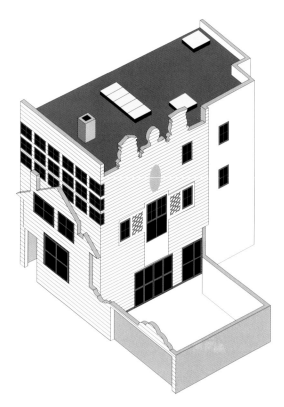

FAT (standing for Fashion, Architecture, Taste) is a design collaborative accustomed to infringing the rules of 'good' taste, so one would expect a house designed by partner Sean Griffiths for his own occupation to be anything but conventional. In fact, Griffiths's house at Garner Street, Bethnal Green, is deliberately populist and pop, designed to communicate with the surrounding community. It opens up to the gritty streets of the East End as if they were located in a gentrified New England seaport.

The American theme is to the fore here. American postmodernism has always generated hostility in the United Kingdom, being seen as reactionary, trite and lacking in seriousness, and the output of Robert Venturi (who was responsible for the admittedly lacklustre Sainsbury Wing at the National Gallery, London) has been singled out for special condemnation. Venturi's work is the first comparison that is brought to mind by the extraordinary street elevation of the Blue House. A cut-out house front, complete with chimney and garden hedge, stands in front of a cut-out office-block façade. Along the side elevation the roofline is decorated with cut-out gables imitating those in Amsterdam. The whole edifice is clad in clapboard, painted sky blue.

The plan of the house, too, owes something to Venturi, with a staircase that wraps around the front of the house, creating a double façade and embracing the kitchen inglenook. Griffiths, however, describes his creation as 'Adolf Loos meets South Park … . It is deliberately cartoon-like and representational in appearance and its "pop" references seek to communicate with a wide audience.'

While office and separate top-floor flat are both accessed directly from the street, the house itself is entered from the yard at the side, and has at its heart a kitchen/dining room; bedrooms are on two floors above. The pervasive influence inside seems to be that of the Arts and Crafts Movement: some of the detail refers explicitly to the architect and designer Charles Voysey (1857–1941). Strong colours are used throughout.

All in all, the house is hugely out of step with its environs. Griffiths denies that it is in any way flippant, yet its obvious wit and lack of guile are attractive. This is one of the oddest and most memorable London houses since Piers Gough's residence, completed in 1988, for the journalist Janet Street-Porter in Clerkenwell.

FAT's Blue House externally makes obvious reference to the pop imagery of postmodernism (opposite and above, left), but internally combines free-flowing contemporary space (left) with Arts and Crafts-inspired details (above, right).

BowZED applies the lessons of Bill Dunster's earlier BedZED development to the field of speculative housing. The significance of the scheme lies in its commitment to low-energy design, achieved in the context of a commercial brief.

Bill Dunster, ex-Hopkins Architects and founder of the innovative ZEDfactory practice, is best known for BedZED, the acclaimed low-energy 100-unit housing scheme completed in 2002 for Peabody (pp. 220–21). The scheme has become the focus of continuing debate about eco-friendly design, but has been generally reckoned a success, not least in terms of its strong community spirit.

The far more modest BowZED is privately developed, but aims to demonstrate that the principles of BedZED can be applied to the commercial sector and on a tight urban site. The development contains just four flats, each with its own south-facing terrace and conservatory, fitted with photovoltaic cells that are reckoned to generate at least 50 per cent of the occupants' energy needs. A further source of clean energy is provided by

the roof-mounted wind turbine. High levels of insulation and the benefits of thermal mass mean that no central heating is needed; solar gain and the heat generated by the occupants are sufficient. Hot water is supplied by a wood-pellet boiler, which also provides back-up heating in the case of exceptionally cold weather. It is claimed that the building will thus be self-sufficient in terms of energy. In architectural terms, the block is hardly an eye-catcher: stock brick and render reflect the character of the surrounding streets in an unglamorous area of London. But as an exemplar for the development industry of how low-energy design can be a selling point, the project deserves to be better known.

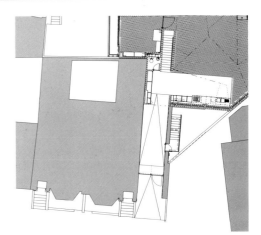

Opposite
The main living space provides a masterclass in the brave and honest use of brick and concrete.

Below and right
Seen in plan and from above, the architect's ingenious manipulation of an uncompromising site becomes clear. The house is rammed between two adjoining properties, and the garden culminates in a jagged point.

Brick House is one of the most celebrated houses to have been built in London in the new millennium: quite an achievement for architect Caruso St John, since it is almost invisible from the street. Occupying an awkward site between the backs of three Georgian terraces and the end of a mews in Paddington, west London, it is hinted at by a ramp and plain timber door. But beyond this checkpoint the project is marked out as one of the capital's exceptional buildings by its extraordinary manipulation of volume and light and its honest display of construction materials.

A nondescript ramped hallway leads from the entrance half a storey up to the first floor. The house's magic becomes apparent with the unfurling of a room that covers almost the entire 185-square-metre floor space. It is topped with a 450-millimetre-thick cast-concrete ceiling, elegantly folded in the manner of a piece of origami and punctuated with triangular roof lights. The scale and sculptural design are remarkable, and the experience has been likened by the architect to wandering into a Baroque chapel in the midst of the crowded streets of Rome.

The origin of the house's name is immediately apparent: virtually every surface is covered in honey-coloured Cambridge brick. Set with unpigmented lime mortar in an ordinary running bond, the brick wraps

around the walls and the floor, even licking up the edges of the bath. The only exception is the kitchen area, where concrete has been introduced. A key reference was the work of the Swedish architect Sigurd Lewerentz (1885–1975), whose church of St Peter, built between 1963 and 1966 in Klippan, Sweden, uses the same running bond for floors, walls and vaulted ceilings. But, while Brick House's austere interior may have monastic undertones, it exudes a definite sense of domesticity at the same time.

The main living space is entirely open-plan, and it is the ceiling plane, rather than partition walls, that defines the kitchen and the zones for eating and living: towards the window, for example, the ceiling dives to create a more intimate dining area. A small study and an even smaller bathroom are also tucked in at this level. Downstairs, the space is more private: a labyrinthine hallway leads to four bedrooms, two bathrooms and a utility room.

The site also contains two courtyards, on to which three of the bedrooms open, and a garden overlooked by the master bedroom and the study above. The irregular shapes of these outdoor spaces, which are squeezed between the building and the property wall, are reminders of how ingeniously the architect has shoehorned this house into a difficult site.

Designed from the inside out, Brick House is like a graceful bunker or, as Adam Caruso puts it, 'both a cave and a tent, at once enclosing and protective, and open and airy'. The house is a unique sanctuary in the busy heart of London, and an outstanding example of what could be done with more of the capital's forgotten yards and alleyways.

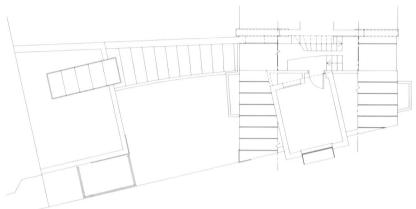

Cargo Fleet is an unusual hybrid of industrial materials and domestic architecture. The house takes its name from an abandoned railway station between Redcar and Middlesbrough, where architect Stephen Chance's father and grandfather worked in the steel factories. Chance grew up surrounded by the industrial buildings of northern England, and their geometric shapes and decaying beauty have had a lasting effect on his work. When he and his partner, Wendy de Silva, found a plot in what was then a neglected part of north London, the industrial undertones both of Chance's past and of the site itself inspired this unique residential project.

The difficult wedge-shaped plot lies on the corner of a cobbled road, which forms a loop around a derelict commercial laundry. It marks the end of a terrace of former lace-workers' houses and is hemmed in by a hill on one side and a railway embankment on the other. Aesthetically, the building is at odds with its surroundings. Inspired by the furnaces, smelting works and signal stations around Redcar, it is a collage of industrial components. The corner windows, for example, resemble signal boxes, while the overhanging timber volume that juts out over the street could be a projecting shed.

The most striking industrial accent, however, is the choice of Cor-ten steel panels as the principal cladding material. This weathering steel, also used by Antony Gormley for his sculpture *Angel of the North*, turns first orange and then brown as it weathers and rusts. The architect chose it to reflect the decay and neglect of England's industrial heritage and to evoke the passing of time. By building with a material that from the beginning signifies its end, they hope to draw attention to the transient nature of any act of creation.

The industrial theme is carried through to the interior, where rough concrete floors and exposed grey plaster contrast with slick wooden panelling and floor-to-ceiling windows. Steel rods connect the free-standing frame to the wall of its neighbour, enabling the removal of the full-length buttresses that previously supported the earlier structure. The resulting gap is now a fully glazed light well, containing the stairs and a dining platform. The buttress scars and bricks of the adjoining house remain exposed.

In contrast to the many references to the past, the layout of the new build is in tune with the increasing fluidity of modern life. Its two volumes are linked by a covered ramp, and the building could accommodate a working studio and a granny annex or flat for an au pair. It could even be split into two separate entities. The house commentates both on the changing nature of England's industrial and built heritage, and on the increasing complexity of people's lives. A bold and challenging statement, it raises as many questions as it answers.

Left and opposite, bottom left
Glazed doors shield the concrete ramp and lead to a courtyard sandwiched between the old and new houses.

Opposite, top left
The exterior bricks of the adjoining house are left exposed in a light well containing the staircase.

Opposite, right
The building confidently addresses its context of Victorian terraces.

Opposite and below
The open-plan living spaces receive generous amounts of natural light from skylights and glazed doors, which lead on to roof terraces.

Above
The ground-floor plan shows the 'notched terrace' concept, which allows the construction of flats with private courtyards despite the awkward, restricted site.

Right
The front doors of the terraced houses are reached by a walled passageway along the boundary of the site.

Colony Mews in north London was in a sense the testing ground for a larger scheme by Peter Barber, Donnybrook Quarter in Hackney (pp. 234–35). Designed in 2002 for developer Colony and completed in 2006, the scheme features the 'notched terraces' that have proved so successful at the Hackney project. They were developed here in response to a restricted site, accessed through an arch in a Victorian terrace fronting Mildmay Grove. Four courtyard houses and one live/work studio have been cleverly slotted into the plot, which measures approximately 550 square metres.

A walled passage, leading to the front door of each property, runs east–west across the site. Beyond each front door is a private south-facing courtyard garden, which is overlooked by a first-floor roof terrace. The houses themselves have been designed to take full advantage of these outdoor areas. The ground floor comprises two bedrooms and two bathrooms, with all principal windows facing the courtyard to prevent the adjacent properties from being overlooked. The first-floor open-plan living space has fully glazed sliding doors, which open on to the roof terrace. At the eastern end of the site, the live/work unit has a roof sloping towards the houses, shielding the entire scheme from the street. Inside, the ground floor has been dropped to semi-basement level to allow for a mezzanine above. The south-facing wall has a window one-and-a-half storeys high to allow in the maximum amount of light.

In a style similar to that of Donnybrook Quarter, the blockwork has been rendered and painted a dazzling white. Crisp lines and neat geometric forms give the project a proudly modern appearance, which is refreshing in an area of London dominated by Victorian brick.

The project is a clever exercise in logistical planning, exploiting every scrap of available space to create houses that, despite being close to one another, maintain an impressive degree of privacy. For a total cost of £1800 per square metre, it demonstrates how odd pockets of land can be transformed into entirely new communities.

David Adjaye's Elektra House in Whitechapel, east London, completed in 2000, created something of a furore: its entirely blank street façade was criticized as an antisocial, defensive gesture. But the form of the house was both a response to a deprived area and a reflection of the needs of the occupants.

The enigmatically named Dirty House, in the same area, is an equally unsettling design, eschewing conventional notions of domestic ease. In common with the Elektra House, it is intended as a live/work space (for artists Tim Noble and Sue Webster). The house is basically a conversion of a plain 1930s warehouse. The internal structure was removed, in consultation with engineer Techniker, to make two double-height studios that occupy most of the ground and first floors. A new residential pavilion, fully glazed, sits on the roof, its own roof cantilevering out to cover an external terrace. The setting back of the pavilion ensures complete privacy. Lighting fitted under the timber decking makes this part of the building appear as a dramatic light beam by night. The main street façades are covered in anti-graffiti paint and fitted with double-glazed mirror-glass windows, so that from the outside the house appears impenetrable and disturbingly anonymous.

There is an air of menace, too, in the very narrow, two-storey-high hallway through which the house is entered. In common with Sir John Soane, Adjaye uses architectural form to elicit strong emotional responses: his is an architecture of sensation rather than of conventional aesthetics, and compression is a device he uses to powerful effect. His skilful use of top-lighting is equally Soanean. However, as a modern architect for whom Soane's classical inheritance is meaningless, Adjaye eschews elaborate detail in favour of a virtuoso approach to the use of materials – whether costly or, as in this house, essentially commonplace.

Below, left and middle
The interior makes skilful use of top-lighting, while an external terrace offers views across the City of London.

Below, right, and opposite
The Dirty House presents an enigmatic, even anonymous, façade to the East End street in which it stands.

Donnybrook Quarter was commissioned in 2003 as a result of 'Innovation in Housing', a competition organized by the Architecture Foundation and Circle 33 housing trust. As part of his competition entry, the architect Peter Barber used a quotation from Walter Benjamin's *One Way Street*, in which the literary critic celebrates the theatrical nature of the cityscape of Naples: 'Buildings are used as a popular stage. They are all divided into innumerable, simultaneously animated theatres. Balcony, courtyard, window, gateway, staircase, roof are at the same time stages and boxes.'

In his design for Donnybrook, which sits on a prominent corner site just south of Victoria Park in Hackney, north-east London, Barber has developed this idea of people activating a streetscape by making shared public space the central element. He describes the project as 'a celebration of the public social life of the street'. Unusually, Barber first built the streets on which the new houses would sit: two tree-lined avenues, an intimate 7.5 metres wide, are laid across the site in a T-shape, with a small square at their intersection. Forty units, ranging from one-bedroom studios to a four-bedroom family house, as well as three live/work units, have been fitted around this plan. Gone are the dark alleys and gloomy stairwells so common in high-density housing schemes, and in their place are the pleasant circulation spaces created by the streets.

The buildings themselves are ingeniously designed to encourage interaction with the public spaces. By developing a new form of housing, the 'notched terrace' (see also pp. 230–31), the architect has provided every home with direct access to the street, as well as a private outdoor area. A typical bay comprises a ground-floor two-bedroom flat with access to a rear courtyard. Above this is a split-level maisonette, which is reached by a gated external staircase leading through a courtyard garden on the first floor. The living area on this level has a fully glazed wall facing south over the courtyard, while the second floor contains two double bedrooms, a bathroom and a balcony overlooking the street. This sectional arrangement satisfies the English planning system's rules concerning overlooking (with specified minimum back-to-back distances) and makes it possible to achieve the exceptionally high density of 400 habitable rooms per hectare in a scheme that is only four storeys at its highest.

In a reworking of the Victorian housing type known as the 'back-of-pavement terrace', the notched terraces have no front gardens and present a hard edge to the street. This allows doors, windows and balconies to overlook the public areas, and gives the scheme an impressive sculptural quality. The style references the work of early Modernists, in particular Le Corbusier, Adolf Loos and J.J.P. Oud, who designed handsome terraces for European cities in the 1920s.

Along the southern edge of the site the gleaming white walls rise to three-and-a-half storeys, and a landmark corner building addresses the junction of Old Ford Road and Parnell Road. Along the eastern edge the terraces curve elegantly along Parnell Road, rising to an impressive four storeys to mark the main entrance to the project.

This is a truly magnificent design in both its logistical planning and its outward appearance. Best of all, however, are the public spaces around which the buildings are configured. By creating safe and attractive communal areas, the architect encourages human interaction and provides a groundbreaking example of how urban regeneration can encourage social sustainability in the capital.

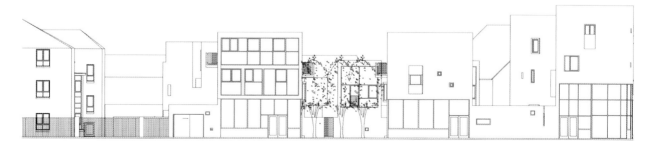

Homes in Donnybrook Quarter are designed to overlook the public street areas, encouraging interaction between neighbours. The buildings take their form from the architecture of the early Modernists.

Opposite
The Frame House is constructed on a lightweight, economical timber frame and is located in a densely built-up quarter of the East End. The essence of the design was to extend the living spaces into the surrounding garden.

Right and below
A highly efficient plan provides flexible internal spaces, generous in scale and with scope for alteration as the needs of the family change.

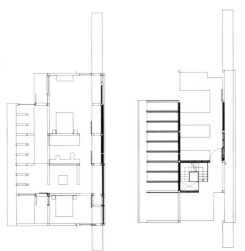

Frame House, designed by Marcus Lee of FLACQ, provides a refreshing contrast to the general run of bespoke new houses in London. A substantial and highly practical family house rather than a minimalist statement, it was built to a modest budget (£300,000), and is located not in a lush suburb but in gritty Hackney, on a constrained site next to a paint-spraying workshop. Formerly with Richard Rogers and now a director of Arup, Lee chose to build in timber not only for its economy and green credentials but also because, he argues, it allows for a 'kit-of-parts' approach: 'You can delay decisions or change things around ... You can get the whole house on a lorry and take it away again.'

Constructed on a frame of laminated Siberian larch and clad in cedar, the lightweight structure has no need for deep foundations. A high level of insulation, grey-water recycling, and heating using wood pellets are part of a low-energy design strategy.

The real strengths of the house become clear inside. The open-plan living area, extending into the kitchen, is a comfortable family space that is also ideal for entertaining. Upstairs, sliding partitions allow bedrooms and bathrooms to be reconfigured, while sleeping space for three young children, along with an office, is provided in the generous loft. A key feature is the way the internal spaces merge with the surrounding – very modest – garden. This is a one-off house, tailored to the needs of one family, but it could provide lessons for large-scale housing design.

The architect Luke Tozer set himself a challenge when he acquired a backland site on Monmouth Road, Bayswater, and set out to build a house for himself and his family. The site, in a conservation area, was occupied by a derelict cottage, the demolition of which was uncontroversial. It was, however, accessible from the street only by a narrow (0.7-metre) passage – a gap between two elegant stucco-fronted villas. The space to the rear now accommodates a top-lit living space and kitchen – the heart of the house – entered on the lower ground floor and flanked by an open courtyard, creating a calm oasis insulated from the street. Bedrooms and bathrooms, as well as a small study, are stacked in three storeys of accommodation in the former passageway and connected by a timber stair, in what is essentially a reinterpretation of the classic London terraced house. The street elevation is self-effacing to a degree, reflecting the planning problems that initially beset the project, its white stucco cladding deferring to its context. As an incident in the street, it hardly stands out.

But the point of the project – apart from building a comfortable and surprisingly spacious family home – was not the creation of an architectural statement but a serious attempt to put into practice rigorous strategies for carbon reduction and green-energy generation. Boreholes 50 metres deep and serving a heat pump provide all heating and hot water for the house. High levels of insulation, rainwater harvesting to minimize water consumption, and the use throughout of sustainable natural materials are other elements in the eco-friendly package, although planners ruled out the use of solar collectors at roof level. The houses architects build for themselves can be exercises in self-indulgence, but Tozer and his practice used this project to develop approaches to low-energy design that they are already applying more widely.

Opposite
Gap House has little impact
on the street.

Below and right, bottom
The top-lit living space at the
heart of the house opens on
to an enclosed courtyard.

Right
The floor plans show how
the project uses a tiny site,
accessed through a gap
between two existing houses.

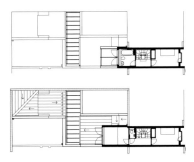

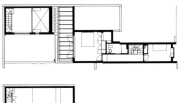

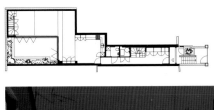

Gazzano House in central London, designed by Amin Taha Architects for developer Solidbau, is an uncompromisingly modern building, and has become an important addition to the Rosebery Avenue conservation area. Standing among a series of Grade II*-listed nineteenth-century warehouses and offices, the building has a simple form – a solid block, with bold lines and sharp corners – that allows it to stand its ground while not overpowering its historically important neighbours. The building consists of ten two-bedroom flats above an Italian delicatessen. The delicatessen had been trading on the site for more than a hundred years, and the brief stipulated that it should not be uprooted.

A steel frame with pre-cast concrete floor slabs is wrapped in Cor-ten steel, which is manufactured from recycled metal and among the most durable of cladding materials. The robustness of the cladding and the small windows reflect the gritty, traffic-riddled atmosphere of this traditionally working-class area. As time passes, the Cor-ten will weather to become darker in tone and richer in texture, further integrating the building with its semi-industrial surroundings. Rugged materials continue inside: exposed concrete and plaster on walls and ceilings, and hard-wearing epoxy finishes on the floor. These not only help to contextualize the scheme, but also improve the thermal performance of the building. The same principle lies behind the aluminium-framed, double-glazed windows, designed to use a minimum area of the exterior.

The brief requested a distinctive building, which Amin Taha Architects have certainly produced. Rather than be overshadowed by its older and more colossal neighbours, Gazzano House stands proudly among them. At a time when high-density living is becoming an increasing priority in London, the scheme provides a brave architectural solution to the use of inner-city spaces.

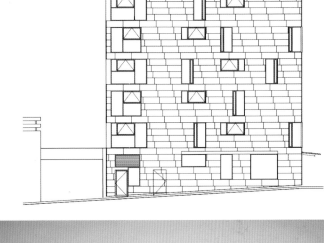

Gazzano House provides desirable and contemporary living spaces in a defensive yet monumental shell. The scattered windows are a striking feature of the exterior.

Opposite
Replacing a house by John
Winter, this luxurious new
dwelling has one of the most
remarkable sites in London,
overlooking Highgate
Cemetery. Fully glazed
elevations capitalize on
views of the landscape.

Right
The house presents a closed
façade to the street, opening
up to the cemetery.

Below
Natural light permeates the
house, and a sliding roof turns
the top floor into an open court.

This is the most spectacular of a number of houses
in and around London by Eldridge Smerin. The site is
certainly as dramatic as virtually any in the capital,
elevated above Highgate Cemetery and with marvellous
views over its surroundings and much of London. It
was previously occupied by a house designed by John
Winter, dating from 1978–82. (Winter's own house, a
classic of the 1960s, is near by.) In replacing a serious,
highly restrained work by a distinguished modernist of
the older generation, Eldridge Smerin has produced a
house that has an almost Californian glamour.

In place of Winter's steel frame, Eldridge Smerin
used concrete: finished to a high quality, it provides a
consistent and potent internal aesthetic while also
allowing for a more sustainable environmental strategy.
The new house, which is constructed on the footprint of
the older building, is arranged over four floors – a storey
higher than its predecessor and with none of the latter's
self-effacing qualities. To the street, admittedly, in the
classic manner of the residences of the seriously wealthy,
it presents a discreet, even anonymous, face, with an
elevation formed of granite, steel and translucent glass.
But in contrast, the elevations facing the cemetery,
which is open to the public only periodically, are largely
of glass, with full-height glazing immaculately detailed.

The extensive use of glass within the house allows
natural light to permeate. A sliding roof transforms the
top floor into an open court. The house is fitted out in
luxurious style throughout, with bespoke joinery and
furniture designed by the architect to create a temple
of minimalism. Sound environmental credentials are
claimed for the project. Reviewing the house, John Winter
generously described it as being 'as near to a faultless
building as I have seen for a long time'.

IROKO HOUSING COOPERATIVE AND COIN STREET NEIGHBOURHOOD CENTRE SE1

This development of fifty-nine dwellings, including thirty-two family houses, by one of London's most dynamic young practices forms the latest segment in Coin Street Community Builders' ongoing development of the 5.6 hectares of land it acquired from the Greater London Council in 1984 (purchase price: £1,000,000). Twenty years ago innovative design and social conviction seemed to be at odds, but this is no longer the case in the London of today. The memory of the earliest work here – uninspired and suburban in character – has now been laid to rest as Coin Street moves on from the excellent mid-1990s contribution by Lifschutz Davidson (twenty-five units, including a nine-storey block) to this latest phase.

Haworth Tompkins won the commission in 1997. The site, formerly occupied by warehousing but used for surface parking for many years, is close to the National Theatre and high-rise IBM headquarters. The character of the new housing is suitably urban, mediating between the cultural/public territory of the South Bank and the modest residential streets beyond. There are four-storey houses on Coin Street and Cornwall Road. On Upper Ground, a busy public through-route, the scale is even bigger, with two-storey maisonettes squatting on top of three-storey houses. Doors are on the street and the houses have private gardens. Both the scale and the layout of the scheme around a central square (with parking underneath) look back to Georgian tradition,

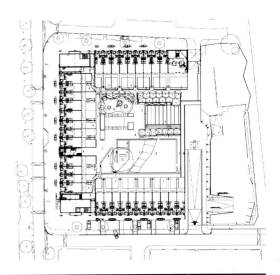

although there is nothing overtly historicist about the architecture. On the street façades, a disciplined and impervious brick cladding is used. On the courtyard side, steel-and-timber balconies with trellises and louvred-timber sun shades create a softer, more lively and informal look. The materials have been used with a view to the conservation of energy. High levels of insulation and roof-mounted solar panels make the dwellings economical to run: this is sustainability in action.

In 2007 the fourth side of the square was occupied by a neighbourhood centre with IT resources, conference rooms and classrooms, exhibition spaces, social facilities and small offices for local arts and community organizations. Facing the heavily trafficked Stamford Street, the building provides an inspiring image of the power of genuinely creative community action to create homes, employment and regeneration in partnership with business and government.

ISOKON FLATS NW3

The Isokon Flats in Hampstead, north London, constitute one of the most important Modern Movement buildings in the United Kingdom. Opened in 1934 and known originally as the Lawn Road Flats, the building was the vision of Wells Coates, a Canadian architect, and his clients Jack Pritchard (a furniture designer whose company Isokon lent its name to the building) and his wife, Molly. All three were devotees of Modernism and the Bauhaus, and, having seen the introduction of communal, high-density living in Europe, they hoped to bring the idea to London.

Coates was fascinated by the efficient, all-in-one layout of ships, and his design for Lawn Road followed that of a giant ocean liner. It had thirty-two compact, cabin-like flats, each kitted out with the latest gadgets and such space-saving solutions as hinged tables and sliding doors. There were balcony 'decks', a large sun lounge on the roof, and a restaurant and bar in the basement. The entire building was constructed from smooth concrete and painted pink. Standing among leafy streets of red-brick Victorian mansion blocks, the Lawn Road Flats proclaimed the Modernist message loud and clear.

During the 1930s the building was a centre for London's bourgeois intelligentsia, with Agatha Christie and Bauhaus founder Walter Gropius among its residents. The Bauhaus teacher Marcel Breuer designed the Isobar (converted into four flats in the 1980s), where sculptors Barbara Hepworth and Henry Moore drank cocktails. After the Second World War the reputation of the Modern Movement started to suffer and the social pulse of the Lawn Road Flats slowed, so Pritchard sold the block in 1969. By the 1970s it was in the hands of Camden Council and, despite being listed Grade II in 1974, was shamefully neglected. By 2000 it was graffiti-encrusted and uninhabitable.

In 2001 the Isokon Trust, a campaigning group set up by a local architect, Chris Flannery, and Notting Hill Housing purchased the block from the council and brought in Britain's foremost expert in restoring Modern Movement icons, John Allan, and his practice, Avanti Architects. Between May 2003 and November 2004 the firm sympathetically restored the fabric of the building, while ensuring that it had a sustainable and secure future. At a total cost of £2,300,000, the scheme provided twenty-five flats for sale under shared ownership, exclusively to key workers, with eleven further flats for sale on the open market.

The work included the repair and restoration of the reinforced-concrete envelope of the building; replacement of the asphalt waterproof coverings and upgrading of insulation; and renewal of wall, ceiling and floor finishes, and of windows and doors. Light metalwork elements and fitted joinery were refurbished where possible and replaced to match the original where not. Mechanical and electrical services have been fully re-engineered to comply with current standards, and new communication, signage and security installations have been sympathetically integrated. The immediate environs of the block have been completely rehabilitated, with a carefully detailed scheme of external works and soft landscaping.

As the building was listed Grade I (upgraded from Grade II in 1999), the layout of the rooms could not be altered. Flat 15, Gropius's old abode, has been restored to provide an authentic historical record of the original rooms, while the plywood panelling in Jack Pritchard's penthouse has been refurbished by cabinetry specialist Nick Goldfinger. The remaining flats have been finished with such modern additions as washing machines, refrigerators and cookers, with the greatest possible respect being accorded to the original design. The former garage houses a permanent exhibition presenting the history of the building and promoting understanding of the radical ideas that led to its creation.

The Isokon Flats building once again stands as a landmark to the Modern Movement and, by providing keyworker housing, it supports the social ideals of the Bauhaus movement that inspired its development. In addition, the incredibly well-researched and rigorously executed work of Avanti Architects is an exemplar of how historic buildings can be rehabilitated without their integrity being destroyed. Such impressive work is essential if the architectural heritage of London is to be maintained.

Opposite, top left
The east elevation. Circulation is concentrated to one side of the building.

Opposite, top right
Flat 15 is a one-bedroom flat. The original sliding door has been restored and the flat furnished with contemporary Isokon furniture.

Opposite, bottom
Restored to its former glory, the building stands as a true beacon of the Modern Movement.

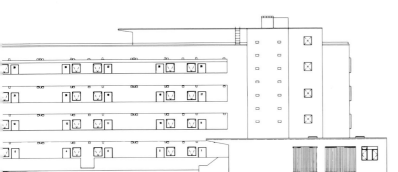

Opposite, top left
The garden wing of the Long
House contains a swimming
pool in the basement.

*Opposite, top right, centre
right, and bottom*
Externally the house is faced
in brick, but it opens up with a
glazed elevation to the garden,
which forms the focus for the
principal living spaces.

Below
The section shows the house's
generous scale, which is not
apparent from the street.

Making ingenious use of a triangular site – marking
the point where the boundaries of two London estates
rather awkwardly met – the Long House is, as a modern
building in an established historic context, a worthy
successor to pioneering London projects of the inter-
war era by Maxwell Fry, Ernö Goldfinger, Walter Gropius,
Mendelsohn & Chermayeff and others. Just as Goldfinger
faced fierce local opposition to his terrace of houses at
Willow Road, Hampstead, so Keith Williams's client had to
win approval from the secretary of state, overruling the
local planners, before the discreet and well-mannered
Long House could be built.

The site is on the eastern side of a mews behind
Hamilton Terrace, in a conservation area. A long, single-
storey garden wing, with a subterranean swimming
pool, sits behind a rebuilt brick boundary wall to the
mews. Family accommodation is in a three-storey
block adjoining nineteenth-century terraced houses of
similar scale on Hills Road, and is faced in white render,
presenting a largely blank face to the mews but opening
with large areas of glazing to the garden. Framed by the
L-shaped plan, the garden forms the focus of a house
designed to allow internal and external spaces to merge.
Staff/guest accommodation is provided over garage
space at the acute end of the triangular site. The aim
was to create a 'secret' house, and it has been realized
to the extent that the qualities of the project are fully
apparent only to those privileged to be invited inside.

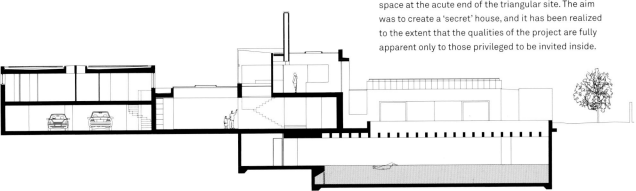

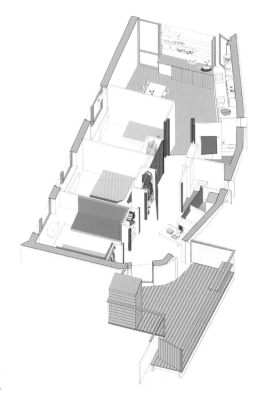

Opposite
The rectilinear golden façade that borders the street (top) creates a dramatic contrast with the curved rear of the building (bottom), clad in a silver membrane and glass-reinforced plastic.

Right
The interiors make the most of a small area, with generous living spaces and good storage.

In December 2002 the Peabody housing association launched a competition, 'Fresh Ideas for Low-Cost Housing', which centred on three sites near London's Royal Victoria Dock in Silvertown, east London. Two outstanding projects have emerged from this contest, one by Niall McLaughlin (pp. 252–53) and the other by Ash Sakula. The latter's prize was an awkward infill site on Boxley Street, with the tracks of the Docklands Light Railway close by to the north and London City Airport to the east. Here four flats in two adjoining buildings form part of a low-cost shared-ownership scheme.

By far the most eye-catching aspect of the project is the lightweight rainscreen cladding that wraps around both timber-framed buildings. The right-angled walls facing the street are clad in a pale-yellow-tinted reflective breather membrane with translucent, profiled glass-reinforced plastic (GRP) laid horizontally over the top. At the rear, where the walls are curved rather than angular, the cladding is silver and the GRP is laid vertically, so that the corrugations run upwards and reach beyond the top of the building. The surfaces glisten as light bounces between the foil wrapping and the outer skin. Ash Sakula worked with the artist Vinita Hassard, who suggested hanging twisted pieces of wire between the two layers to animate the surfaces further. The architect wanted the residents of the project to feel as though they were living in a real-life work of art rather than a low-cost housing scheme, and this treatment is a striking improvement on traditional cladding materials.

The four flats are near-identical units stacked on top of each other in two pairs. Challenged with a floor space of just 69 square metres in which to accommodate four people and provide two bedrooms, the architect rejected both the traditional Victorian template and an open-plan scheme (often perceived as a lazy solution). Instead the practice designed the spaces around a range of modern scenarios: the unusually wide entrance hall, for example, doubles as a laundry area or workspace with built-in cupboards and box shelves, and allows natural light to reach the rest of the interior. The main social space is the kitchen, where all units and appliances are fixed to one wall and the space opposite is free for either a playpen or a table and chairs. The drawing room can be used as a family room, home office or guest bedroom, while the living room is less flexible, its built-in perimeter seating inspired by the Ottoman salon and transport cabins. The bedrooms are small and can be used only for sleeping, but the separate WC and bathroom are both large and naturally lit. Outdoor space is provided in the form of an entrance yard or second-floor deck. The only awkward part of the design is the prefabricated deck and staircase structure, its balustrades formed from timber posts and simple chainlink fencing. One feels that a greater elegance here might have been more fitting.

The cladding and internal layout of this scheme subvert traditional expectations of the home and raise questions about the future of low-cost housing. For a final cost of £1498 per square metre, Ash Sakula has replaced a brownfield site with four flexible homes, making a strong architectural statement in the process.

The cladding incorporates radiant light film, enabling natural light to reach the interiors while providing a radical exterior with a constantly changing appearance. The interiors are simple but elegant, a combination not usually found in low-cost housing.

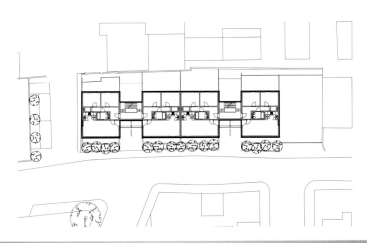

In December 2002 Niall McLaughlin Architects won the Peabody housing association's 'Fresh Ideas for Low-Cost Housing' competition (see also pp. 250–51) with a scheme to build twelve flats on Evelyn Road in Silvertown, east London. The project was inspired by the history of the area, which by 1900 was one of the largest industrial complexes in the world, producing such consumer goods as sugar, matches and dye. The site itself was once occupied by the warehouses that stored these commodities, but by the 1990s the area had become wasteland. McLaughlin's scheme plays a key role in the area's regeneration.

The building contains four flats on each of three floors. Its prefabricated frame and walls are constructed from timber, with an eye-catching, decorative street frontage that has caused a stir. The architect collaborated with light-artist Martin Richman to develop a system never before used in construction, which employs ribbons of radiant light film to create a 'chemical flare' across the building's façade. Iridescent as a peacock's feather or petrol on water, radiant light film is used in the manufacture of packaging, ribbons and shoes. The architect encased the material in modified double-glazing units – one face is cast glass, the other aluminium – and attached strips of film to slats of glass, set alternately to the front and back of the cavity. These varying depths create contrasting reflections, and the screen changes with different light and weather conditions, times of day, and viewpoints.

The interior has unusually high ceilings for low-cost housing, and makes the most of the sun and outlook. Each flat has two bedrooms and a bathroom, with the kitchen, dining and living areas accommodated in one large space on the south side. The flats on the ground floor have a back garden, while those above are provided with a south-facing terrace and corner windows to give views along the street towards the O2 and Canary Wharf in the distance. By encouraging collaboration between architect and artist this scheme projects an impressive sense of place while challenging preconceptions of low-cost housing.

It is difficult to miss Prewett Bizley Architects' first new-build project, a brick oddity with unevenly placed windows. Built over a gruelling six years by Graham Bizley as a home for himself and a base for the practice, which he established with Robert Prewett in 2005, the house is attached to the end of a Victorian terrace in the gritty enclave of Newington Green in north-east London, and is progressive yet sympathetic to the surrounding traditional brick buildings. Whereas the choice of Ibstock brick was informed by these and by a desire to keep the cost down, the form of the building was dictated by the irregular 60-square-metre plot. Hemmed in by a road, two properties and a private garden, it presented a challenge in terms of both the physical boundaries and rights of light. The response is a four-storey, turret-topped house that turns its back on its neighbours but embraces the street.

The west façade has no fenestration (natural light is instead allowed in through a glazed roof), but the street façade is dominated by apparently randomly spaced, exaggerated, plain-glass windows. Most impressive is the strip window to the office, which wraps around two sides to give views on to the street and down to the green.

Bottom, left
The glazed roof dissects the exterior brickwork at an angle, allowing for an unexpected interior window, which gives views over the ground floor from the bedroom above.

Bottom, right
The bespoke latticed staircase runs the height of the building and allows light to filter through to all areas.

Opposite, bottom
The project is a modern take on the quintessentially British building material: brick. An unusual strip window lights the office from two sides, emphasizing the horizontal proportions of the blocky building, but the boldest element of the house is the pavement-level window, which allows views directly into the living area.

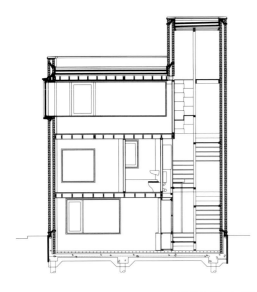

A window at street level encourages passers-by to peer into the living area, thus severing the barriers between the public and the private and creating a dialogue between the house and the street. For Bizley that is one of the most important functions of the building.

Throughout the interior, the emphasis is on simplicity and economy, with basic building materials and exposed joints. The ground floor contains the living, dining and kitchen area; above are the bedroom and bathroom; and stacked on top of these is the office. The fourth-floor tower provides a laundry and shed area leading on to a roof terrace. Connecting these floors, and creating the spine of the building, is a latticed staircase of plywood and Douglas fir. Such details as this, combined with the functional appearance of the exposed construction, render the house an elegant solution to a difficult site. By creating such a building for just £212,000, Bizley has proved that the economical brick terrace is still a relevant form.

This £7,700,000 student-housing scheme by Haworth Tompkins for Shaftesbury Student Housing on a 4800-square-metre site marks a refreshing departure from the stereotypical brick accommodation blocks to which Britain's students have become so accustomed. Located in the Newington Green conservation area in Islington, north London, the project provides rooms for 200 students from City University London. Its construction consisted of two distinct phases: the first was the renovation of the four-storey Edwardian China Inland Mission building fronting Newington Green, and the second the demolition and replacement of Alliance House, a five-storey Victorian building to the rear. The resulting scheme demonstrates how student accommodation can be both architecturally exciting and beneficial to the surrounding community.

The grand façade of the China Inland Mission now provides a double-height covered archway into the site. Alterations have been relatively slight, the only major change being the replacement of two shoddy brick extensions with two small single-storey buildings. These 'bookend' the retail units on either side and re-establish the symmetrical composition of the main arch. The extension to the south houses a shop and that to the north a restaurant, integrating the scheme into the existing streetscape. The remainder of the building provides eleven maisonettes, accessed via the original stair cores to the front of the building: one core has been altered to provide lift access for disabled occupants and visitors.

The bulky Edwardian building restricts the visual impact of the new scheme on the surrounding area, giving the architect much greater creative freedom than it might otherwise have been granted. Permission to demolish the Victorian building was obtained by demonstrating that redevelopment could significantly enhance the quality of the environment for residents near by. Whereas the Victorian block extended the full length of the site, leaving only a narrow strip of land along each of the longer elevations and drastically restricting light to and views from the neighbouring houses, Haworth Tompkins' scheme is conceived as free-standing buildings integrated into a garden setting. Four blocks are positioned irregularly down the plot, giving the neighbouring properties views across the site and considerably improving the amount of daylight for those immediately to the north.

The design was significantly influenced by the fifteen mature trees that punctuate the site. The four blocks are positioned around the trees and reach to a similar height. But the presence of the trees, most importantly, resulted in a pronounced verticality in the scheme, with service cores expressed as a cluster of three vertical elements: a lift, a stair and kitchens stacked one on top of the other. Each element is treated with a different material. The staircases are left partly

The scheme has a pronounced verticality, emphasized by the exterior treatment of the three service cores for each block.

open with a perforated screen of vertical larch boarding to provide protection from the rain. This not only reduces construction costs and heating bills, but also encourages a more direct relationship between the occupants and the community. The kitchens are partly embedded in the main blocks, but their core-side exteriors are clad in larch boards. The surface of the lift cores is *in situ* concrete, the shuttering pattern mimicking the grain of the perforated screens. When the untreated larch weathers, the colour of all three core elements will be similar.

In contrast, the accommodation blocks are rendered in a brilliant white polymer, which reflects light around the site, and the windows and spandrel panels are faced in naturally anodized aluminium. The façades are configured as a series of vertical strips: narrow floor-to-ceiling windows alternate with bands of render. According to the architect, this irregularly spaced glazing reflects the way in which the trees meander upwards, although the glazed elements terminate not in leaves but in butterfly roofs.

Inside, a series of flats leads off from the main core, with either five or seven en suite study rooms sharing a kitchen and dining area. The windows of the student rooms face east or west around a series of open courtyard gardens. This arrangement enhances the sense of community, while preventing the neighbours from being overlooked. Beyond the austere entrance arch facing the traffic surging through Newington Green, this is a secret green enclave. There cannot be many better places in London in which to study.

One Centaur Street is progressive both in its form and in its use of prefabricated materials. The interior is equally modern, and designed for open-plan living and working.

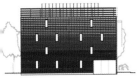

One Centaur Street has transformed an unpromising site into a model for future urban housing. Designed by dRMM (de Rijke Marsh Morgan Architects) in collaboration with the progressive developer Roger Zogolovitch of Solidspace, the building has been slotted into a 368-square-metre gap between a railway viaduct and a row of listed buildings. In order to protect the inhabitants from the noise of the trains, the four-flat building is constructed from *in situ* concrete. This also allows for flexibility in the spatial arrangement of the interior: the architect has replaced a standard stacking system with duplexes arranged back-to-back on the lower floors, and three-storey maisonettes arranged similarly above. These basic units are designed to extend both horizontally and vertically, and would allow much greater urban density than conventional housing if the scheme were to be repeated elsewhere.

Externally, the project demonstrates the architect's research into new building solutions, in particular cost-effective prefabricated materials. The concrete frame is clad in a rainscreen of the wood-grained fibrous cement boards most usually seen in North American kit houses. The gaps between these chocolate-brown planks widen as the eye moves up the façade, revealing more of their vertical support structure and the aluminium-faced thermal insulation behind. Toughened glass punctuates these surfaces, generously lighting the living spaces of each flat. A glass stairwell, which provides a communal

space and access to all four flats, juts out from the side of the building to within inches of the brick of the railway arches. This bold addition integrates the old with the new, as the viaduct becomes the visual backdrop of the building's central circulation space.

The interiors of the flats give the impression of great spaciousness and openness, although the fact that they are arranged over different vertical levels creates clearly defined zones. In each a jagged concrete staircase leads to the encapsulated bedrooms and bathrooms, which hang like viewing platforms over the living areas. The north-facing flats have double-height winter gardens and the larger units benefit from an additional room on a third storey. Roof decks sit at the same level as the railway line and allow inhabitants to peer down into the garden below or watch the trains curving out of Waterloo station.

One Centaur Street complements its gritty urban setting perfectly, while suggesting a cost-effective solution to London's housing shortage. The project has received a number of awards, including the RIBA London Building of the Year Award in 2003, when the judges commented that 'to achieve this sense of special delight in a one-off house would have been commendable; to get it on a tight urban site for speculative private housing is really remarkable.' DRMM itself is clearly delighted with the scheme, as it has moved its office into one of the lower units.

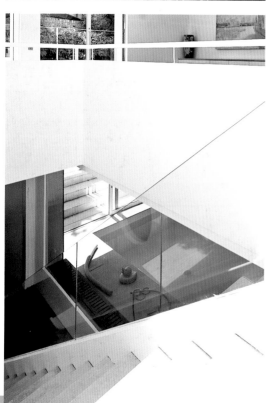

The concrete structure inserted into the ground was designed so that as much natural light as possible reaches the interiors. The sedum roof (opposite, top left) and indoor swimming pool (opposite, bottom left; below), which acts as a heat sink, are just two of the building's many ecological features.

When Alex Michaelis (the favourite eco-architect of prime minister David Cameron) bought a plot of land in Notting Hill, west London, he faced an unusual challenge. The site, wedged between two Edwardian terraced houses, was subject to an unusual planning regulation, which stipulated that any building constructed on the site could rise no more than 2 metres above the ground. Few architects would relish the thought of designing a house smaller in stature than themselves, but Michaelis had been coveting the spot for fifteen years and refused to be put off.

In place of 1000 cubic metres of London clay, which was removed from the site along with abandoned fridges and other such detritus of illegal fly-tipping, he built a two-floor, five-bedroom house. The building is completely hidden from the street behind a nondescript brick wall, beyond which a curvaceous ramp leads down into a crisp white concrete cube. The interior gives very little clue that it is below ground level. The open-plan living, dining and kitchen space is generously lit by a vast roof light and glazed doors leading to a paved terrace. Smaller skylights built into the patio that surrounds the house provide light for the basement bedrooms. In this way every room, with the exception of the utility room and the bathroom, enjoys at least a glimpse of natural light. The downstairs bedrooms are further illuminated by light reflected from the glass-enclosed swimming pool, around which they are arranged.

The sleek white walls and clean lines of this sophisticated modern house mask its impressive ecological credentials. Michaelis is a staunch believer in reducing energy consumption and investing in renewable energy sources. The house is remarkably well insulated, and windows, doors and roof lights with the same insulation properties as brick were sourced from Denmark. The walls are laced with Kingspan thermal wool insulation, and a sedum roof traps heat while releasing oxygen into the environment. A bank of solar panels above the carport fuels the family's electric car. Another set works a heat pump to bring water up through a borehole that taps into the earth's aquifer 100 metres below the surface. This arrangement provides all the house's hot water – including that for the underfloor heating and the pool – while a filtration system ensures that the tap water is drinkable. The pool also acts as a heat sink, regulating the temperature throughout the house.

As environmental sustainability forces its way on to the agenda of the construction industry, Michaelis has proved that helping to preserve the planet's resources does not preclude the creation of a stylish home.

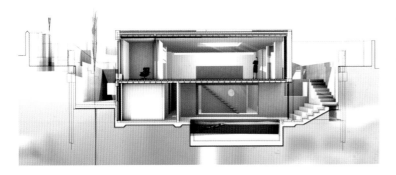

Left and below
The Parkside project responds
to a context of largely
Victorian housing, and the
scale of the blocks equates
to that of the surviving big
nineteenth-century villas.

Opposite
This solid, even monumental
architecture contrasts with
the flimsiness and apparent
ephemerality of much recent
housing in both the private
and the 'social' sectors.

'Frighteningly austere' was one description of this project, commissioned as affordable, mixed-tenure housing by the Circle Anglia housing trust for a site close to Finsbury Park. The architect's stated desire to create 'housing that felt solid and substantial' – in contrast to the insubstantiality of so much recent residential development in London and beyond – finds clear expression in the completed £4,800,000 scheme. Sergison Bates' work certainly eschews rhetoric (as did that of Peter and Alison Smithson – a strong influence) in favour of a rigorous response to site and context. Jonathan Sergison worked for David Chipperfield and Tony Fretton – clearly kindred spirits – before founding the partnership with Stephen Bates in 1996.

The site is in an area characterized by large Victorian villas (now flats), interspersed with later developments of variable quality. The project consequently takes the form of three new 'villas', two located on Seven Sisters Road and the third, smaller in scale, set back beyond a central shared garden space. The blocks are faced in red brick, flush-jointed, with windows deeply recessed, their rhythm responding to the elevations of neighbouring Victorian houses. Internally, the two larger blocks are arranged around circulation cores, while the smaller block has flats that, with the exception of two on the top floor, have their own front doors. Constructed on a concrete frame, the development has a solidity that is more than an aesthetic device, contributing equally to its impressive environmental credentials.

While much of the 'social' housing of the last decade or so condescends to its residents with cheap veneers of coloured metal and high-maintenance timber, Sergison Bates offers housing that, for all its austerity, has the potential staying power of the Peabody flats of the Victorian era and London County Council's early housing schemes, which are still working well in the twenty-first century.

This rooftop house on top of a former warehouse has magnificent views. It is designed for open-plan living, and its detachment from the street makes it the ultimate city loft.

Family connections underlie the involvement of Richard Rogers in this project, originally designed by Tonkin Liu for Rogers's son and daughter-in-law and their four children. The project epitomizes Rogers's gospel of urban renaissance and 'greening the city'. Wanting to live in this part of London, but finding it impossible to secure a vacant site for a new house, the clients opted to build on top of an existing building, a solidly constructed four-storey warehouse typical of the area. As a result, the two-storey house has marvellous views to the south and west through generously glazed elevations. The structure is extremely economical, creating an impression of lightness and transparency and allowing natural light to flood into the interior. Shading is provided by external blinds and by the generous planting envisaged as an organic foil to the rational minimalism of the architecture; the mesh that cloaks the house is designed as an armature for climbing plants. Five of the six bedrooms, each with a small external terrace, are on the lower level. An open-plan living space fills the upper floor. The master bedroom and a spectacular bathroom are in a central tower, and an open terrace deck forms the roof level.

The house – which is accessed not through the warehouse on which it sits but via a lightweight bridge from an adjacent building – is hung from a central ring beam, which transfers its weight to the external walls of the warehouse below. None of this came cheaply, but the attractions of living in a calm oasis high above the city streets are obvious. This is a new take on loft living.

Stealth House sits between a Modernist detached house dating from the 1960s and an 1890s Edwardian terrace. The site, bombed during the Second World War, was formerly occupied by a 1950s building that was abruptly set back from the terrace and that, with its dark engineering bricks and roof of cement tiles, jarred with the rest of the street. In contrast, the new house, designed by Robert Dye for clients Geof Powell and comedian Jenny Eclair, enhances its surroundings. It creates a smooth transition between its disparate neighbours, in particular through being set back in two stages from the street.

This was an architect-assisted self-build project: Dye produced the plans while Powell and his builders undertook the construction work. The house is timber-framed, with stressed plywood panels to allow a double cantilever at the corners. The black-stained Russian redwood cladding was a contextual response to the black timber balconies on the flats opposite. The cladding is fixed to an inner core, rendered in pale grey K-rend (a traditional Irish building material made of crushed rubble), but there is a slight gap between the two so that the outer skin seems to 'float'. The interior walls are plywood, forming a breathable 'skin' for the building.

The roof, made from a grey-green mineralized felt, carries on the line of the brick house to one side. From the street the building appears to be a two-storey black house with a grey pitched roof, but the monopitch hides a third storey with a double bedroom and en suite bathroom opening on to a hidden roof terrace, visible only from the rear.

The house has an internal area of 200 square metres, making superb use of a tight site. With a cost of £260,000, it also represents value for money. But most impressive is its contextual sensitivity and the way it has re-established cohesion in the street. In 2005 it received an RIBA Award and the Manser Medal for the best one-off house designed by an architect for a private client. It proves that contextually sympathetic buildings do not have to rely on pastiche.

The reconstruction of Elephant & Castle in south London, scheduled to be completed by 2020, is one of the most ambitious urban regeneration projects in Europe. It will involve the demolition of most of the widely despised post-war housing in the area as well as the drab shopping centre, and the creation of new public spaces and parks. The proposed transformation is likely to cost more than £1,500,000,000 and will include more than 5000 new homes, along with landmark commercial developments. A masterplan for the project was drawn up initially by Foster + Partners, and has been further developed by Make.

BFLS's scheme provides the first of a number of new landmark towers at Elephant, identified as a suitable location for a cluster of tall buildings. Built for developer Multiplex, it replaces Castle House, which dated from the 1960s. The new 43-storey, 147-metre-tall apartment building was given planning consent in the spring of 2006. Superficially, it appears to be yet another of the many high-rises built or planned in London for an affluent urban elite. In fact, the project has some radical aspects. The building's striking profile derives largely from the aspiration to make it a 'green' tower: three large wind turbines, each 9 metres across and mounted at roof level, power the building's lighting all year round. The aerodynamic form of the tower is designed to maximize the benefits of wind power. This investment in environmentally friendly energy is a response to recent changes in building regulations, which also dictated the solid shape of the tower, cut away where necessary. The confined nature of the site necessitated a triangular form.

Inside the building, in place of cramped corridors and lift lobby spaces, mini atria give a sense of space and light. By installing sprinklers, an unusual feature in a residential building and one that imposes a further cost, the architect was able to remove internal fire lobbies. But the greatest attraction of the tower to prospective residents, apart from its proximity to the City and the West End, is that it offers spectacular views: some of the flats have a direct view of St Paul's Cathedral from the front door.

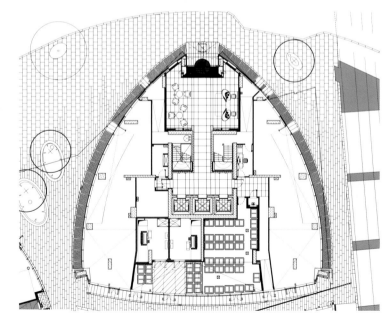

The striking tower, with its three enormous wind turbines, forms an important part of the visual identity of the revitalized Elephant & Castle area.

STUDIO HOUSE E2

Sergison Bates is known for its reductive approach to architecture, by which the authenticity of construction methods and the nature of the materials are expressed directly and with rigour. Such projects as their Prototype Social Housing in Stevenage (1998–2000) and the Assisted Self-Build Housing in Tilbury, Essex (2001–2002), are bold and functional, and display a rare honesty in their use of materials. Studio House, in the previously semi-industrial area of Bethnal Green, east London, is in this vein, and its position on a piece of derelict land on a street of light industrial buildings and large pre-war housing blocks reiterates the firm's continuing commitment to regeneration.

In response to a complex brief combining four programmes – two flats, a studio for an artist, and a space for a joint therapy practice – the architect has used a form that does not immediately announce its purpose. The geometric, 'no-frills' street façade, with its porch covered by a mesh screen for security and semi-privacy, reads as an urban house or a small industrial building. The form was largely generated by two constraints: the extraordinarily narrow site (4.5 by 20 metres) and the planning department's dictates on massing and sightlines. The client asked for a fluid floor plan, with an unorthodox arrangement of interconnected rooms and changes of level, very similar to the spatial qualities of Kettle's Yard, the house and gallery in Cambridge.

The timber-framed structure of Studio House allows both the stacking of a variety of spatial volumes and a compact, elongated form to fit the site. The rooms are arranged around an open courtyard, with staircases placed along one side in long flights. The high-pitched roof lends an attic-like feel to the top-floor flat. The rear of the building is one storey high with a roof terrace above it on the first floor. The elevation here is visually complex: external timber cladding alternates with bands of semi-reflective glass that cover the solid walls as well as the windows and doors. In contrast, the rest of the building is clad in brick washed over with a mortar slurry. On two of the walls a brick slip system – thinly cut bricks bonded to rebated strips and slotted together in the manner of shiplap boarding – has been used. This monolithic yet delicate surface adds to the building's contradictory nature, lending it an imperfection that fits well with the fragmented nature of the surrounding streetscape. Studio House may seem nondescript and slightly defensive at first sight, but on closer examination it is intricate in appearance as well as structure, paying homage to its context.

Below
The plan is narrow but well organized, allowing ample room for the living areas. The first floor (shown here) leads on to a generous terrace.

Opposite, left
The front of the compact building is unfussy in its design.

Opposite, right
At the back, wood and semi-reflective glass combine in an attractive but inscrutable façade.

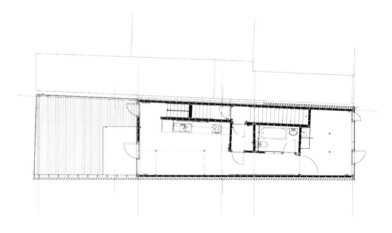

Left
The housing in Vassall Road combines flats and maisonettes in a socially mixed development that includes a health centre.

Below
The blocks are faced in brick, and take their scale from nearby nineteenth-century terraces.

Opposite
Floor plans and sections reveal an intelligent adaptation of the traditional terrace to modern needs.

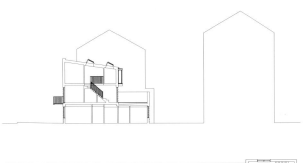

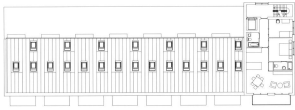

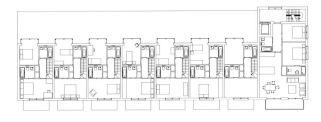

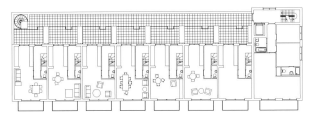

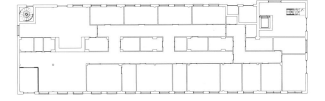

Vassall Road mixes restored ninteenth-century villas with social housing of the 1960s and 1970s; the local landmark is G.E. Street's magnificent church of St John. Tony Fretton Architects' project, commissioned by the enterprising developer Baylight, manages to be contextual and appropriate by studiously avoiding modish gestures. The use of red brick as an external material – over-painted to simulate ageing (an eccentric measure) – and the profile of the windows provide points of reference to the neighbouring villas.

The three-and-four-storey development, which replaces an abandoned pub, contains a much-needed facility for the local community: a new health centre occupying the entire ground floor. The commercial element of the scheme, to fund the health centre, provides ten flats for sale, seven of them maisonettes designed for possible family occupation.

The development is conceived as a formal terrace standing in its own enclosed garden. The flats have their own garden space to the rear, while the surgery has a dedicated entrance on Vassall Road. The street corner is marked by the elevation of the block to four storeys – a device familiar from Georgian and Victorian residential developments. Generous external balconies are another attractive addition to this reworking of an established form of urban architecture.

Alison Brooks's VXO House is essentially a reworking of an unremarkable 1960s house. Hamfistedly extended during the 1970s – gaining space at the expense of convenience and legibility – the earlier structure now forms the core of a remarkable residential complex in which wit and lightness of touch are the distinguishing themes.

The original house, which had been damaged by fire when Brooks was commissioned, stood in a generous garden in Hampstead, set back from the street behind an enclosing wall. The initial brief was one of repair, conversion and extension, with the addition of a bedroom and a more generous entrance space. The project subsequently grew to include a radical reconstruction of the existing house, new structures in the garden and a reconfiguration of the landscape. The architect describes the completed project as 'a domestic campus of enclosed, semi-enclosed and open structures'. The changes are far from cosmetic, and exhibit – for a relatively modest project costing under £600,000 – considerable structural bravura by the consultant engineers, Price & Myers.

The additional space needed for the existing house could only be provided on the garden front, where it forms a timber-clad volume hovering over a new glazed terrace and supported on a single 'V' column, painted bright red. Inside, a new suspended staircase, contained within steel mesh, hangs from the first floor in a central atrium that forms the focus of the house. A free-standing screen wall, the work of artist Simon Patterson, conceals the cloakroom, and there is now a dining room where there was formerly an outdoor terrace. New timber decks connect internal and external spaces.

The separate X-pavilion (which replaces a double garage and contains a gym and guest accommodation) is conceived as a pure glass box, sitting on a folded *in situ* concrete plate that provides the base for the building and a retaining wall. Inside, a folded timber plate forms both a floor and a screen wall. The earth-covered roof of the pavilion is carried on two 'X' members. Finally, the existing carport has been replaced by a new 'O port': just a roof, dramatically cantilevered, sitting on a light steel O-shape and slender columns.

Inside the house, high-quality materials, including aluminium, choice woods, etched glass and limestone, are used freely. The essence of the project seems to be the attempt to erode the barriers between the highly tactile interior and the openness of the garden beyond.

The VXO project – the initials of which derive from the boldly painted steel structural members – includes the refurbishment of an existing house, the construction of a new glazed pavilion containing a gym and guest accommodation, and a replacement carport. The three buildings form a family of structures in the lush garden.

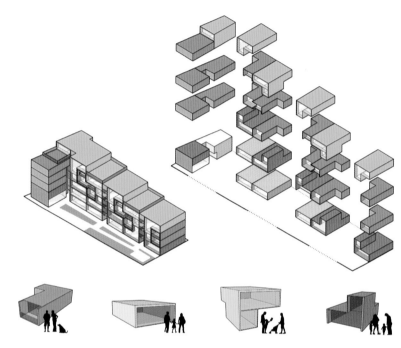

The Elephant & Castle project is the largest component of the ongoing regeneration strategy for the London Borough of Southwark, involving the demolition of substantial areas of failed post-war housing (see also pp. 268–69). Wansey Street lies just south of the notorious Heygate Estate, which is being knocked down as part of the programme, undertaken by Elephant & Castle Regeneration. De Rijke Marsh Morgan Architects (dRMM) won a competition for the Wansey Street housing – thirty-one units, 60 per cent of them affordable, developed by freeholder Southern Housing Group – in 2004. The scheme is seen as a pilot project for the redevelopment of the surrounding area, and is in essence a twenty-first-century reinterpretation of the traditional London terrace, taking into account present-day concerns over sustainability, ownership and security.

Occupying a classic urban gap site linking surviving nineteenth-century terraces with the town hall on Walworth Road, the scheme is carefully integrated: there are shared stairs and a communal garden, and none of the rigid division between private and 'social' housing seen in many recent residential projects in London is present here. Four blocks, ascending in height from east to west, contain a mix of flats and maisonettes, with between one and three bedrooms. The coloured street façade makes the development something of a local landmark. The southern (garden) elevation features more glazing, plus sun screening, balconies and access stairs. Some of the detailing is crudely done, but as a piece of urban architecture, sensitive to place – in contrast to the mega-structures of the 1960s and 1970s – the scheme deserves to be studied.

Opposite, top
The diagram of the Wansey Street housing mixes flats and maisonettes to provide units suitable for a variety of residents.

Opposite, bottom, and right
The southern elevation makes extensive use of shading.

Below
The street façade is boldly coloured, a contrast to the grey concrete of the failed housing schemes in the area, now being demolished.

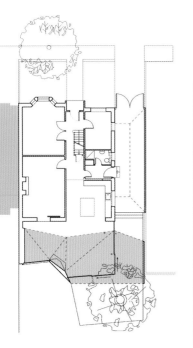

Seen from the street, this appears to be an ordinary Chiswick town house, with the stained glass and elaborate detailing characteristic of a Victorian building. Yet the back of this west London home presents a drastically different view. A jagged glass-and-timber structure hovers over the garden, a wooden deck sprawls over the lawn, and the roof extends upwards in numerous directions. Striking, intelligent and completely original, this project by Alison Brooks Architects is one of the most impressive residential extensions recently built in the capital.

The 100-square-metre extension is constructed predominantly from ipe timber, manipulated into triangular forms. The aggressive angles of the roof mimic the forms of the original Victorian structure. At one end the timber surface swoops down to create a low dining space with a floor-to-ceiling glass wall framing the outlook over the garden. At the other end, the structure folds upwards to provide more expansive views around and up to a large copper-beech tree.

Light seeps inside through a narrow, glass-encased opening, which runs the width of the building between the original house and the ipe roofing. Despite requesting extensive glazing to maximize light, the clients were concerned about the building overheating in the summer and about being overlooked by a row of houses to the south. The solution was to extend the timber roof beyond the line of the glazed enclosure to connect with the far edge of the deck and create a sculptural outdoor archway. As well as forming a covered outdoor dining portico, this wooden projection protects the interior from both the midday sun and prying eyes.

In the middle of the garden-facing façade, the roof folds down to form an internal fireplace. The timber roof and wall surfaces also wrap around to form the internal floor and external decking, giving the entire extension a solid sense of cohesion. The complex three-dimensional geometry results from the use of traditional setting techniques, along with strings and lasers, to position the rigorously accurate triangular roof planes and the precisely converging lines of the internal ceiling. Throughout the project the traditional inspires a dramatically modern result.

Opposite and below
In contrast to the mews house's appearance by day (below), the interior is illuminated at night by an array of vibrant colours (opposite). A counter in the kitchen on the first floor hides the 4-metre shaft for the shower below.

Below, right
Notoriously cramped, mews houses are plentiful – and increasingly popular – in London. Here, the three towers replace a badly designed interior arrangement and organize the tight space.

It comes as something of a surprise to see an RIBA plaque nailed to the front of this house in Notting Hill, west London. Seen from the exterior, it appears to be an ordinary mews house, shabbily constructed during the 1980s. But step inside and the building's award-winning credentials become immediately apparent.

When the architect first laid eyes on the house it was dark, dingy and impractically designed. A garage on the ground floor was so narrow that it was impossible to open a car door inside, and a bulky staircase blocked out most of the natural light. Granted permission by the client to do exactly as they pleased, Tonkin Liu gutted the building, even removing the floors. The firm then constructed three internal towers built from prefabricated medium-density fibreboard and slotted together like a giant Meccano set. The services are contained in one of the towers: on the ground floor is the bathroom, with a dramatic 4-metre-high shower, and above is the kitchen, with the shower shaft hidden under a worktop. The second storey has been cut away above the kitchen to provide a double-height space lit by a roof light.

The second tower accommodates the sleeping and living areas, with a bedroom on the ground floor and the living area above. Although the living area receives most of the natural light, its floor is made from reinforced glass, through which light can penetrate to the level below. A switch beside the bed activates a horizontal blind to separate the two visually. The third tower provides room for the staircase, storage and a third-floor area where the client keeps his DJ equipment. Cables run from here into every room of the house, creating a sophisticated surround-sound system.

Tonkin Liu is known for its innovative use of light, and the scheme for Young House was inspired by the practice's Q Restaurant in Hong Kong, where lights are used to differentiate between daytime and evening meals. The interior of the London project has no doors and no blinds, so during the day it is incredibly bright. The second floor is painted white and the first and ground floors darkening shades of blue to create the effect of looking into a pool of water. At night the house is transformed by colour-changing neon lights that illuminate almost every surface. All the lighting elements have at least two settings and each tower is wired separately to allow a bewildering array of colour combinations at any one time.

The mews house is a tiny 70 square metres, but Tonkin Liu's inventive layout and use of lighting allow the space to be manipulated to suit a variety of occasions. Despite the appearance of the exterior, the interior is far from drab.

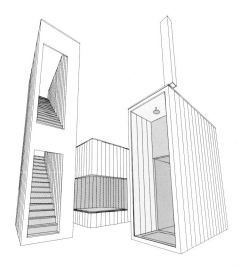

OFFICES

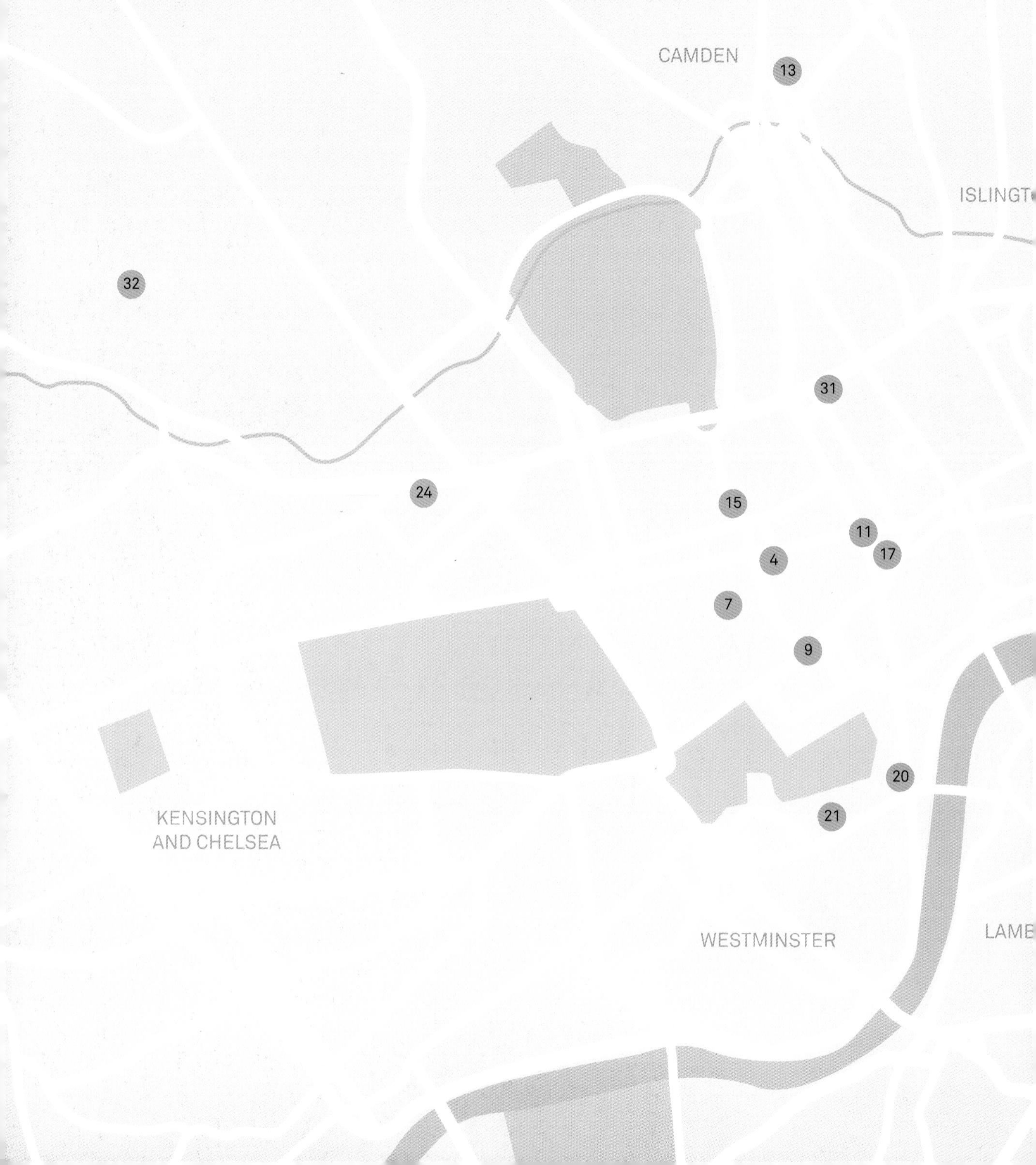

CAMDEN
13
ISLINGT
32
31
24
15
11
17
4
7
9
20
21
KENSINGTON
AND CHELSEA
WESTMINSTER
LAMB

HACKNEY

SOUTHWARK

Described by one critic as a 'blingtastic homage to Seifert', 1 Coleman Street is an eye-catching addition to the architectural zoo created as a result of the ongoing redevelopment of London Wall in the City, where few buildings now remain from the reconstruction that took place in the 1950s and 1960s after devastating wartime bombing. The scheme replaces Austral House (1961), described by Nikolaus Pevsner as 'particularly attractive' but by the 1990s seen as functionally obsolete and ripe for redevelopment. In fact, proposals for a new structure on the site date back to the early years of that decade, although the scheme was radically redesigned ten years later, and won planning consent in 2005.

Whether or not the comparison with Richard Seifert's work of the 1960s is fair – the architects prefer to cite the inspiration of the Banque Lambert in Brussels by Gordon Bunshaft of Skidmore, Owings & Merrill – the fluid form of 1 Coleman Street marks a break with the orthogonal aesthetics of the 1960s (and of most recent City office buildings, Foster's 30 St Mary Axe – pp. 294–95 – being one notable exception). Austral House had marked the entrance to Coleman Street from London Wall with a depressing ramp to an underground car park. The form of its replacement has allowed the street, now pedestrianized, to open out to create an attractive public space at its northern end. City planners initially wanted the new building to be clad in Portland stone, but subsequently approved the use of highly polished pre-cast concrete, with windows framed in stainless steel; on a sunny day the façades sparkle. Shapely and sculptural it may be, but 1 Coleman Street (eight storeys, with 20,000 square metres of office space) makes highly efficient use of the site and is a rational, as well as a highly contextual, example of the new City style.

Below
1 Coleman Street is part of the ongoing redevelopment of London Wall. The building in the background is Foster + Partners' replacement for the 1960s Moor House.

Opposite
The cladding has a precise, diamond-like quality and is executed in pre-cast concrete and stainless steel, while the form of the building neatly frames the entrance to Coleman Street.

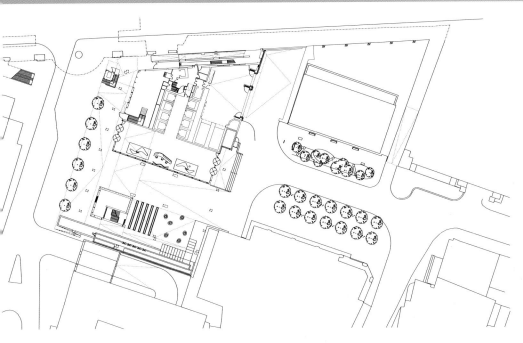

Opposite
Set in an extraordinary
context of buildings by
Richard Rogers, Norman
Foster, Terry Farrell and
twentieth-century classicists
McMorran and Whitby,
5 Aldermanbury Square, which
replaces an undistinguished
building dating from the
1960s, is part of the ongoing
redevelopment of London
Wall. The building is clad in
stainless-steel panels, with
the structural frame in front
of the glazing.

Left
The site plan shows the
relationship of the building
to the recast square, and the
pedestrian route from the
latter to Wood Street.

An earlier office project by Eric Parry, completed in 2002 on the eastern side of Finsbury Square (pp. 292–93), sought to impart a 'civic' feel to a large commercial block overlooking an important public open space in a conservation area. Parry's Finsbury Square office floors are standard column-free spaces, but the handsome load-bearing stone elevation reflects Parry's belief (in tune with the preferences of planning officers) that 'spaces need weight'. In comparison, the stone framing of Foster + Partners' block on the south-western corner of the square looks a rather token gesture.

5 Aldermanbury Square has similar civic ambitions. It, however, is steel-framed and clad in large stainless-steel panels, with the structural frame clearly expressed in front of the glazing, and a second layer of glass allowing natural light to penetrate the office floors while baffling solar gain and glare.

The new nineteen-storey building, which consists of two parallel blocks linked by a central section that includes a triple-height reception area, replaces the tired Royex House (1962) by Richard Seifert, one of the last of the boxy slabs that once lined London Wall. Since the mid-1980s, Wood Street has been almost totally redeveloped, with buildings by Richard Rogers and Norman Foster and, on London Wall, Terry Farrell's extraordinary Alban Gate prefacing the entrance to the Barbican. Immediately south of Parry's building is the listed police station by McMorran

and Whitby; coincidentally, the structural engineer for 5 Aldermanbury Square was Whitbybird (now Ramboll), in which George Whitby's son Mark was a partner. The tower of St Alban's church, all that survived of the original fabric after wartime bombing, is the other historic presence in the street, which originally led north to Cripplegate, one of the ancient points of access to the City.

The gentle tapering (or entasis) of the new building echoes that of McMorran and Whitby's adjacent tower, although its materials form a deliberate contrast with the brick and stone of the latter. The structure of Parry's façade, with a double-height rhythm above the triple-height ground floor, further reduces its apparent scale. Parry's building also re-establishes the building line on to Wood Street, lost in the development of the 1960s, with a colonnade that shelters the pavement.

The project has all the subtlety and attention to context that one expects of Parry, but also offers an additional benefit in the form of a new public space, Aldermanbury Square. This connects Wood Street to Basinghall Street and links with the upper-level walkways that are a legacy of post-war planning prescriptions and a fundamental ingredient of the Barbican. Trees and other planting, new paving, street furniture and lighting create what the architect envisaged as an 'enchanted garden', a real oasis of calm in the heart of the City.

Opposite
The stepped atrium at
10 Gresham Street is a
familiar device from earlier
Foster projects, including the
Willis Building of the 1970s.

Left
The corner service cores
are clad in stone, framing
curtain-walled façades of
Miesian elegance.

Below
The glazed screen to the
reception area is set back to
create a paved area in front
of the building.

Gresham Street remains part of the City's historic core: the Guildhall and Corporation church of St Lawrence Jewry form the key features of the conservation area next to the site of 10 Gresham Street, with the magnificent Grade I-listed Goldsmiths' Hall immediately to the west.

The commission for 10 Gresham Street dates back to 1996, but construction did not begin until 2001, following the demolition of the twelve-storey 1950s buildings on the island site. The location, in a protected view corridor, limited the height of the new building to 50 metres, and the planners' initial preference was for the use of a natural stone cladding in deference to the established character of the area. The completed scheme, however, uses stone only for facing the service cores, which are perceived as towers at each corner framing four storeys of curtain walling set above the double-height ground floor. Two more floors of offices are contained in a set-back mansard.

The building makes full use of the site, filling it up to the street boundaries and re-establishing the sense of enclosure that is a vital part of the City's character. Internally, a stepped atrium – a classic Foster diagram, first seen in the iconic mid-1970s Willis Building in Ipswich – allows light to penetrate to the heart of the eight-storey building, illuminating the surrounding office floors, which are 18 metres deep. The rigorous discipline of this building is as frankly Miesian as any of Foster's buildings. Eschewing display in favour of solid dignity, it is, for all its American inspiration, rooted in sound City traditions, and a worthy neighbour to the surrounding venerable institutions.

Left and opposite, bottom left
The façade of 10 Hills Place
has a slightly surreal quality.

Opposite, top
The project is an addition
to an existing building in
a narrow side street.

*Opposite, centre and
bottom right*
The windows, which appear
eccentric in form, are designed
to channel natural light into
the building.

Judging by this extraordinary building, which introduces an element of the surreal into the mundane hinterland of Oxford Street, Amanda Levete's studio looks set to continue the tradition of radical innovation that characterized her work with the late Jan Kaplicky at Future Systems. In fact, the project is essentially an addition (three storeys high and just over 1300 square metres in area) to an existing building, itself an extension (dating from the 1970s) on a narrow side street to a handsome early twentieth-century block with its front on Oxford Street.

The existing building was retained beneath a new skin with a strikingly sculptural appearance achieved using technology more familiar from shipbuilding. The façade was assembled, rather than constructed, on site using profiled aluminium sheets finished with a high-performance paint commonly used for yachts. Levete cites the work of artist Lucio Fontana, famous for his 'slashed' canvases, as the inspiration for the form of the windows, which emerge as great scoops of glazing, drawing light from above into the offices. At street level, the façade is formed of laminated glazing, incorporating stainless-steel mesh, which is lit from behind using fibre optics to create patterns that animate the elevation and add visual interest to the narrow street. On a fine day the façade shimmers and reflects the sun. This far from costly project, making good use of an existing structure, has turned Hills Place from a backwater into an eye-catcher.

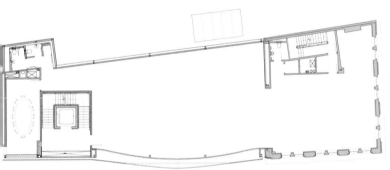

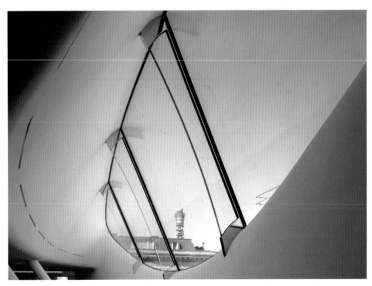

27–30 FINSBURY SQUARE EC2

Eric Parry's redevelopment of 27–30 Finsbury Square (on the edge of the City but just within the borough of Islington) highlights many of the problems underlying the politics of development in the business heart of London. The site was previously occupied by two buildings: an undistinguished 1960s block deemed obsolete for present-day commercial use, and an inter-war building in a dignified, if commonplace, classical manner, which was 'locally listed'. Both stood in a conservation area. Finsbury Square, originally a Georgian development, was – and remains – a collection of diverse post-1900 frontages, but these are now unified by the prevalence of solid masonry façades: even Foster + Partners' recent building on the corner of Finsbury Pavement bows to this pattern.

Parry's project to redevelop the site was linked to a masterplan by Latz + Partner for the reconfiguration of the square, a rather confused space that contains a bowling green, filling station and underground car park. The aim was to make the new building 'a wall to a square', and to give it a distinctly civic presence.

Parry's response was a sophisticated façade of load-bearing stone, engineered with Whitby & Bird (now Ramboll); it incorporates shading and drainage, and is integrated with the column-free office floors behind.

This is a subtly understated building by an architect with a thoughtful approach that is increasingly influencing the London commercial scene. Parry sees the danger of a decreasing area for architecture in a market that demands standardization and economy. 'Spaces need weight', he insists. At Finsbury Square he has produced a convincing model for a new masonry-fronted City architecture that is compatible with the spatial demands of the twenty-first-century office.

Below, left
The interior, in common with the façade, is simple but strong and elegant.

Below, right, and opposite
The façade could be seen as an optional, even a dispensable, feature of the modern office building, but at 27–30 Finsbury Square Eric Parry has transformed it into a potent civic and public presence.

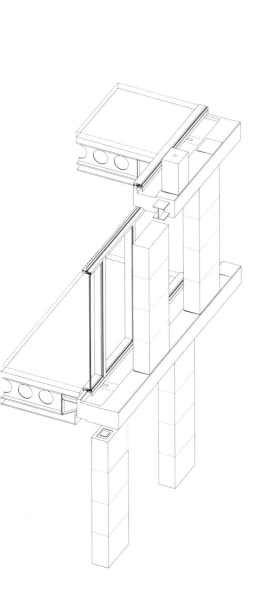

Opposite
30 St Mary Axe is conceived as a series of vertical 'villages', with mini atria at the perimeter providing social space and connecting the floors.

This page
The building has a distinctive and dramatic presence on the skyline, its shapely form contrasting with the more conventional geometry of earlier buildings in the City.

30 St Mary Axe ('the Gherkin') is one of half a dozen or more City of London office schemes by Foster + Partners that have been planned or built since 2001. It stands out from the rest not only for its prominence on the skyline – at forty-one storeys, it competes for attention with the slightly taller Tower 42 (formerly NatWest Tower) – but also, and even more, for its technical and environmental innovation. Indeed, it is one of the key Foster projects of the new century and was a worthy recipient of the coveted Stirling Prize in 2004.

The site is that of the Baltic Exchange, a sumptuous but rather dim Edwardian commercial palazzo damaged beyond repair by an IRA bomb in 1992. Foster's first proposal for the site was the London Millennium Tower, but this aroused strong opposition from amenity groups and found little favour with the City Corporation. With Swiss Re (a major reinsurance company) as client, Foster developed a new scheme for 'London's first ecological tall building'.

The 40,000-square-metre project has its origins in Norman Foster's exploratory work with Buckminster Fuller on the Climatroffice concept, which integrated green garden spaces into the workplace. It also develops ideas seen in the seminal 1970s Willis offices in Ipswich and, more recently, in the Frankfurt Commerzbank with its 'sky gardens'. The sky gardens re-emerge here as mini-atria, facilitating ventilation largely by natural, non-mechanical means; air conditioning is used only in a supplementary role and windows are made to open. The office floors spiral around the atria, forming vertical 'villages' that are intended to generate the interaction increasingly seen as vital to creative office work. Lifts, stairs and other services are concentrated in a central core, leaving the fully glazed perimeter free of intrusions.

At street level the painstaking aerodynamic modelling of the tower has been calculated to avoid downdraughts and to ensure benign conditions in the new piazza that surrounds the building.

30 St Mary Axe has injected a new element into a continuing debate about the place of high buildings in London. It reinforces the point that office towers can be distinctive, even beautiful, objects that complement rather than deface the skyline. It also undermines the contention that tall buildings are environmentally irresponsible, dependent on huge amounts of energy. For all this, it was a prestige commission, a bespoke work for a client whose name and reputation can only have benefited from an act of enlightened patronage.

50 NEW BOND STREET/14 ST GEORGE STREET W1

Eric Parry's emergence, in mid-career, as an important player in the commercial sector has been marked by substantial projects in the City of London, including 5 Aldermanbury Square (pp. 286–87) and 60 Threadneedle Street (2009). Parry's discreetly contextual modernism seems, however, to have found particular favour in the City of Westminster, where the prevailing planning orthodoxy rules out the extreme and the expressionistic. He was a natural choice for the highly sensitive St Martin-in-the-Fields project (pp. 96–97) and equally for the controversial redevelopment of 23 Savile Row (2009), where his elegant and undemonstrative masonry street elevations enclose highly efficient office floors.

At 50 New Bond Street/14 St George Street, the firm was commissioned in 2004 to address the challenge of a much larger site, in a conservation area. The starting point of the scheme was the demolition of an unloved 1960s block on New Bond Street designed by Michael Rosenauer, allowing a new office building to be inserted. Other buildings on the site – including the ebullient Grade II*-listed Edwardian Pinet building, a nineteenth-century terrace extending along Maddox Street and a group of Georgian town houses on St George Street – had to be retained, although an unsympathetic 1970s insertion on the corner of Maddox Street and St George Street was a candidate for remodelling.

With a disused industrial building in the backland removed, the new office development extends in two blocks from New Bond Street to St George Street, where the town houses have been sympathetically converted. An internal light well allows the offices to be naturally ventilated. The Maddox Street terrace has been renovated as flats, reflecting Westminster's policy of reinstating Mayfair as a residential district. The most striking element of the project, in terms of the public realm, is the new façade on New Bond Street, vigorously modelled with projecting oriel windows and clad in green faience. It is altogether an excellent piece of street architecture and a suitable complement to the adjacent Pinet building.

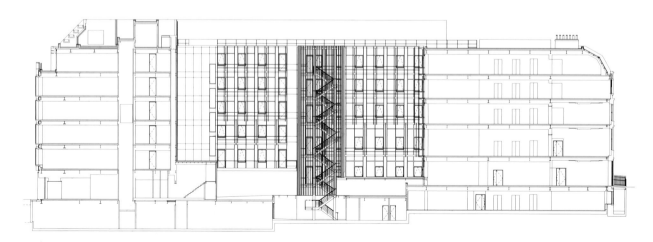

Opposite
The New Bond Street/
St George Street project
involved the restoration
and reconstruction of an
entire block at the heart
of the West End.

This page
Parry's new façade on Bond
Street uses green faience to
achieve a luxurious effect with
echoes of the late Victorian
era. Its scale and rhythm
respond to the adjacent
listed Pinet building.

110 Bishopsgate – also known as Heron Tower, after its developer – might appear to be a relatively uncontroversial project after Norman Foster's 30 St Mary Axe (pp. 294–95) sailed through the planning process with backing from the City, English Heritage and the government. In the spring of 2001, however, a call-in order by then environment secretary John Prescott stopped the scheme in its tracks and threw its future into question. Prescott subsequently gave consent for the scheme in 2002, following a public inquiry, and construction began in 2007.

It is the second City project by Kohn Pedersen Fox (KPF), a practice originating in the United States but rapidly gaining serious credentials in Europe (Thames Court, Upper Thames Street, was finished in 1998). Another major office development by the practice was completed in 2001 just outside the City on High Holborn. Comparable in scale to 30 St Mary Axe and markedly less high than the 1970s Tower 42 (formerly NatWest Tower), KPF's building replaces a group of utterly banal 1970s buildings at Houndsditch, on the eastern boundary of the City. Far removed from the St Paul's Heights control zone, it forms part of a cluster of towers in this part of London, close to excellent public transport facilities. At street level the scheme produces real public benefits, with part of Houndsditch closed to traffic and turned into a new square, framing the church of St Botolph. The lower levels of the building are given over to shopping and restaurants, creating a public domain that demonstrates a marked contrast to the typically private City office lobby. There will be a public restaurant on top of the tower – a response to the former mayor Ken Livingstone's call for high buildings to be accessible to all.

The aim was to produce a highly transparent structure, light and elegant in form, and to instil seriously green ideas into the high building form. The south side of the tower, which faces a busy road, houses a concentration of services that baffle solar gain. On the north side, the building opens up with stacked three-storey atria that serve a series of office 'villages'. The east and west façades provide natural ventilation for the office floors. Intended for multiple occupation by international businesses, the tower addresses the needs of the City as an international financial centre.

Although smaller in scale than some recent or proposed additions to the London skyline, Kohn Pedersen Fox's Bishopsgate tower reflects a serious environmental and urban agenda, with façades designed to capitalize on natural light and ventilation, internal gardens and public amenities, including a new square and rooftop restaurant.

In the late 1980s, when the Prince of Wales's campaign to revive traditional architecture was in full flood, there seemed every possibility that several major London sites would be redeveloped by a new generation of classicists. But John Simpson's proposals for 'Venice on Thames' (on the site of what is now More London) and his masterplan for Paternoster Square, inspired by Leon Krier and developed with Terry Farrell and a bevy of British and American traditionalists, remained unbuilt (see pp. 334–35), as did the curious designs by Gabriele Tagliaventi for the site in Marsham Street, Westminster, now occupied by Farrell's Home Office complex (pp. 324–25). Even Quinlan Terry, whose Richmond Riverside scheme of the 1980s seemed to be a harbinger of big things to come, has subsequently built relatively little in London: a set of villas in Regent's Park (1990–2009), a modest office scheme on Baker Street (2002), the infirmary wing at Chelsea Royal Hospital (pp. 136–37) and a mixed-use building on Tottenham Court Road (pp. 304–305). John Simpson's Queen's Gallery at Buckingham Palace (2002) is perhaps the most conspicuous traditionalist project of recent years in London.

The principal elevation of 198–202 Piccadilly (below) is unashamedly decorative. With a profusion of sculptured ornament and a showy corner tower, it provides a striking contrast to the simplicity of Joseph Emberton's Simpson's building (to its left). The other elevations (opposite), addressing St James's Church and Jermyn Street, are less assertive, with a mix of brick and stone cladding.

Robert Adam's Piccadilly project is, in the circumstances, a significant expression of what was once called New Classicism. The scheme (which provides nearly 6000 square metres of offices and 2500 square metres of retail space) replaces a dull block dating from the first decade of the twentieth century adjacent to Joseph Emberton's Simpson's building (now occupied by Waterstone's), a listed Modern Movement landmark. Sir Christopher Wren's church of St James's, Piccadilly, is immediately to the west across a narrow pedestrian alley, with the former Midland Bank by Edwin Lutyens beyond. Constructed on a steel frame – Adam has no qualms about using modern structural solutions, and the office spaces are of a conventional nature – the building is composed to a classical formula of base, centre and attics. The double-height base, set behind rusticated pilasters, houses shops. Four storeys of offices are above, with additional accommodation in two set-back attic floors. An octagonal corner tower marks the entrance to the narrow Church Place.

A special feature of the project is the involvement of Scottish sculptor Alexander Stoddart, with whom Adam previously collaborated on a library for the Ashmolean museum in Oxford. Capitals by Stoddart form a prominent element in the Piccadilly elevation, which is shamelessly decorative. The side and rear elevations are altogether less assertive.

Purists of all persuasions will not take to this building. It is shamelessly historicist, with a swagger that is anything but Palladian and more than a hint of Alexander 'Greek' Thomson in its proportions and details. But the piquancy of the contrast it provides to Emberton's horizontality can be enjoyed regardless, and there is none of the air of compromise that seems to characterize much recent commercial development in Westminster.

Opposite, left and bottom right
The Broadgate Tower forms
a striking addition to an
office quarter that has been
in development since the
mid-1980s.

Opposite, top right
A glazed galleria links
the tower to the adjacent
201 Bishopsgate.

Below
The buildings are elegantly
detailed in the best SOM
tradition.

The Chicago office of Skidmore, Owings & Merrill (SOM)
has been involved with the planning and development
of the Broadgate office quarter since the mid-1980s,
replacing Arup as lead architect for the later phases of
the project. If SOM's postmodernist styling, applied to
the massive blocks extending along Bishopsgate, found
little favour with British critics, the latter warmed more
to Exchange House (1990), a building where engineering
and architecture merged, expressively cantilevered
to span the tracks out of Liverpool Street station and
sparely detailed in the best Miesian tradition.

The Broadgate Tower and 201 Bishopsgate,
completed in 2008 for British Land, are similarly air rights
developments, constructed on a concrete raft over the
railway tracks (which remained in operation throughout
the construction period). The thirty-five-storey,
165-metre-tall tower and the thirteen-storey block at
201 Bishopsgate, which features a central atrium, are
linked by a glazed galleria suggestively pointing north-
east towards areas of likely expansion of commercial
development on the City fringe. The strongly expressed
structural bracing of the tower recalls that of an SOM
classic, the John Hancock Center in Chicago (1970).
Internally, the entrance lobby is an imposing space.

While other proposals for tall buildings in the City
have generated intense controversy, the Broadgate Tower
won planning consent without debate after its height
had been reduced in discussion with the planners, and
was constructed to a fast-track programme while other
schemes were bogged down in the planning process.
Clearly it would have been a more striking landmark, and
visually more satisfying, had it been half as tall again.

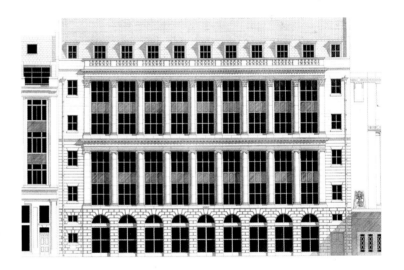

The Terry practice is perhaps best known for its private house projects – the group of villas on the western edge of Regent's Park, for example (1990–2009) – but as long ago as the 1980s Quinlan Terry successfully married classical architecture with modern office and retail space in his Richmond Riverside scheme. More recently, the firm has completed an office development on Baker Street (2002), and the Tottenham Court Road project further reflects its willingness to work within the constraints of the London office market. In all these instances, classical elevations are combined with internal spaces of an entirely contemporary character. At Tottenham Court Road, the interior architecture is by ESA. There are four floors of offices, with residential units at roof level and shops on the ground floor.

Tottenham Court Road has a remarkably varied townscape, with few buildings of great individual merit, but planners saw a strong case for a traditional masonry-fronted building on this site, close to the junction with Oxford Street. The street elevation has a rusticated base (housing the retail units) with a giant Ionic order and a giant Corinthian order above, each extending across two floors and together fronting the four office floors. The flats are in a set-back attic. Plain, rusticated 'book-ends' contain the elevation to north and south. The use of metallic panels between the columns on the office floors recalls the traditionalist commercial architecture of the inter-war years.

As usual with the Terrys' work, there is no hint of 'progressive' classicism in this project. Details are freely taken from Andrea Palladio's *Quattro libri dell'architettura*, and craftsmanship is of high quality. However, this building contains few clues as to how classical architecture can be more widely adapted to the needs of the commercial sector.

Opposite
The mixed-use development, close to Centre Point, seeks to impose a new classical discipline on the visual anarchy of Tottenham Court Road. The use of the Orders is fundamental to the work of the practice.

Above
The elevation is an exercise in neo-Palladianism, applied to the demands of modern commercial development.

ALLIES AND MORRISON STUDIOS SE1

Occupying an irregularly shaped site on Southwark Street, Allies and Morrison Studios incorporates landscaped spaces to the rear, while the main street façade is highly transparent and animated by bold use of colour.

Allies and Morrison's move to Southwark reflected both the remarkable growth of the practice to more than 150 staff, necessitating the abandonment of increasingly cramped offices in W1, and the rise of SE1 as a stylish business address. A site for the firm's new building was secured on Southwark Street, directly opposite the Bankside 123 development (Allies and Morrison's biggest job to date; pp. 310–11) and a short walk from Tate Modern (pp. 100–101).

The building makes a positive addition to Southwark Street, which can seem a monotonous thoroughfare, by day and by night. The street elevation (which faces north) is fully glazed and elegantly detailed, with brightly coloured internal shutters to deflect sunlight when necessary or simply to secure privacy. Its transparency is a relief in the context of the heavyweight brick façades of adjacent warehouses, and it is a beacon of light and colour on a dark winter afternoon.

Internally, the building focuses on the stepped atrium formed on the south side of the irregularly shaped site and providing a visual and operational connection between the six storeys of offices. The character of the interior is defined by the use of high-quality fair-faced concrete, left exposed throughout (there are no suspended ceilings and a virtual ban on plasterboard). The main staircase is a tour de force. Metalwork is finished to a heavy-duty industrial grade, and the floors are of black granite (in the ground-floor reception/exhibition area) or grey resin. A roof garden, facing south, is an amenity in fine weather. The ground-floor plan incorporates a through route from Southwark Street southwards, a recognition of the need to open links between the riverside and the hinterland.

The private gallery and archive for artist Philip Hughes at the end of a garden in Kentish Town 'provided the opportunity to incorporate somewhat conflicting programmes that extended the influence of the garden', according to Francesca Hughes, his daughter, whose practice collaborated with Sanei Hopkins Architects on the project. The aim was to create not just a space for reflection 'but also the very urban possibility of anonymity to the point of disappearance, of becoming sublimated into context, the brick and buddleia of Kentish Town'.

The project was initiated when the client acquired the redundant workshop at the bottom of the garden of his Victorian house. The shell was retained, and the building presents a secure, blank face to the lane at the rear. On the garden side, however, there has been a total transformation, with a great wedge-shaped glass enclosure framed by a soffit of mirror glass. The new glass roof extends the line of the existing workshop roof. There are views into the space from the house, with the original brick elevation visible beyond the glass enclosure. A sauna and steam room are contained respectively in a glazed box and a ceramic 'blob' that are free-standing objects within the space. 'A very peculiar, but nonetheless charming wonderland in which to escape', commented the *Architectural Review*.

Above, below and opposite
A tranquil space for reflection, the studio retains a visual link with the house but is separate from it. Large glass doors blur the boundary between the interior and the garden.

Right
The studio is subsumed into its context by virtue of an expanse of mirrored glass.

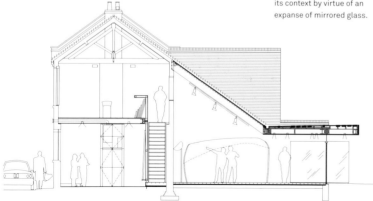

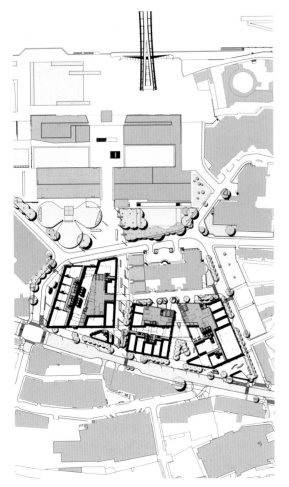

St Christopher House, which formerly occupied this site, was described by Nikolaus Pevsner as 'the largest office block under one roof in Europe' when it was completed in 1959. Long occupied by the civil service, it was certainly one of the largest (and ugliest) buildings of its type in London, and its demolition in 2003 was uncontroversial.

In addition to the blankly utilitarian character of its architecture, St Christopher House was disastrous in terms of urban design: it was a monolithic block providing an impermeable obstacle between Southwark Street and the River Thames. With the opening of Tate Modern on the riverside (pp. 100–101), the need for new routes across the site became more pressing. Allies and Morrison began work on a masterplan in 2000, with Land Securities as client. A key theme was to create these routes and to mix office use with retailing, restaurants and bars serving the local community and visitors to the area as well as those working on the site.

The three buildings of Bankside 123, which provide about 110,000 square metres of space, are conceived as city blocks penetrated by two new pedestrian routes. The architectural language of the scheme contrasts crystal translucency and distinctive aluminium sun-shading fins, in Building One, the 'Blue Fin', with the more solid aesthetic of the other two blocks. Perhaps more significant than the architecture – which is typical of the better end of early twenty-first-century commercial development – is the quality of the landscape around and between the buildings, where paving, planting and street furniture reflect a generous budget.

Winning the competition held in 2000 for a comprehensive reconstruction of Broadcasting House in Portland Place, the BBC's historic London flagship, was a landmark victory, even in a career as distinguished as that of Sir Richard MacCormac of MJP (MacCormac Jamieson Prichard) Architects. Other architects shortlisted included Alsop Architects, Stanton Williams and Eric Parry. It was also a landmark for the BBC, which had for a time seemed content to leave imaginative patronage to other broadcasting institutions. (ITN had commissioned Norman Foster, for example, and Channel 4 Richard Rogers, to design new headquarters.)

Broadcasting House, now a Grade II*-listed building, opened in 1932, a striking expression of the BBC's growing status as a national institution. The building, designed by Val Myer, with interiors by Serge Chermayeff, Wells Coates and others (all now lost) and external sculptural adornment by Eric Gill, was a subtle, Modernistic response to the site, on the bend of Langham Place, opposite John Nash's church of All Souls. The *Architectural Review* described it as nothing less than 'a new Tower of London'.

Over the next fifty years, with the development of the BBC's Television Centre at Shepherd's Bush and subsequently its vast White City building, both in west London (after the abandonment of Norman Foster's visionary project for a new radio headquarters at Langham Place), the future of Broadcasting House became uncertain. MacCormac's project was designed to reinstate it as the base for all BBC radio and music services and news operations, as well as the headquarters of the World Service.

As part of the project, initially developed in partnership with Land Securities and project-managed by Bovis Lend Lease, Myer's building was restored and updated. The awkward 'catslide' roof that Myer had been forced to introduce along its eastern edge because of rights of light was replaced by practical new floorspaces. Phase 1 of the new-build element of the scheme was completed in 2006, to MacCormac's designs, replacing a 1960s block to the east of the original Broadcasting House. The new building is clearly a contextual response to the latter, with Portland stone cladding and a rounded prow addressing the church of All Souls. The development incorporates a generous new public space with cafes and shops. Conscious of the pioneering tradition established by Lord Reith in the 1930s, the BBC commissioned art consultant Vivien Lovell to develop a well-funded public-art strategy for the new building, which is an assured and appropriate addition to the West End scene.

The second phase of MacCormac's project, involving the redevelopment of the 1960s block immediately north of the Myer building, included the scheme's most radical elements. Bovis's decision (approved by the BBC) to appoint Sheppard Robson – admittedly a practice with an excellent design record – to progress this phase involved the deletion of some of the more innovative aspects of the scheme. More recently, the Broadcasting House project has become enmeshed in a wider debate about the role of the BBC and the way in which it spends funds raised largely from the television license fee. The second phase of the Portland Place project is now £55,000,000 over budget and four years late, and its total cost will top £1,000,000,000. How far it will live up to the vision set out by MacCormac remains to be seen.

Spitalfields was the scene of a three-decade battle between the development industry and the conservation/community lobby. The Spitalfields Trust, founded in 1977, was responsible for saving dozens of fine early Georgian houses in the area, while a National Lottery-funded project by architect William Whitfield, succeeded by Purcell Miller Tritton, has rescued Nicholas Hawksmoor's magnificent Christ Church from utter dereliction. Nothing, however, could save the historic fruit-and-vegetable market, which was founded in the 1680s and finally closed in 1986. The removal of the market opened the way for commercial redevelopment of the site, and schemes by MJP Architects, Leon Krier, Quinlan & Francis Terry, Swanke Hayden Connell Architects, Benjamin Thompson Associates and Farrells, among others, grappled with the problem of inserting a large complex of modern offices into the fine-grained historic context.

After a long hiatus during the recession of the 1990s, Foster + Partners became involved. The practice's first scheme proposed two large office buildings on the site of the market buildings (which date from the 1920s), retaining and restoring the original, listed portion of the market, which had been colonized by small businesses. The final development, completed in 2005, is radically different in character, but, with 72,000 square metres of offices and 3700 square metres of retail space, marks the absorption of Spitalfields into the City. The East End now starts at Commercial Street rather than Bishopsgate.

Bishop's Square consists of four long fingers of offices, separated by atria and stepped in form, allowing the creation of attractive roof gardens on three of the blocks. The architecture of the office buildings is restrained and rational, in contrast to the flamboyance of some of Foster's recent City buildings.

The most positive aspect of the project, however, is its comprehensive approach to the planning of the site. A new landscaped space, complete with gardens and a lily pond, has been created to the west, on what was a lorry park. A second public space, with a steel-and-glass roof, connects the new buildings to the retained Victorian market. Along the southern side of the development a glass-roofed galleria, angled to focus on Hawksmoor's spire, contains shops and cafes. The pavilions of the market on Brushfield Street have been retained, with flats on the upper floors, providing a welcome element of continuity. In addition, the generosity of scale and semi-industrial character of the new covered spaces are in tune with the old market beyond, mitigating the

dramatic change wrought by the development, which houses 5000 City workers, half of them employed by a single law firm. A progressive element is provided by the largest installation of photovoltaic cells in any commercial development in Europe, although they will generate only a tiny fraction of the complex's energy needs.

For some, lawyers' offices, expensive shops and wine bars will never belong in Spitalfields. Yet the character of the area changed for ever when a new breed of affluent residents colonized the restored Georgian houses that form a piquant contrast to the ethnic bustle of Brick Lane. Not even Spitalfields can resist the dynamic of change that is fundamental to London.

Below
Although controversial, the Bishop's Square development provides valuable, tree-filled public space for residents, tourists and office workers.

Opposite
The rationale of the scheme is the provision of a large area of state-of-the-art office space (middle and bottom left). The scheme also offers public benefits in terms of new open spaces (top) and an elegant glazed arcade that focuses on the spire of Nicholas Hawksmoor's Christ Church, itself recently restored (bottom right).

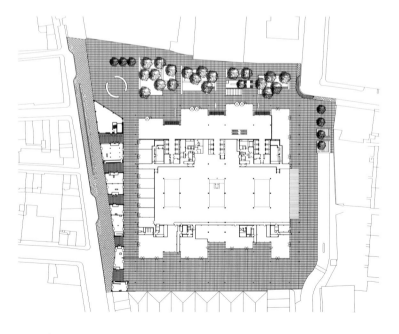

Opposite
Renzo Piano used brightly
coloured terracotta panels
to animate the new blocks
at Central St Giles, in an
area of London likely to be
transformed by Crossrail.

Below
The blocks are arranged
around a square, and include
housing as well as offices.

Central St Giles has certainly generated controversy. Its
scale is clearly appropriate to its context and nobody
regrets the loss of the bleak 1950s office complex that
previously occupied the site, close to the Georgian
church of St Giles-in-the-Fields and Richard Seifert's
Centre Point, in an area where the advent of Crossrail
is likely to have a dramatic, and positive, impact
(pp. 24–27). It is the bold use of colour in the form of
red, orange, yellow and green terracotta panels on the
façades of the blocks that has offended some critics,
who condemn it as alien to London. Piano is, of course,
renowned for his inventive use of a great variety of
materials, and here stone, glass and timber animate
the buildings, alongside the terracotta, which is used in
such a way as to emphasize its function as a decorative
veneer. The façades seem to rest on thin columns or rise
above fully glazed ground floors.

 This is a mixed-use scheme: 80 per cent of the
65,000 square metres of space is given over to offices,
with large but generously day-lit floorplates, but there
are also 109 flats (almost half of them 'affordable'), as
well as shops, bars and restaurants. A public square,
providing new pedestrian routes through the site, forms
the central focus of the development, and the frontages
of the blocks enclosing it are clad in a less strident grey
terracotta. The commercial success of this scheme,
which doubled the density of accommodation on the site,
seems assured – this rather shabby area of London is
changing fast – but its urban impact is equally positive.

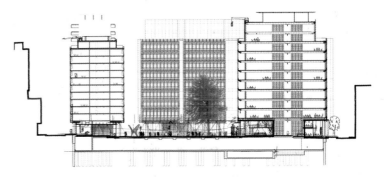

Below and opposite, top
A ramp links all floors of the building, which contains generously day-lit office spaces, and, on the top floor, a public space for special events. The assembly chamber at the heart of the building is a transparent and open space that echoes Norman Foster's Berlin Reichstag.

Opposite, bottom
The landscaping around the building includes an amphitheatre that can be used for meetings and performances.

The new headquarters for the Mayor of London and the Greater London Authority (GLA) was commissioned, controversially, well in advance of the elections held in 2000 that restored to London a measure of strategic local government. In 1998 competing proposals were put forward to house the GLA in Royal Victoria House, Bloomsbury, where a conversion by Will Alsop was on offer, or in a custom-made building developed as part of the London Bridge City development. The latter option was selected by the government.

After a classical revival 'Venice on Thames' scheme designed by John Simpson was abandoned, a new masterplan for the second phase of London Bridge City was commissioned from Foster + Partners. The building can therefore be seen as a spin-off from a commercial development, located in an office ghetto removed from the 'real' London. Yet Foster's building, caricatured as a 'glass testicle' or 'fencing mask', is a carefully considered and highly symbolic structure that draws on his experience with the Berlin Reichstag. In total it provides 17,000 square metres of space on ten levels, with offices for the mayor, GLA members and their staff, as well as committee rooms and public space.

At the heart of the building is the assembly chamber, enclosed in glass, with views across the River Thames to the Tower of London. The intended symbolism is clear: this was to be seen as a centre of transparent, democratic local government. In practice, the building is far less accessible than the former County Hall and less welcoming than the Reichstag.

The form of the building reflects a determined effort to secure optimum energy performance. Cladding is designed to respond to patterns of sunlight falling on the building. Active and passive shading devices are part of a programme of natural ventilation, with cooling provided using groundwater pumped from boreholes below the building. City Hall has become an instantly recognizable London landmark.

The renaissance of the Bankside quarter of Southwark has been driven as much by the reuse of old buildings (most obviously Tate Modern – pp. 100–101 – and Borough Market) as by new architecture, and the most popular new building is probably Theo Crosby's remarkable re-creation of the Globe Theatre. A short walk from More London and the site of the rapidly rising 'Shard' (pp. 326–27) – reflections of Southwark's growing role as a prime business district – narrow, atmospheric streets hug the river. Edward Cullinan Architects' Clink Street project occupies a site (long used as a car park) that was sensitive in many respects. In particular, it contained the fourteenth-century rose window and fragment of medieval wall that are all that survives of the lost palace of the bishops of Winchester. Scheduled as an ancient monument, these remains had to be rigorously protected but also given a more appropriate setting.

Cullinan's mixed-use scheme, which was finally completed, after long delays, in 2009, provides offices, housing and retail units in a series of blocks that take their inspiration from the nineteenth-century 'functional tradition' expressed in the area's surviving warehouses and market buildings. The only existing building of

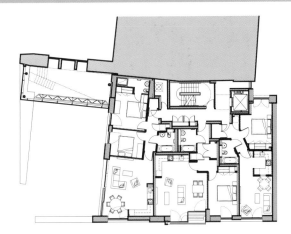

interest on the site was retained and converted to new use. Winchester Square, which marks the site of the central court of the bishops' palace, has become a new public space, with a small piazza created at the junction of Clink Street and Stoney Street from which the rose window can be viewed. This project exemplifies Cullinan's contextual modernism, sensitive to place and history but entirely lacking in needless sentimentality.

Opposite and above
The Clink Street project forms a new public square as well as an appropriate setting for the precious medieval fragment of Winchester Palace.

Below
The fourteenth-century rose window.

The Treasury complex (originally occupied by other government departments) was built between 1899 and 1915. It is one of the most prominent buildings in central London, extending along the northern side of Parliament Square and framing the entrance to Whitehall. It is big, bold and confidently neo-Baroque, a key landmark of London in the age of empire.

By the end of the twentieth century, however, the Treasury building, listed Grade II, was seen as something of an embarrassment, providing poor working conditions for staff, with large areas of under-used space that could potentially accommodate other departments then housed further from the centre of power. Sensibly, the government turned to the commercial development sector for a strategy to rationalize the complex, and a public–private partnership was formed to carry it through.

The public face of the building is unchanged. Inside, however, previously unused courts and light wells have been transformed into circulation, social and recreational spaces, with cafes, a library and, in the larger areas, planting and pools. Some of these spaces are capped by lightweight roofs in the tradition of Foster's Great Court at the British Museum (pp. 86–87). Colour is used freely, particularly in large banners by Danish designer Per Arnoldi, a regular Foster collaborator. The great circular court at the heart of the building, long used as a car park, is landscaped as a pedestrian piazza. Offices have been radically revamped, with an estimated 11 kilometres of partitions stripped out to provide open-plan workspaces. In the process, it was possible to rationalize the Treasury's occupancy, and the department now holds only the western half of the building, leaving the rest for use by other departments.

Sustainability is a key theme of Foster's architecture and one that the government was keen to endorse. The light wells and courts also function as thermal chimneys, with opening vents extracting stale air from the offices. Opening windows have been retained and upgraded to improve their security. 'Windcatchers' mounted on the roof supplement the natural ventilation system.

The Treasury project is a further example – less conspicuous than the Great Court but in its way just as significant – of Foster's expertise at making new and old work together, a skill first demonstrated in London with the Sackler Galleries of the Royal Academy of Arts in the early 1990s.

Massive in scale, the Treasury building was transformed by Foster + Partners to create new circulation and communal spaces in previously disused courts and light wells, some of them topped by glazed roofs. Office spaces were reconfigured, with corridors and partitions removed in favour of open-plan space.

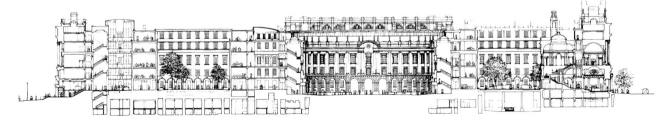

Farrells prepared a masterplan for the redevelopment of this project's Marsham Street site, occupied by three high-rise office slabs, as long ago as 1991, when it was assumed that it would be sold for commercial development. A competition held in 1996 resulted in victory for a cumbrous classical scheme by Italian architect Gabriele Tagliaventi. But this was set aside by the new Labour government in 1997, when a decision was made to demolish the original complex and build the new Home Office. Farrells began to develop the present scheme in 1998, and it was incorporated into a Private Finance Initiative (PFI) bid in 2000. The building opened in 2005.

The existing towers were designed by Eric Bedford for the then Department of the Environment and completed in 1971. At 67 metres tall, they had long been reviled for their impact on distant views of the Palace of Westminster. A maximum height of eight storeys was set for the new, 70,000-square-metre development, and allowance was made for increasing accommodation on the site by 50 per cent in the future. The principles of the scheme are essentially those laid down in the masterplan of 1991: the reintegration of the site, permeated by public spaces, into the city fabric, with three buildings conceived as a series of distinct blocks rather than as a megastructure. Residential accommodation is provided in a block to the west, underlining the commitment in the masterplan to mixed-use provision.

The new Home Office draws on the best practice of the commercial office sector to create a working environment for more than 3000 civil servants that is far removed from the drab confines still inhabited by many government departments. Workspaces are largely open plan, and benefit from generous natural light and views out to the 'pocket' parks formed between the buildings. An internal 200-metre-long 'street' running the length of the buildings on the first floor contains shared resources, including cafes, meeting areas, a print shop and space for the interaction now seen as fundamental to team working. Large atria enhance the sense of connection and communication. Colour is used throughout, and funds for artworks were generous, although the overall budget for the project, which was delivered on time and to cost, was strictly controlled under the PFI scheme. A glass canopy, designed in collaboration with artist Liam Gillick, who also coordinated the display of art throughout the building, is the defining feature of the street elevation.

The PFI system has been widely criticized as undermining the quality of design in the public sector. If broader issues of cost and control are left aside, the Home Office is one project where PFI seems to have worked, at least in terms of providing a distinctive and practical building with a benign impact on the public domain.

Opposite
Artwork is a crucial part of the design of the complex. The street façade, with its striking metal cut-outs, is topped by a glass canopy designed in collaboration with Liam Gillick.

Below
The three buildings are linked on the first floor by an internal walkway. Their relatively low-rise, stepped construction defers to the historic buildings in the area.

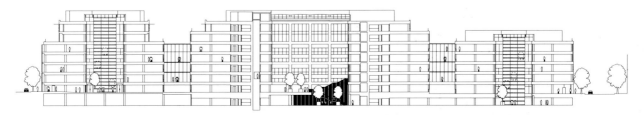

LONDON BRIDGE TOWER SE1

Following initial proposals by Broadway Malyan, Renzo Piano was brought in by developer Irvine Sellar during 2000 to work on plans for a mixed-use tower next to London Bridge station. The 'shard of glass', as Piano named it, finally won planning consent in November 2003, following a public inquiry at which English Heritage was a key objector. (Then Mayor of London Ken Livingstone and the Commission for Architecture and the Built Environment were strong supporters of the project, which won the backing of Southwark Council.)

Replacing an undistinguished 1970s high-rise, the tower was initially conceived as a structure 420 metres and eighty-seven storeys high. The actual tower will be 306 metres and sixty-eight storeys high, but it will still be the tallest building in Europe. In common with Norman Foster's 'Gherkin' (30 St Mary Axe; pp. 294–95), it will certainly become as much a symbol of London as are St Paul's Cathedral or Big Ben. Demolition of the existing buildings began in 2007, and completion (excluding fit-out) is scheduled for 2012. The tower will contain 54,000 square metres of office space; a 200-bed five-star hotel on the top eighteen storeys; and fourteen storeys of flats. Some 7000 people will live or work in the building.

'The Shard' uses advanced glazing technology to achieve not only exceptional aesthetic effects – reflections of light and changing cloud patterns will make the form of the tower elusive – but also outstanding environmental performance. The ventilated double skin of the building, incorporating extensive shading, is designed to reduce heat gain. Excess hot air from the offices will heat the flats and hotel. Winter gardens with

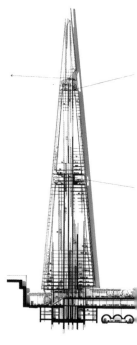

opening louvres will provide access to fresh air and connect with the world outside (similar examples can be seen in Piano's Aurora Place tower in Sydney, completed in 2000). It is claimed that the building will consume 30 per cent less energy than a conventional structure of comparable size.

One of the project's strongest selling points, in environmental terms, is its close proximity to major public transport facilities, which will be augmented by the Thameslink rail project. The Shard offers only forty parking spaces, but the gains for rail and Underground users – including a generous new railway station concourse, a relocated bus station and an external public square – are hugely significant.

London Bridge Place (nicknamed the 'Baby Shard' or 'Gem') won planning consent in the spring of 2006. Located west of the Shard, close to Borough High Street, it defers to the historic context of Borough Market and Southwark Cathedral, and forms almost a foothill to the Alp-like mass of the Shard. Its faceted form is partly dictated by the proximity of the railway viaducts, but Piano has capitalized on that to produce a structure of memorably sculptural qualities. He envisages the building floating 'like the rock of Magritte above the ground, liberating space and creating a vibrant public environment'.

Opposite and right
London Bridge Tower will
be a slender presence on
the skyline south of the
River Thames.

Below
Sophisticated glazing
technology allows maximum
transparency to be combined
with low-energy servicing.

The New Street Square project has transformed the area between Fleet Street and High Holborn. Heavily bombed during the Second World War and somewhat bleakly rebuilt in the 1950s and 1960s, this area now forms part of the quarter that is being promoted as Midtown ('where the City meets the West End'). Developer Land Securities at first planned a huge groundscraper office scheme on the site, but a radical rethink produced a far more satisfying mix of offices, shops and restaurants – and precious public space.

The resulting four large office buildings form a pleasing sequence, varied in their treatment yet clearly related to one another. The eighteen-storey block, a dramatic wedge framed in the view along New Fetter Lane from High Holborn, ingeniously sidesteps a protected view corridor. The smallest of the buildings, 3 New Street Square, is elegantly framed in limestone, deferring in its scale and materials to adjacent buildings in the Fleet Street conservation area, notably Dr Johnson's House in the tranquil enclave of Gough Square.

But it is as a piece of urban planning more than for its architecture (the latter notable for the restraint and careful detailing typical of Bennetts Associates) that New Street Square triumphs. The plan has been very carefully considered in the context of the irregular grain of this quarter of the City, right down to the deliberately narrow and inviting points of entry from adjacent streets. New Street Square has already established itself as a destination in an area not noted for decent restaurants and shops. High-quality landscaping and subtle lighting after dark add to its attractiveness. This is a generous addition to the City's fabric, far more appealing in its consistency than the architectural 'zoo' of Paternoster Square (pp. 334–35).

Opposite and below
Carefully detailed and appropriately scaled, New Street Square is one of the developments that is transforming 'Midtown' into a major business hub.

Left
The scheme provides a large new public square, with shops and restaurants, and opens up new routes across the site.

The development of Paddington as an important business location might seem an obvious move, given the area's transport links – Underground, mainline railway, Heathrow Express and the prospect of Crossrail (pp. 24–27) – but the development of derelict railway and canalside land around Paddington station was slow to take off. A masterplan with up to 110,000 square metres of offices won planning approval in 1992 but fell victim to the recession of the early 1990s. The basin project was relaunched in 2000 by a new developer partnership (Godfrey Bradman of European Land and Chelsfield's Elliott Bernerd), with a fresh masterplan by Terry Farrell providing a more dynamic mix of uses than was envisaged in the early 1990s.

The first building to be completed, the ten-storey, 20,000-square-metre Point, was designed by Farrells and forms a gateway to the site. Its sleek styling is typical of Farrells' recent work. Two further blocks were designed by Richard Rogers Partnership (now Rogers Stirk Harbour + Partners). In 2005 a substantial but not especially distinguished housing development by Munkenbeck + Marshall (now separate practices Munkenbeck + Partners Architects and Stephen Marshall Architects) was completed.

The latest phase of development focuses on Merchant Square at the eastern end of the basin, where a residential tower by The Kalyvides Partnership and office tower by Mossessian & Partners were under construction in 2010. Yet the area still seems strangely lifeless, perhaps because it is boxed in by the A40 road, the St Mary's Hospital campus and the station. Plans to demolish the easternmost part of the latter (a later addition to Isambard Kingdom Brunel's terminus) and replace it with a commercial development by Grimshaw, providing a new route to the basin, have been abandoned. Meanwhile, the development of Paddington Central, on the former goods-yard site north of the basin, continues, with buildings planned by Allies and Morrison, Kohn Pedersen Fox, Sheppard Robson and Sidell Gibson Architects.

Opposite
The Point, by Farrells, was the
first building completed at
Paddington Basin and forms
a gateway to the site.

This page
A number of other practices
have been commissioned
for further buildings as part
of the development, which
surrounds the canal basin.

PALESTRA SE1

Palestra is formed of horizontal volumes that fit together to provide highly flexible office space. The monumental building is given a skewed appearance by a tilted ground-floor layer, which rises to accommodate public areas.

Palestra is a heavyweight of a building. The site once contained a renowned boxing ring, but more recently was occupied by Orbit House, an unremarkable block designed in the 1960s by Richard Seifert. The advent of the Jubilee line – MJP Architects' Southwark Underground station is just across the road – and Tate Modern (pp. 100–101) made this an attractive locale for new commercial development. The Palestra project launched the idea of Blackfriars Road as part of London's 'South Central' quarter, and has led to the emergence of a number of schemes for sites in the area between Southwark station and the River Thames. A large part of the building has been let to the London Development Agency, a prestigious tenant.

Will Alsop first made his mark on Southwark with Peckham Library (pp. 84–85), a building that became a symbol of the borough's regeneration programme and won the Stirling Prize in 2000. Palestra tested Alsop's ability to put his stamp on a large (25,000-square-metre) commercial development. He envisaged the building as a series of horizontal planes, the lowest of which is tilted upwards from ground level to provide a covered public space with shops and cafes. Palestra would have had an even more forceful impact had not plans for a top layer of offices, contained in a transparent slab, been removed on the insistence of planners. The application of strong colour, using advanced glazing technology, gives the building a highly distinctive look. Yet it is also a very practical structure, with flexible 30-metre-wide, column-free floors enhanced by double-height cut-outs, mezzanines and terraces.

Palestra is a powerful, even slightly intimidating, addition to the Southwark cityscape and a harbinger of much more to come. It confirms Alsop's ability to transform functional buildings into urban icons – and even into works of art.

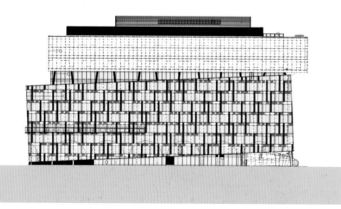

PATERNOSTER SQUARE EC4

The opening of the rebuilt Paternoster Square in 2003 was rather an anticlimax after years of heated debate about the future of the site. Flattened by wartime bombing, the area immediately north of St Paul's Cathedral was rebuilt in 1961–67 to designs by Trehearne & Norman. Nikolaus Pevsner saw merit in the resulting development, but it was generally disliked and its central public space, elevated on a raised service deck extending beneath the entire complex, was little visited. The City rebuilding boom of the 1980s generated plans to redevelop the whole area anew, and a high-profile architectural competition launched in 1988 (involving Norman Foster, Richard Rogers and others) was won by Arup. The winning scheme was abandoned in the face of strident criticism from the Prince of Wales, who encouraged John Simpson to produce alternative plans, classical in style and aiming to reproduce something of the long-lost streetscape of the area. With a new developer in charge, Simpson was commissioned, along with a bevy of traditionally minded architects, to produce a new masterplan. It obtained planning consent in 1993 – and was then abandoned.

In 1997 William Whitfield was drafted in to produce a scheme that was both buildable and acceptable to a wide range of tastes. Its greatest strength was the decision to bring the area back to street level, with new service roads in basements. The square now forms part of the City's network of pedestrian routes and is entered from St Paul's via the rebuilt Temple Bar, finally restored to the City. The buildings around the square include work by leading contemporary practices (Allies and Morrison, MJP Architects, Sidell Gibson Architects, Eric Parry Architects and Sheppard Robson), but Whitfield's cumbrous stripped classical colonnade compromises their clarity.

Neither hard-line moderns nor traditionalists will ever love a development that is essentially a compromise in architectural terms, and the new square somehow fails to be particularly inviting; the Arena at the Broadgate Centre has far more of a buzz. But the creation of a substantial area of traffic-free space and a decent setting for St Paul's is an achievement in itself.

To a masterplan by Whitfield Partners, the redevelopment of Paternoster Square includes buildings by a number of major architectural practices in a contextual modern manner, framing views of St Paul's Cathedral. An irregular square forms the centrepiece of the scheme. St Martin's Court (opposite), by Allies and Morrison, connects the square to Newgate Street by way of a glazed atrium.

Replacing Fitzroy Robinson's Standard Chartered Bank, completed as recently as 1985 and once boasting the most spectacularly planted atrium in London, the Pinnacle or DIFA Tower (named after the German firm that commissioned it) will be the tallest building in the City. At 288 metres high, it will provide a dramatic riposte to Renzo Piano's 306-metre-high London Bridge Tower across the River Thames in Southwark (pp. 326–27). The Pinnacle is one of several completed or projected towers in this sector of the City, which is not subject to the constraints of planning regulations that protect 'corridors' giving views of the historic London skyline. The group includes Tower 42, Foster + Partners' 30 St Mary Axe (the 'Gherkin'; pp. 294–95), the projected Leadenhall Building by Rogers Stirk Harbour + Partners and 110 Bishopsgate (the Heron Tower; pp. 298–99), also by Kohn Pedersen Fox (KPF).

KPF won an invited competition for the project in 2003; the scheme secured planning consent in the spring of 2006 and, with significant areas of offices pre-let, started on site in 2008. The tower provides 80,000 square metres of offices on floorplates of up to 2380 square metres, as well as three levels of retail and public 'sky lobbies', with a restaurant at level 43. The striking form of the building is an unashamed exercise in composition (its highly sculptural top floors contain nothing more than plant), a pinnacle to the growing cluster of towers that capitalize on the increasingly positive public response to tall buildings in London.

At ground level the character of the tower as two interlocking volumes is apparent. Accessed beneath a flowing 18-metre-high canopy, a public route, surrounded by shops and cafes, leads to the long-neglected Crosby Square to the east. This will be landscaped as part of the project, and may be linked to the recast public domain around the Leadenhall scheme by Rogers. The Pinnacle's office areas are entered from first-floor level.

The design of the façade was the subject of intense study, as it was imperative to meet the requirements of stringent building regulations and the mayor of London's guidelines on sustainability, while maintaining the tower's transparency. The building is wrapped in a ventilated façade, using framed glazing, that reduces solar heat gain and allows natural ventilation. Internal louvres counter direct sunlight, while allowing natural light to illuminate the workspaces. A battery of photovoltaic cells is provided at high level – a token

gesture, it might be argued, but at least a step in the right direction.

The Pinnacle is clearly a product of the 'Gherkin effect': 30 St Mary Axe gave planners and the public a taste for towers of unusual shape. KPF's Heron Tower, designed a few years earlier, is strictly orthogonal, but this product of the same architectural stable has been variously nicknamed the 'Helter-skelter' and the 'Mexican wrap'.

Left
Meeting the ground in spectacular fashion, the tower will have a highly sculptural form typical of London's new generation of tall buildings.

Below
A section through the base of the tower shows the very large area of covered public space, an unusual commodity in the City.

Opposite
This perspective from the South Bank shows completed and projected City towers, including (from left to right) KPF's 110 Bishopsgate, Richard Seifert's Tower 42, the Pinnacle, Foster + Partners' 30 St Mary Axe, and Rogers Stirk Harbour + Partners' Leadenhall Building.

PLANTATION PLACE EC3

Plantation Place is one of the largest new office developments in the City, and offers considerable benefits for the public realm. It is one of a series of recent office buildings along Fenchurch Street, including Richard Rogers's Lloyd's Register, designs by John McAslan + Partners and Kohn Pedersen Fox, and a new tower by Rafael Viñoly that is set to replace the undistinguished 1960s Kleinwort Benson building at 20 Fenchurch Street.

The 1-hectare site of Plantation Place, bounded by Fenchurch Street, Rood Lane, Mincing Lane and Eastcheap/Great Tower Street, was formerly occupied by Plantation House, a 'remarkable, incoherent building' (according to Nikolaus Pevsner) constructed in phases between 1935 and 1954 to house commodities markets. It was comprehensively refurbished in the early 1990s, but in 1996 developer British Land commissioned Arup to prepare plans for redevelopment. The complex (not listed) was demolished and replaced by about 100,000 square metres of new office space.

The scheme comprises two buildings: a fifteen-storey block on Fenchurch Street and a ten-storey block to the south, each with a distinct character. The northern block is clad in a double skin of glass, while the southern has a load-bearing stone façade with limited glazing. Stone fins are a feature of both buildings, a response to the planning requirement that the development have a 'solid' character at street level. The upper levels of the northern block, in contrast, are a transparent presence on the skyline. Between the two buildings is a new east–west pedestrian route, Plantation Lane, a welcome addition to the City's traditional lanes and alleys.

The project involved complex planning negotiations, and required significant archaeological and historic-building issues to be addressed: Sir Christopher Wren's Grade I-listed church of St Margaret Pattens stands at the south-western corner of the site. The modelling of the scheme defers to the neighbours' rights to light and views, with setbacks to reduce its impact on the narrow streets of the City. All in all, it is an ingenious piece of design and a rational retort to the tendency towards 'iconic' structures, offering much that is technically innovative, notably a mixed-mode ventilation strategy that reduces dependency on air conditioning.

As part of the scheme, the client commissioned artist Simon Patterson, well known for *The Great Bear* (1992; a reworking of the London Tube map), to collaborate with Arup on a major work of public art. Entitled *Time and Tide*, it consists of a glass screen, 41 metres long and 6 metres tall, forming one side of Plantation Lane. The screen is a giant light box – a painting in light – featuring close-up images of the surface of the Moon in constantly changing colours. Patterson also designed lettering on the pavement, a 'carpet of words' that relate to the history of the site and the City. This is a bold and effective piece of architectural art, properly integrated into the project.

The context of the Plantation Place development includes the church of St Margaret Pattens by Sir Christopher Wren. The skilful composition of the two new office buildings provides a neutral backcloth to the Wren spire.

Opposite
The external skin, which
incorporates a double layer
of glazing and extensive
shading, is part of a
sustainable services strategy
that is, by British standards,
highly innovative.

Below
The form of the building,
conceived as interlocking
cubes, was dictated by the
location, in which a tall
building was rejected.

Proclaimed as 'one of the most sustainable buildings ever developed in the City', Ropemaker Place certainly has impressive environmental credentials: solar heating panels, photovoltaic cells, rainwater collection and 4650 square metres of planted external terraces, which, it is claimed, encourage biodiversity as well as providing a pleasant 'garden in the sky' for the occupants of the 56,000-square-metre office building. Less sustainable, perhaps, was the decision to demolish the 1980s block by Covell Matthews Wheatley that previously occupied the site, immediately north of the Barbican, but other City buildings of the 1980s are likely to bite the dust as the office market revives and rents escalate.

The architect compares the building, which rises to a maximum of twenty storeys, to 'a simplified Chinese puzzle where the sum of the parts defines the whole'. The idea of a really tall building on the site was soon ruled out, and planning consent was gained quickly as a consequence. Six interlocking cubes form a staggered tower, with the planted terraces at levels 8, 12, 16 and 20. Typically innovative cladding technology, incorporating double glazing and shading, forms part of the low-energy services strategy and gives the building its slightly anonymous appearance; in this location, there was no need for the more obvious response to context of Arup's earlier Plantation Place project on Fenchurch Street (pp. 338–39). Colour is used internally to provide a sense of place.

For all its size, this is a building that is easily overlooked, and makes no attempt to impose its presence on the City townscape. In the Arup tradition, it provides a rational response to the practical brief rather than extraneous display.

'Modern in design, frugal in operation, evangelical in purpose': that was the client brief for Sheppard Robson's new City building housing the international headquarters of the Salvation Army, an organization known for its religious and charitable activities across the globe but firmly British in origin.

The Salvation Army came to Queen Victoria Street in 1881, three years after its foundation by William Booth. Its first headquarters was destroyed by German bombs in 1941. A replacement building designed by H.M. Lidbetter was eventually completed in 1963, but in 1999 the organization's British operation was relocated to a site near Elephant & Castle in south London, leaving much of the relatively undistinguished Lidbetter block empty and clearly ripe for redevelopment. Indeed, the Army seriously considered selling the Queen Victoria Street building and moving its international headquarters to its training college in south London. But with the opening in 1999 of the Millennium Bridge, which became a prime tourist route linking St Paul's Cathedral to Tate Modern, the site, flanking the northern end of this route, acquired a new prominence. The organization's leader at the time, General John Gowans, saw the potential for the building to become 'a window to the world', promoting the Army's message to millions of passers-by.

Advised by space planner Andrew Chadwick, the Army conceived a strategy to redevelop the site, capitalizing on its value for commercial development and, in the process, shrewdly providing the organization with a new building of about 3200 square metres, in line with its practical needs but at minimum cost. The Army's new premises occupies the western end of the site, and the remainder has been redeveloped into speculative offices. Sheppard Robson won the project in a developer/architect competition in 1999, and planning consent was given in 2001, although the events of 11 September that year put the scheme on hold for a time. The new headquarters finally opened in 2004.

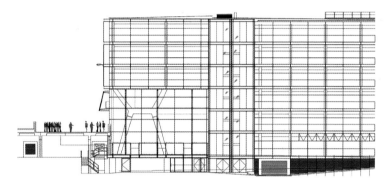

This building exemplifies the best of Sheppard Robson's work: it is purposeful, elegant and immaculately detailed. The architecture is essentially that of the world of business, but then, as Booth insisted, 'the devil should not have all the best tunes'. The offices that occupy the top three floors of the building are indeed state-of-the-art City workspaces, a vast improvement on those previously occupied by the Army's staff. Offices for senior staff are on the first floor in a series of glazed enclosures flanking the chapel. Services – stairs, lifts and WCs – are pushed to the eastern edge of the building, where they form a natural boundary to the commercial development that lies beyond. But it is the lower levels that form the headquarters' public face: meeting rooms, a generous lobby and an attractive cafe on the lower ground floor are all clearly visible to passers-by through the glazed façade. William Booth is remembered as a prime exponent of 'muscular Christianity', and this strength is symbolized by the exposed structural steel frame, painted brilliant white, seen throughout the interior and forming a dramatic feature in views from outside.

Opposite, top left and bottom Elegantly transparent, Sheppard Robson's Salvation Army Headquarters gives this international organization a new public face.

Opposite, top right, and above Internally, the building opens up to a series of communal spaces, visible to passers-by and in tune with contemporary commercial practice. Offices are on upper floors.

Opposite and right
The Gibbs Building is a dominant presence, a symbol of the significance of the trust as a funder of medical research. The restaurant is at the top of the building, with views over Bloomsbury.

Below
The Trust's 1930s headquarters has been converted into an exhibition and conference centre, and its interior given a new lightness and accessibility.

Abutting the 1930s Wellcome Trust building, coldly Palladian and designed by Septimus Warwick, the Gibbs Building, completed in 2004, is essentially a prestige 22,000-square-metre office building housing the 500-plus staff of an organization that hands out over £400,000,000 annually for medical research.

The building consists of two blocks – 18 metres wide and ten storeys high to the north, 9 metres wide and five storeys high to the south, facing University College – joined by a 9-metre-wide full-height atrium. The whole is covered by a glazed roof that sweeps down to the rear of the site to enclose a restaurant on top of the southern wing, and features solar blinds and fritted glazing to exclude direct sunlight. Staircase cores and recessed bays containing double-height social spaces punctuate the Euston Road frontage, where the double-skin façade is part of a low-energy services strategy.

The interior character is formed by an exposed steel frame, but derives warmth and texture from the extensive use of timber. Offices up to the fourth floor are open to the void (with moveable screens for when privacy is needed), generating a sense of community in a large building. A striking installation by artist Thomas Heatherwick terminates the atrium to the west. Full-height external triple glazing reflects the theme of transparency.

With the Trust's staff rehoused in the Gibbs building, Hopkins later converted Warwick's headquarters into a library, conference centre and exhibition space, opened in 2007. The clarity of the original internal spaces, blurred by later alterations, was restored, and the interior opened out to be more welcoming and accessible. The most significant spaces, including the handsome library, have been treated with respect as part of a project that has injected new life into a significant but tired landmark building.

HUNTER   JENNER   DARWIN   BERNARD   MENE

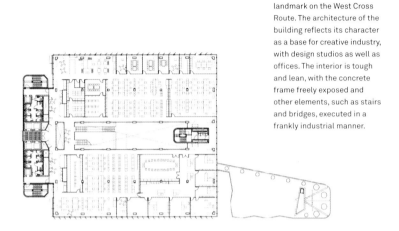

Notting Hill may be world-famous, but where on earth is Notting Dale? This hitherto obscure location, once a notorious slum, now hemmed in by the Westway, with the vast Westfield shopping centre just across the road, is becoming the base for 'creative industries', which initially colonized redundant industrial properties. The Yellow Building, the headquarters of fashion chain Monsoon Accessorize, is part of 'Nottingdale Village', with two subsequent phases of development also designed by Allford Hall Monaghan Morris (AHMM) as part of a masterplan including offices, studios, a hotel and housing. The practice first worked for Monsoon in 2000, when it restored a listed former maintenance depot next to Paddington station as the company's headquarters. Monsoon quickly outgrew its Paddington offices, however, and turned to the same architect for its new flagship building.

The 15,000-square-metre Yellow Building (cost: £32,000,000) is hardly a typical office block. According to Simon Allford of AHMM, the aim was to create something 'rough, robust – we wanted to strip out the fluff that covers most office interiors'. The ethos of the building is essentially creative, housing designers as well as finance and administrative staff. Office floors open on to a full-height atrium, with the concrete structural grid, elegantly and economically engineered by Adams Kara Taylor, frankly exposed: the omission of suspended ceilings and other finishes is part of a low-energy services strategy. The top (fifth) floor, where the designers work, has the feel of a factory, with pitched roofs capping a 6-metre-high, generously day-lit space. The ground floor acts as a gallery to display items from Monsoon's extensive collection of contemporary art, as well as housing the staff restaurant. Whereas in the interior, the vital element of colour is largely provided by people (mostly young and all fashionably dressed) and swathes of fabric, externally bright yellow cladding makes the building a marker for the ongoing transformation of the surrounding area.

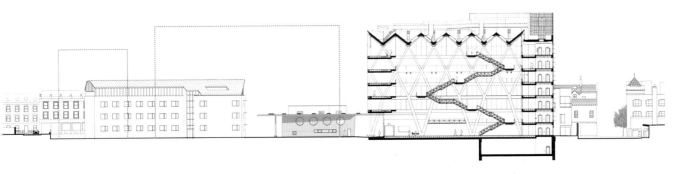

FURTHER READING

Allinson, K., *London's Contemporary Architecture: A Visitor's Guide*, 5th edn, London (Architectural Press) 2009

Allison, P. (ed.), *David Adjaye: Houses*, London (Thames & Hudson) 2005

— (ed.), *David Adjaye: Making Public Buildings*, London (Thames & Hudson) 2006

Bayley, S., *Work: The Building of the Channel Tunnel Rail Link*, London (Merrell) 2007

Bennetts Associates: Four Commentaries, London (Black Dog) 2005

Bradley, S., *St Pancras Station*, London (Profile Books) 2007

Building the BBC: A Return to Form, London (Wordsearch Communications) 2004

Chapman, T., *The Stirling Prize: Ten Years of Architecture and Innovation*, London (Merrell) 2006

The Complete Zaha Hadid, London (Thames & Hudson) 2009

Davies, C., *Hopkins 2*, London (Phaidon) 2001

Foster + Partners, *Foster Catalogue 2005*, Munich (Prestel) 2005

Gumuchdjian Architects: Selected Works, London (Eight Books) 2009

Hines, M., *The Story of Broadcasting House: Home of the BBC*, London (Merrell) 2008

Jackson, A.A., *London's Termini*, Newton Abbot (David & Charles) 1969

Jenkins, D. (ed.), *Norman Foster: Works*, Munich (Prestel) 2000–

John, R., *New Classicists: Robert Adam, The Search for a Modern Classcism*, Mulgrave, Vic. (Images Publishing) 2010

Jones, E., and Woodward, C., *A Guide to the Architecture of London*, 4th edn, London (Seven Dials) 2009

Kerr, J., and Gibson, A. (eds), *London, from Punk to Blair*, London (Reaktion Books) 2003

Long, K., *New London Interiors*, London (Merrell) 2004

McKean, J., *Royal Festival Hall*, Buildings in Detail, London (Phaidon) 1992

Nairn, I., *Modern Buildings in London*, London (London Transport) 1964

—, *Nairn's London*, Harmondsworth (Penguin) 1966

Eric Parry Architects, vol. 1, London (Black Dog) 2002

Powell, K., *30 St Mary Axe: A Tower for London*, London (Merrell) 2006

—, *City Reborn: Architecture and Regeneration in London, from Bankside to Dulwich*, London (Merrell) 2004

—, *Richard Rogers: Complete Works*, vol. 3, London (Phaidon) 2006

Schumacher, P., and Fontana-Giusti, G. (eds), *Zaha Hadid: Complete Works*, London (Thames & Hudson) 2004

Sheard, R., *The Stadium: Architecture for the New Global Culture*, Sydney (Pesaro) 2005

Stanton Williams: Volume, London (Black Dog) 2010

Sudjic, D., *Future Systems*, London (Phaidon) 2006

Summerson, J., *Georgian London*, London (Pleiades Books) 1945, and subsequent editions

Transformations: The Architecture of Penoyre & Prasad, London (Black Dog) 2007

Veseley, D., and Wang, W., *Eric Parry Architects*, vol. 2, London (Black Dog) 2011

Watkin, D., *Radical Classicism: The Architecture of Quinlan Terry*, New York (Rizzoli) 2006

Wilkinson, C., and Eyre, J., *Bridging Art and Science: Wilkinson Eyre Architecture*, London (Booth-Clibborn Editions) 2001

Wright, H., *London High*, London (Frances Lincoln) 2006

INDEX

PICTURE CREDITS

First published 2011 by

Merrell Publishers Limited
81 Southwark Street
London SE1 0HX
merrellpublishers.com

British Library Cataloguing-in-Publication data:
Powell, Ken, 1947–
21st-century London : the new architecture.
1. Architecture–England–London–History–21st century.
2. Architecture–England–London–History–21st
century–Pictorial works. 3. London (England)–Buildings,
structures, etc. 4. London (England)–Buildings,
structures, etc.–Pictorial works.
I. Title
720.9'421'090511-dc22

ISBN 978-1-8589-4537-8

Produced by Merrell Publishers Limited
Designed by Alexandre Coco
Project-managed by Rosanna Lewis
Maps by Adam Meara
Proof-read by Philippa Baker
Indexed by Hilary Bird

Printed and bound in China

Front cover: London Bridge Tower (pp. 326–27)
Back cover, clockwise from top left: Tate Modern
(pp. 100–101); Terminal 5, Heathrow Airport (pp. 46–47);
Clapham Manor Primary School Extension (pp. 168–69);
Newington Green House (pp. 254–55); Wembley Stadium
(pp. 152–53); Twenty Fenchurch Street (pp. 7–8)
Page 4: Darwin Centre, Phase Two, Natural History
Museum (pp. 54–55)

ACKNOWLEDGEMENTS

I should like to thank Hugh Merrell of Merrell Publishers
for commissioning this book, and, also at Merrell,
Rosanna Lewis, Alexandre Coco and Alenka Oblak for
seeing the project to fruition. Architects, clients and
building users too numerous to mention provided
information and drawings, Adam Meara contributed
the maps, and without the excellent work of VIEW –
Yvonne Peeke-Vout, Sophia Gibb and the many
photographers – the book would not have been possible.

Kenneth Powell
London, November 2010